Warren N. Stilbert

William Hageman

Chicago Cubs: Seasons at the Summit

Warren Wilbert
William Hageman

Sagamore Publishing
Champaign, Illinois

Book design: Michelle Summers
Cover Design: Deborah Bellaire
Editor: Susan McKinney
Cover Photos: Center photo: Warren Wimmer Photography; Top right: Photo File;
          Top left, bottom left, and bottom right: George Brace
Interior Photos: Unless noted, all photos courtesy of George Brace

ISBN: 1-57167-110-2
Library of Congress Catalog Card Number: 97-65485

Sagamore Publishing
804 N. Neil St. Suite 100
Champaign, IL 61820
www.sagamorepub.com

Printed in the United States.

To my grandsons, Jake and Alan
—WW

For Dona and the girls, Julie, Kelly, and Katie
—WH

CONTENTS

ACKNOWLEDGMENTS

Acknowledgments are in order, all right. Having completed *Chicago Cubs: Seasons at The Summit*, I'm aware now, more than ever, just how much we stand on the shoulders of those who have gone before. Many a baseball writer, many a baseball historian, and many a baseball researcher have paved the way with countless bits of information just waiting for a theme. To all of them, I tip my cap.

Some time ago I picked up Donald Honig's *Baseball America*. I'm not above admitting that his prose stirred and inspired me. Though I've never had the privilege of meeting him, I hope that day comes, because I'd like to acknowledge personally the lift his writing has given me.

Then, too, I owe a personal debt of gratitude to one of my fine Christian friends, Ernie Harwell, who has been supportive and helpful in his own kind way. Always cheerful and forward-looking, Ernie has been an inspiration not only to me, but to legions of baseball fans throughout the continent.

For a baseball writer to have the expertise and information of a Pete Palmer available when those extra touches are needed, or when accuracy and precision are demanded—that's good fortune beyond description. Thanks, Pete, for your patience and insight and for just plain being available.

Our catalyst and major domo, Mike Pearson, of Sagamore Publishing, deserves special kudos. His upbeat, can-do attitude and selfless dedication to all the "necessaries" kept us on track and on target.

—Warren Wilbert

This book would not have been completed without the help and support of many people: Eddie Gold, for his assistance in uncovering players' uniform numbers; Marion Grimm, for her stories about her late husband, Charlie, and his players, and for granting us access to her book collection; George and Mary Brace, for their help in securing photos; the peerless people at Sagamore Publishing; and my family: my wife Dona, and my daughters Julie, Kelly, and Katie.

—Bill Hageman

INTRODUCTION

The Chicago White Stockings, later to become Wrigleyville's loveable Cubbies, were charter members of the National League, and the only original franchise that has operated continuously in the same city between the first game played on April 22, 1876, and today. During that time, upwards of 1,750 ballplayers have pulled on Cub uniforms, and out of that number we've taken the players who have put together individual seasons of such magnificence that they've merited our top 50 billing.

From Al Spalding to Cap Anson to the Peerless Leader, Frank Chance, and on to 'Ole Pete Alexander and Hack Wilson; from Gabby Hartnett and Billy Herman on to Ron Santo and "Let's Play Two," Ernie Banks; and on to the more recent past with Billy Williams and Mark Grace, the famous and the not-so-famous are presented in rank order from the very best of the creme de la creme, on down through No. 50.

The first question that will come to mind is a real toughie: How did we come up with the top 50? The next, equally bothersome, is: How did the top 50 get lined up in a 1 to 50 "batting order?" The answers will take a little explaining and will no doubt be as debatable when all is said and sorted out, as the final listing presented in these Seasons at the Summit.

So we'll begin with a given: you're going to disagree with some if not many of the selections. And, as you look into the record book for yourself, you'll no doubt disagree with a particular player or a particular season we've chosen. That's OK. The call on a lot of these legendary heroes is going to generate some heat.

Be that as it may, let's get at some of the answers with a few of the "ground rules" we've established in narrowing down and then rating a glittering array of more than 200 exceptional seasons to the 50 at the summit.

To begin with, grandstand and Bleacher Bum favorites like Ryno, Ernie, Three Finger and Fergie are but four among others on the honor list who had a number of outstanding seasons in a Cubs uniform that would have merited mention at two or more spots among the all-time 50. Ground rule No. 1, however, stipulates one listing per player.

So, for example, Billy Herman's greatest Cub seasons, strung together in a 1935-37 cluster, might have appeared in the listing at three different places. Instead, we took the best of the three, 1935, as the single Herman entry. Consequently, 50 different franchise players, stretching from Al Spalding's 1876 all the way through to the 1992 season contributed by Greg Maddux, comprise the listing.

Another principle that guided our choices specified that, for example, batting averages, slugging averages, or low ERA's are *not necessarily* indicators, by and of themselves, of super seasons, however important a part of the total picture of one season they may be. To get a well-rounded, more comprehensive look at what was going on in a given season, we considered:

1) How the league in general, and the Cubs in particular, fared in the player's big season.

2) The hitting and pitching characteristics of the league overall during the season. For example, 1930 and 1994 were "hitter's years" and 1908 wasn't. The 1908 NL team batting average was a paltry .239. Those kinds of factors have tremendous influence on rating the performance of hitters and pitchers.

3) The characteristics and idiosyncrasies of the various franchise ballparks, particularly, in its early years. Half the schedule is played on the home field, and that made 1884 a real haven for the White Stockings because of the "short porch" down the foul lines, at a mere 216 feet. That was dinger heaven, if ever a ballplayer saw it, and

if Ned Williamson, who set a home run record that lasted for 35 years until Babe Ruth broke it in 1919, were still around, he'd no doubt tell you all about it—over a cool brew.

4) The statistic line that represents, in numerically quantifiable terms, the player's productivity, along with the numbers in some relatively recent and highly significant categories that have emerged from the work of sabermetricians*. Batting runs, fielding runs, pitching runs and pitcher's defense are some of these newer statistics that have been extremely helpful in getting behind the meaning of a player's contribution to his team's play. These newer numbers are reviewed in sample seasons a bit further on.

Still other factors, like All-Star games, the World Series, and in the case of the Chicago teams, the old City Series (1903-1942), which may to a certain extent be reincarnated in the form of interleague play in 1997, also have special meaning, and are, when appropriate, called into play as we attempted to take a searching look at Mordecai Brown's 1906, Phil Cavarretta's 1945, or Ryne Sandberg's 1984.

Because the object of the game is to win by scoring more runs than the opposing team does, the run is of basic importance in determining the worth of a player's contribution to the team. The run is, as it were, the coinage of the realm. What a player does to enhance the possibility of the team to score more runs, or to prevent opponents from scoring, turns out to be the essential unit of worth in the 'ole ballgame. From it, judgments as to how much a player's productivity is worth in a given season as compared to others, can be made. This is the sabermetrician's basic insight. The linear weights and measurements he uses furnish the wherewithal to rate Orvie Overall's 1909 better than Hank Sauer's 1952, and on through the list. We'll see how that works in sample cases just ahead.

Let's take a look at a position player and a pitcher to familiarize ourselves with the terms and abbreviations used throughout the book. To do so, we're going to review the statistical data on Don Kessinger's 1969 season (a position player, and a 1969 Gold Glover, at that), and the 1926 season of pitcher Charlie Root, a Wrigley Field favorite during the '20s and '30s.

Don Kessinger, Shortstop, 1969 Season:

AB-R-H	BA	OB%	SA	EXBH	HR	RBI	BR	FR	SB	TPR
664-109-181	.273	.335	.366	48	4	53	-13	25	11	2.9

OB% .335   On-base percentage, a figure compiled by dividing Kessinger's hits plus walks plus times hit by pitches, by his number of at-bats; .335 is a decent, but by no means outstanding, percentage.

SA   .366   Calculated by dividing Kessinger's total bases (he had 243) by the number of official times at-bat (664), or .3659 (.366) = his slugging average (SA).

EXBH   48   Extra base hits (48)

BR   -13   Batting runs, a linear weights measure of runs contributed *beyond* those contributed by league-average players (the league-average player is rated at 0 in all sabermetric calculations), which is a measure of the player's contribution to his team's run scoring productivity. In Don's case, the BR rating is poor, detracting from an otherwise fine season. Compared to some of the more outstanding single season figures of, e.g.: Ron Santo's 1967, 43, or Hack Wilson's 1930 figure of a huge 74, Kessinger's 13 puts his weaker stick into sharp perspective for 1969.

FR   25   Fielding runs (FR) is another linear weights measure that computes the number of runs *saved* beyond what a league average player might save in a given season (rated at 0). The rating number given as the result of the mathematical formula's calculation can be used as a measuring stick to determine just how much better or worse one player's rating is than another's. Kessinger's is a superior rating. Ivan De Jesus' rookie Cub season figure of 36 (1978), Johnny Evers' 1908 rating of 36, and Stan Hack's 18 FR in 1945 are other superior Cub ratings.

TPR	2.9	Kessinger's Total Player Rating (TPR) for the 1969 season is a very good one, despite his low, -13 batting runs productivity. If a player were capable of putting together 10 or 12 out of 15 seasons of 2.5+ ratings, he would be well on the way to Cooperstown. Checking over the Hall of Famers in *Total Baseball*, the sabermetrician's "Bible," one notes career averages among Cub players like Pete Alexander (3.25 for 20 years); 2.49 for 14 years for Mordecai Brown; Ernie Banks' 1.36, 19 years; and 1.73 TPR /18 seasons, for Billy Williams. Babe Ruth? The all-time first at almost everything "baseball" rolled up a 124.7 (107.6 as a position player plus 17.1 as a pitcher), for a 22 season average of 5.67. That's beyond awesome!

Charlie Root, Pitcher, 1926 Season:

W-L	W%	IP	CG	SH	SV	BB/K	OBA	PR	DEF	ERA	TPI
18-17	.514	271.1	21	2	2	127/62	.264	30	-1	2.82	3.2

W-L-W%	Games won, lost, and winning percentage: Despite what might be considered a so-so W-L record, this was Charlie Root's best Cub season, *all things considered*. That takes into consideration the league's and team's year in 1926, other statistics and some linear statistics that bring new insights to bear on the pitcher's contribution in a given year. Two of these, pitcher runs and pitcher's defense, are explained below.
CG-SH-SV	These three tabulate the number of complete games (CG), shutouts (SH), and saves (SV) logged. In Root's 1926 that came to 21 CG, 2 SH and 2 SV. For the 1920s, those are very respectable figures.
PR	Pitching runs (PR). Another linear measurement that calculates runs saved *beyond* what a league-average pitcher might save (rated 0). Some of the better Cub PR numbers include Kenny Holtzman's 21 in 1970, Johnny Schmitz's 35 in 1948 and Pete Alexander's 50 in 1920 (that's orbital). Charlie Root's 30 ranks right up there among the Cub all-time highs.
DEF	Pitcher's defense (DEF). A linear weights measure of runs saved *beyond* what a league-average pitcher might have saved. It's a statistic that takes into consideration different positions (like the pitcher) because of the demands and individuality of the various positions, assists, errors, putouts, double plays and the pitcher's strikeouts. All of these factors contribute, in one way or another, to getting the side out and preventing runs (or in permitting them). Anything above a 4 as the DEF figure represents outstanding pitcher's defense. These are *really* the "fifth infielders" around the league. Rick Reuschel's 5 in 1974, John Clarkson's 8 in 1885, and Larry Jackson's 7 in 1964 are examples of great pitcher defense numbers. Charlie Root's -1 figure for 1926, a tad below average, is still in all a relatively decent figure.
TPI	Total Pitcher Index (TPI). The TP correlates to the position player's TPR. The figures are comparable as a measure of the player's contribution to the team's winning capabilities in a given season. Both will be given further attention below. The 3.2 Root ranking for 1926 is just a shade better than Kessinger's 2.9 (1969).

Note that in the Charlie Root statistic line, the strikeout/bases on balls figures are stated to indicate a ratio, whiffs as compared to walks. For Root, the 1926 ratio was 2 to 1. In other words, he was sending twice as many hitters back to the dugout as he was putting on first base via a free pass. That's good. In fact, it was his best ratio in 16 Wrigleyville seasons.

If you look up Charlie Root's career record, his 1927, 26-15 record will stick out like a sore thumb, at least as far as win-loss record is concerned. At first blush that would be an odds-on favorite for his best Cub season. Remember, however, that we've tried to explain at some length the "all things considered" factor in rating individual seasons. In Root's case, his 1927 season was actually in the neighborhood of three times *less* valuable in sabermetric terms than

1926, a year in which the North Siders barely avoided the second division, finishing fourth. It took some outstanding pitching to win 18 times with a mediocre ballclub and tough competition in the league's first division.

Before turning to your Cub favorites and all those extraordinary seasons in the fascinating history of the franchise, there remains one other important consideration. That would be what sabermetricians like Pete Palmer, John Thorn, Mark Alvarez and Bill James (the Society for American Baseball Research numbers over 5,000), call the "MVP of Statistical Analysis," the Total Baseball Ranking (see Kessinger and Root above). Expressed in terms of Total Player Ratings (TPR) for position players and Total Pitcher Index (TPI), the ranking reveals the most valuable players, and results in season ratings given point values ranging from ca. -10 to +10. Position players and pitchers' ratings are, of course, calculated by using a different mix of variables, but the result is a rating that is consistent in its assigned value. Thus, a pitcher's 5.0 is on a par with a position player's 5.0. In either case the player's contribution to his team's win total for a given year is the same. To get from the player's ranking (5.0, as in our example) to victories, we simply equate each point along the spectrum with a win. A 5.0, which extends from 4.5 to 5.4, translates to 5 victories during the course of a season. Here's an example: Phil Cavarretta's 1945 TPR was figured at 3.8, or 4 victories above what a league-average player might have contributed that season. Teammates Lennie Merullo (-.3), pitcher Paul Erickson (0.1) and outfielder Peanuts Lowery (0.0) were at or near average seasons in 1945. In the case of Cavarretta, we have the difference between a final season tally of 98 wins and 56 losses and a 94-60 record, which would have dropped the Cubs into second place behind the Cardinals. That's one of the reasons Philibuck's 1945 is in the summit 50.

The individual contributions of position players and pitchers certainly make a difference. Sabermetricians quantify those differences, enabling them to make value judgments about their calculations in an evenhanded manner across positions and decades. Consequently, shortstop Joe Tinker's 1908 4.8 rating is on a par with relief pitcher Lee Smith's 1983 4.9 rating. Note the difference in both position and year. Both players, rated a full notch above Cavarretta, brought five extra wins to the Cubs in their summit seasons.

But enough already. Time left for a confession: We've left room in the midst of all this higher math for a researcher's instinct, and we've taken some liberties here and there about the who, where, and how good. There was no way that players like Cap Anson or Johnny Evers were going to be left behind—nor Kenny Holtzman or Mark Grace, for that matter.

Let the great debate begin. But let's celebrate these legendary Cubs along the way!

* Sabermetrician: from SABR, an acronym for Society of American Baseball Research, referring to the mathematical and statistical analysis of baseball records.

AT THE SUMMIT OF THE SUMMIT: AN INTRODUCTION

THE TOP 10

1) John Clarkson, 1885, P
2) Rogers Hornsby, 1929, 2B
3) Grover Alexander, 1920, P
4) Ron Santo, 1966, 3B
5) Mordecai Brown, 1906, P

6) Ernie Banks, 1959, SS
7) Ryne Sandberg, 1984, 2B
8) Ferguson Jenkins, 1971, P
9) Jack Taylor, 1902, P
10) Greg Maddux, 1992, P

The superbly gifted ballplayers who fashioned the Top 10 greatest single seasons in Cubs history stretch across a century of baseball in the Big Show. Standing at the head of that distinguished group of six pitchers and four position players is an 1880s vintage, crafty right-hander, all but unknown today and relegated to the yellowed and brittle pages of the National League's earliest history. That fellow, John Clarkson, who in 1885 established the Cubs record for most victories in a single season at an incredible 53, is perched atop the summit, unassailably No. 1. As you take a look at the Cubs up there in the 1-10 spots, don't skip over Clarkson to get at Greg Maddux or Ryne Sandberg, whose more recent achievements may still be fresh in your mind. Clarkson's 1885 reads like one of Paul Bunyan's better hunting days, and it's worth a longer look. It's crammed with barely believable numbers that hoist him a notch above the others in the Top 10.

Clustered tightly behind the pace-setting Hall of Famer Clarkson are two Cub infielders, the Rajah, second baseman Rogers Hornsby at No. 2, and third baseman Ron Santo, who holds down the No. 4 spot on our honors list. Rounding out the top five are Grover Cleveland Alexander, the pitcher's pitcher, and Mordecai "Three Finger" Brown, ace of those incomparable Cubs pitching staffs of the early 1900s. Three of these four are Hall of Famers, and Santo certainly should be, adding more luster to their greatest seasons in a Cub uniform.

Standing at a level of excellence just a hair's breadth below the sparkling seasons registered by the top five are two NL MVPs: Ernie Banks, the most popular Cub of them all, and the much respected Sandberg. Another pair of award winners, Cy Young pitchers Fergie Jenkins and Maddux, hold down the Nos. 8 and 10 positions, respectively, on the honors list.

Sandwiched between Jenkins and Maddux is the fiercely combative "Old Iron Arm," Jack Taylor, who will probably hold in perpetuity the record for consecutive complete games, including his banner 1902 season, which added 33 to his staggering total of 187 straight between 1901 and 1906. That's beyond contemporary comprehension.

Yup, there's room for argument here. But one thing stands out: There *is* discernible space between the top five and the seasons ranked between six and 10. We've ranked them like this: Banks (6), Sandberg (7), Jenkins (8), Taylor (9) and Maddux (10). For those of you who are, at least in spirit, true believers in Chicago's North Siders, there'll no doubt be a fuss raised over the ranking order.

OK, you Bleacher Bums, take your best shot.

John Clarkson—1885

Chicago Cubs Summit Season
Number 1

No. 1
JOHN CLARKSON

BORN: July 1, 1861; Cambridge, Massachusetts
DIED: February 4, 1909; Belmont, Massachusetts

Chicago White Stockings: 1884-1887
Hall of Fame: 1963

SEASON AT THE SUMMIT: 1885

W-L-%	IP	CG	SH	SV	K/BB	PR	DEF	ERA
53-16 .768	623.0	68	10	0	318/97	67	8	1.85

The archetypal ballplayer of the late 19th Century was a rough-and-tumble character, brawling and brash, someone who relied on raw physical strength and size to overcome his opponents.

Then there was **John Clarkson**.

Clarkson was the game's premiere pitcher of his day, winning 207 games over one five-year span, leading Chicago's White Stockings to two National League championships. He did it not by overpowering enemy batters or through trickery, but by using intelligence, excellent control and a wicked drop curve.

In an era when baseball was considered a less than noble profession, Clarkson seemed out of place. Quiet, reserved and relatively small at 5-foot-10 and 155 pounds, he was the son of a well-to-do Boston businessman. The 20-year-old Clarkson broke into the National League with Worcester in 1882, appearing in three games before a sore arm forced him to the bench. In late 1884 he was signed by White Stockings manager Cap Anson, who was looking for help for his team.

Student of the Game

Anson's ballclub had finished fourth, 22 games behind Providence in the 1884 race. The problem was pitching: Aside from Larry Corcoran (35-23), Anson had none. For 1885, Chicago figured to have an effective 1-2 punch with Corcoran and Clarkson.

The season opened on April 30 with a 3-1 loss in St. Louis, Corcoran suffering the defeat. Clarkson made his 1885 debut the next afternoon, allowing just three earned runs in a 9-5 victory. The two pitchers alternated through the first 3½ weeks of the season, Clarkson winning seven of nine decisions and Corcoran five of seven as the Whites and New York battled for first place. By the middle of May, though, Corcoran had developed arm trouble and was shelved, leaving the pitching in Clarkson's hands.

Unlike most other pitchers of his day, Clarkson relied on intelligence to get the job done. He studied opposing batters to learn their weaknesses, then exploited them. And his drop curve—a sinker—took less of a toll on his arm than a constant barrage of fastballs. Another thing

Clarkson had going for him was Anson. The young pitcher was extremely sensitive, and would become quiet and withdrawn after losing. Anson did his best to keep Clarkson in a good mental state, constantly encouraging him, praising him in the press, and bending team rules to accommodate him.

Clarkson lost his last two decisions in May, dropping his record to 8-4 and setting the stage for one of the most memorable months in franchise history.

Clarkson started June in quick fashion, beating Detroit three times in four days (the other game was rained out). The best of the bunch was a five-hit shutout on June 1, his third whitewash of the young season. The club's lack of pitching depth may have been troubling the baseball writers and fans, but Anson seemed unconcerned. "Oh, Clarkson is all right," he told the *Chicago Tribune*, "and, barring accident, he can pitch in every game for a month to come and it won't hurt him."

The Man They Relied On

And Anson wasn't kidding. Clarkson became the team's iron man, starting 17 of the team's 24 games, the other starts being split among Ted Kennedy, second baseman Fred Pfeffer and third baseman Ned Williamson. The recipe worked, as Chicago won 18 in a row at one point, and Clarkson put together a 15-1 record for the month.

Among his highlights was a 9-2 six-hit victory over St. Louis on June 6 to open the White Stockings' new $30,000 ballpark at Congress and Loomis, a 5-0 one-hitter against Buffalo on the 20th, a 5-3 three-hitter against Philadelphia on the 23rd for his 20th victory, and a 12-2 two-hitter over the Phillies the next day. Clarkson's only loss in June—and the game that ended Chicago's 18-game winning streak—came on the 25th when he lost to the Phils 2-0. He allowed just seven hits, one a homer by Joe Mulvey, but Philadelphia's Ed Dailey stopped the Whites on three hits.

Clarkson finally got some help in mid-July when Anson secured right-hander Jim McCormick from Providence, where he had struggled to a 1-3 record. He would go on to a 20-4 record for the Whites, alternating with Clarkson and giving Anson the 1-2 pitching punch he had been looking for.

Still, Clarkson was the big gun in July—beating Buffalo three times in as many days on the 13th, 14th and 15th; stopping Boston 6-5 on the 18th with a five-hitter to run his record to 30-8; and winning his last 10 starts. His most impressive win came on the 27th when he no-hit Providence, striking out four and not walking a batter.

The Race With New York

The Whites had moved into first in May, but could never put any distance between themselves and New York. The Gothams, led by sluggers Roger Connor (he was hitting well over .400 through the middle of August) and Mike Dorgan and pitchers Mickey Welch and Tim Keefe, beat Chicago two of three in a key early August series to draw within one game of first.

Down the stretch, it was again Clarkson who carried the Whites. He beat Buffalo three times in the first five days of September—his September 5 win a 13-strikeout five-hitter—to run his record to 44-12 and leave Chicago 2½ games ahead of New York. He won seven of his next eight decisions as well, including a 2-1 three-hitter over New York on September 30, to finish the month 52-13.

Chicago wrapped up the NL title on October 6 by beating Philadelphia while New York was losing to St. Louis. The Whites then coasted through the final week—Clarkson lost his last three outings, a combination of a tired arm and having to pitch in meaningless games—winning the pennant by two games and earning a spot in a postseason playoff series with American Association champion St. Louis.

The series was a disappointment for Chicago and Clarkson, by now exhausted after a busy season. He struck out nine and didn't allow an earned run in the first game, which ended in a 5-5 tie. He took the loss in Game 3, and didn't pitch again against St. Louis. The series ended with each team winning three games, a huge moral victory for the supposedly inferior American Association.

Clarkson's final mark of 53 victories was tops in the league, as was his number of games (70 of Chicago's 112), complete games (68), innings pitched (623, more than 130 more than his nearest rival), strikeouts (318) and shutouts (10)—astonishing numbers he would never duplicate.

He spent two more fruitful years in Chicago before asking to be traded to his hometown Boston club. He spent 4½ seasons there and 2½ in Cleveland before retiring, not so much the victim of diminishing skills, but largely because of a rule change that moved the pitcher's mound from 50 feet from home plate to 60 feet 6 inches. He was unable to adjust to the new distance and was out of baseball at the age of 33.

JOHN CLARKSON'S

Two Other Great Cub Seasons

	Yr	W-L	IP	GS	GC	SH	SV	PD	K/BB	OBA	OB%	ERA	PR
1.	1886	36-17	466.2	55	50	3	0	4	313/86	.229	.264	2.41	47
2.	1887	38-21	523	59	56	2	4	9	237/92	.246	.281	3.08	58

Two bantam-sized hurlers sparkled during the White Stockings' early years. They were Larry Corcoran and John Clarkson. Their imposing numbers were instrumental in a string of Chicago pennants. Clarkson's gargantuan 1885 effort is beyond the usual Mount Everest comparisons. It's clearly the greatest single season ever contributed by a Wrigleyville ballplayer. His No. 1 single season, however, is almost matched by the pair listed above. In fact, his second best in 1887, an 8.3 TPI just under his 8.9 franchise high (1885), is better than Rogers Hornsby's 1929 season, ranked at No. 2 among the Top 50 Summit Seasons.

"John Clarkson never had a superior as a pitcher and never will. I have stood behind him day after day and watched his magnificent control, as confident of his success, especially in tight places, as if he had the United States army behind him. He was a master of control and that was his long suit. In addition he had everything a pitcher had in the way of curves, with a thorough knowledge of his opponents."

—Former White Stockings' second baseman Fred Pfeffer on John Clarkson

CLARKSON: A NOTEWORTHY BOX SCORE

July 27, 1885

Clarkson throws a no-hitter against Providence, outdueling Old Hoss Radbourn.

Chicago	AB	R	H	PO	A	E	Providence	AB	R	H	PO	A	E
Dalrymple, 1f	4	0	1	0	0	0	Hines, cf	4	0	0	5	0	0
Gore, cf	2	0	0	1	0	0	Carroll, 1f	4	0	0	2	0	0
Sunday, cf	2	0	0	1	0	0	Daily, c	3	0	0	1	0	2
Kelly, rf	3	0	0	3	1	0	Start, 1b	3	0	0	6	0	0
Anson, 1b	4	1	1	12	1	0	Radbourn, p	3	0	0	0	0	3
Pfeffer, 2b	3	2	1	1	2	1	Farrell, 2b	3	0	0	1	4	2
Williamson, 3b	3	1	0	2	2	2	Denny, 3b	3	0	0	2	2	0
Burns, ss	3	0	0	0	1	0	Radford, rf	3	0	0	1	0	0
Clarkson, p	3	0	0	1	7	1	Bassett, ss	3	0	0	6	0	0
Flint, c	3	0	2	6	0	1							
TOTALS	30	4	5	27	14	5	TOTALS	29	0	0	24	6	7

Providence	0 0 0	0 0 0	0 0 0	--0
Chicago	0 2 0	2 0 0	0 0*	--4

Earned runs--Chicago, 1. Double--Flint. Passed ball--Daily, 4. Wild pitch--Radbourn. Bases on balls--Chicago 2. First base on errors--Chicago 3, Providence 3. Struck out--Providence 4. Double plays--Chicago, 1. Umpire--Bond. Attendance--1,100 (est.)

Other Baseball Highlights of 1885

▪The National League's New York Giants, part owners of the American Association's New York Metropolitans, pluck Tim Keefe from the Mets' roster. He goes on to win 32 games for the Giants.

▪Roger Connor of New York is the NL batting champion with a .371 average; Louisville's Pete Browning wins the AA title at .362.

▪Chicago's Abner Dalrymple leads the NL in homers with 11.

Rogers "Rajah" Hornsby—1929

Chicago Cubs Summit Season
Number 2

No. 2
ROGERS HORNSBY

BORN: April 27, 1896; Winters, Texas
DIED: January 5, 1963; Chicago, Illinois

Chicago Cubs: 1929-1932
Hall of Fame: 1942

SEASON AT THE SUMMIT: 1929

AB-R-H	BA	OB%	2B	3B	HR	RBI	BR	FR	SB
602-156-229	.380	.459	47	8	39	149	74	1	2

The original Cub Wrigley, William, was no piker. He drew on his chewing gum fortunes often and lavishly to spruce up both his ballpark and ballclub. The Cubs were the apple of his eye, so when he had the opportunity to pry 1928 NL batting champion **Rogers Hornsby** from the struggling Boston Braves, Wrigley wrote out a $200,000 check without a whimper, bringing the Rajah to the Friendly Confines. The deal put in place the last and most powerful cog in the machine that club president William Veeck Sr., manager Joe McCarthy and Wrigley had been patiently assembling since 1925.

All three were fully aware of what Hornsby's presence would mean, and all three were willing—Veeck a little less so—to take their chances on whatever that might bring. No one had to tell them that with Hornsby you got more than an offensive wrecking crew. There was more than a hawk's eyes, a baseball mind par excellence, and a burning desire to dominate. The cold, icy stare, the disdain for mortal baseball shortcomings, an "around-here-I'm-top-dog" attitude—it would also mean friction and frayed tempers. But with a pennant race just ahead

and a world championship within their grasp, they signed their man and never looked back.

Immediate Dividends

The Cubs opened their season at home with a three-game series against the Pirates. They lost the opener on April 16, 4-3, but then won the next two, big—13-2 and 11-1, with Hornsby going 3 for 8. Hornsby had his first big day of the season on the 21st, going 4 for 4, two of the hits doubles, in a 4-0 victory over St. Louis before some 45,000 fans at Wrigley Field.

But then he slumped, going 1 for 13 in a subsequent three-game series against Pittsburgh, and ended April at .365. The tailspin continued through the first two weeks of May as his average fell below .300. "Just about everybody now has awakened to the fact that the great Rajah is considerably behind in his bat work," wrote Irving Vaughan in *The Sporting News*.

Fortunately for the Cubs, Riggs Stephenson (.418 through May 16), Charlie Grimm, Kiki Cuyler and Hack Wilson picked up the slack until Hornsby got back on track. And he did. On May 31 he was up to .347—and climbing. He reached the halfway point of the season in July at .356 with 64 RBIs.

With Hornsby, Wilson, Stephenson and Cuyler all hitting over .330, and Guy Bush (15-1) and Pat Malone (15-7) anchoring the pitching staff, the Cubs were in the driver's seat by mid-August. They clinched the NL pennant on September 18—not with a victory, but by virtue of a loss by second-place Pittsburgh.

To take nothing away from a Cub lineup already sizzling with punch, it was the 33-year-old Hornsby who made the difference between a very good and an absolutely devastating 1929 pennant-winner. Uncorking a dozen three-hit games and five more four-hit contests, he led the way, paying immense and immediate dividends on Wrigley's investment. And as the Cubs hit the home stretch, it was Hornsby who led the way, hitting over .400 through the last six weeks of the season leading to the World Series (his performance against the AL champion Philadelphia A's wasn't vintage Hornsby: a .238 average as the A's beat the Cubs in five games).

MVP Numbers

Hornsby finished the season with a .380 batting average, 229 hits and 156 runs—all all-time Cub records. His slugging average was .679 and he had 409 total bases, both league-leading figures, and he had 149 RBIs and a .459 on-base percentage. He also led the league in assists with 547. After the season, Hornsby was chosen National League Most Valuable Player in a vote of NL writers, taking home $1,000 in gold and a bronze medal. (Philadelphia's Lefty O'Doul was a close second, Billy Terry of the New York Giants third.)

But for all Hornsby's stats and accomplishments, there was another huge contribution to the Cubs' 1929 success story: his influence on his teammates.

Individually, there was shortstop Woody English, who, by his own admission "learned the trade" in the field and

at-bat from Hornsby, who never tired of talking about the ins and outs of the game. They were ideal roommates on the road, one a willing instructor, the other a willing pupil.

And Hornsby—all business, all baseball—also influenced the Cubs as a team. Starting with Stephenson at .363, there followed in descending order Wilson, Cuyler and Grimm, all over .300. English, who would come into his own in 1930 at .335, hit .276. The Cubs averaged 6.3 runs a game, leading the league with 982 runs scored, and hit .303 as a team. They also led the NL in walks (589) and tied for the lead in doubles (310).

As the 1929 season wore on, National League hitters seemed more and more intent on a wholesale rewrite of the record book. And the Cubs took a back seat to no one: a team-record nine grand slams during a single season; a major-league record-tying 10 straight hits in a September 7 game against the Braves (Hornsby was 3 for 4 that day, and 4 for 5 a day later). That kind of hitting helped produce winning streaks of four or more games 11 times, including one of nine games.

He Made Everyone Better

There is a point to be made here. While Hornsby may have scared some people and alienated others with his manner, one thing was bound to surface with him in the lineup or dugout: You were going to hit to the best of your ability or you were going to have to answer to him.

All of that was a huge part of the Cubs' story in 1929. The entire effort was raised to a higher level of championship play. While the front office and McCarthy contributed mightily to the season, it was Hornsby who translated it all into the kind of action that registered victories and a championship. It was still another reason to place his 1929 campaign so high as to mark it the finest ever by a Cubs' position player.

ROGERS HORNSBY'S

One Other Great Cub Season

	YR	GP	AB-R-H	BA	OB%	SA	K/BB	HR	RBI	SB	FR	BR
1.	1931	100	357-64-118	.331	.421	.574	23/56	16	90	1	-15	32

In 1929 the Rajah won his second MVP award on the strength of an awe-inspiring season. It was his last hurrah. He had terrorized the National League since 1915 with sizzling ropes and extra-base power, but by the time he settled into his Chicago togs, the wear and tear began to show. Nonetheless, he fashioned one more "unbelieveability," leading the Cubs into the '29 World Series on the heels of his No. 2 Cub Summit Season performance. Though his 1931 numbers would be envied by players in either league, they weren't Hornsby numbers—and that's about the only thing that mattered to "His Bluntness."

"Once he stepped into the batter's box, he was in another world. His concentration was so intense you could have shot off cannons around him and he wouldn't have heard it."
—Pitcher "Wild Bill" Hallahan, a 1926 Cardinal teammate, regarding Hornsby's intense concentration in the batter's box.

HORNSBY: A NOTEWORTHY BOX SCORE

August 8, 1929

Hornsby's fourth-inning home run, one of four hits on the afternoon, beats the Reds 1-0.

Cincinnati	AB	R	H	RBI	PO	A	E	Chicago	AB	R	H	RBI	PO	A	E
Swanson, lf	4	0	1	0	3	0	0	McMillan, 3b	4	0	2	0	1	2	0
Critz, 2b	4	0	2	0	0	3	0	English, ss	4	0	0	0	4	1	1
Walker, rf	3	0	0	0	2	0	0	Hornsby, 2b	4	1	4	1	1	2	0
Kelly, 1b	4	0	0	0	12	1	0	Wilson, cf	4	0	1	0	5	0	1
Allen, cf	4	0	1	0	2	0	0	Cuyler, rf	4	0	0	0	2	0	0
Sukeforth, c	4	0	1	0	3	0	0	Stephenson, lf	3	0	0	0	2	1	0
Ford, ss	4	0	1	0	1	0	1	Tolson, 1b	3	0	0	0	4	0	0
Stripp, 3b	3	0	0	0	1	4	0	Gonzales, c	3	0	0	0	8	1	0
Frey, p	2	0	0	0	1	4	1	Root, p	3	0	0	0	0	0	1
May, p	0	0	0	0	0	1	0								
Lucas, ph	1	0	0	0	0	0	0	TOTALS	32	1	7	1	27	7	3
TOTALS	33	0	6	0	24	13	2								

Cincinnati	000	000	000	— 0
Chicago	000	100	00*	— 1

Doubles--McMillan, Swanson. Home run--Hornsby. Bases on balls--off Root, 1. Struck out--by Root, 4; by Frey, 1; by May, 1. Hits--off Frey, 6 in 7 innings; off May, 1 in 1 inning. Wild pitch--Frey. Losing pitcher--Frey. Umpires: Magerkurth, Rigler, McCormick

Other Baseball Highlights of 1929

- Yankees manager Miller Huggins dies on September 25 of blood poisoning.

- Ty Cobb and Tris Speaker retire before the start of the season.

- On July 5, the Giants become the first major league team to use a public address system.

- White Sox first baseman Art Shires, a prizefighter in the off-season, beats up manager Lena Blackburne three times during the season.

Grover Cleveland Alexander—1920

Chicago Cubs Summit Season
Number 3

No. 3
GROVER CLEVELAND ALEXANDER

BORN: February 26, 1887; Elba, Nebraska
DIED: November 4, 1950; St. Paul, Nebraska
Chicago Cubs: 1918-26
Hall of Fame: 1938

SEASON AT THE SUMMIT: 1920

W-L-%		IP	CG	SH	SV	K/BB	PR	DEF	ERA
27-14	.659	363.1	33	7	5	173/69	50	2	1.91

The Cubs opened the 1920 home season on April 22 with 10,000-plus on hand to get their first look at manager Freddie Mitchell's ballclub. And the pitcher? A cagey veteran possessed of more than adequate speed, a nasty, crackling curveball, and, as always, unwavering, pinpoint control.

That would be **Grover Cleveland Alexander**, who on that occasion bested Dutch Reuther (who was 19-6 for the 1919 world champion Cincinnati Reds) 4-3 in 11 innings. The win reversed a loss in the Cincinnati opener, involving the same pitchers and the same 4-3 score.

It was an auspicious home opener for what would ultimately be an inauspicious Cub season. Jim "Hippo" Vaughn (19-6 in 1920) and Ole Pete were the pitching mainstays on a club that settled for a 75-79 mark and a fifth-place tie with St. Louis, 18 games off Brooklyn's league-leading pace. Season-long injuries, illness and sore arms regularly plagued the Cubs almost from the opening of spring camp at Catalina Island, California. The club never really got it all together to make a sustained run at the top. Sporadic hitting and a questionable defense added to the team's woes, and by August both players and fans were looking to a new season.

No Stopping Him

Not so Alexander, who just kept rolling toward still another 30-win season, though stymied by 3-0, 2-0 and 1-0 defeats as well as other assorted one-run losses—not to mention his personal battles with alcohol and epilepsy. He wound up with 27 victories, good enough to place him second behind Miner Brown for the most wins in a season in Cubs' modern history. The 27 wins represented 36 percent of the Cubs' total (Vaughn contributed another 25 percent).

Alexander appeared in 46 games for the Cubs in 1920, employing the same formula that nurtured his Hall-of-Fame career from Day 1: Know the hitter and keep the ball away from his sweet spot. Alexander had it down to perfection: low and away or high and tight, yet slicing the edges of the strike zone just enough to frustrate the best of them. His 1920 log showed 69 walks, one for every 5⅓ innings pitched. Even that miserly sum was countered by his league-leading 173 strikeouts, most of which he saved for tight spots.

Alexander put together an eight-game winning streak early in the season until it was snapped on June 4 by the Cardinals and Rogers Hornsby, who pounded out a pair of triples to lead the way. By June 19, Alexander was back in control, beating Al Mamaux and Brooklyn in 12 innings on Fred Merkle's double. It was a fairly typical outing: Hang on in the tight spots and find a way to win.

The highlight of Alexander's season came on August 27 at Cubs Park (it would be renamed Wrigley Field later). Future Hall-of-Famer Burleigh Grimes, "Old Stubble-beard," and his Brooklyn Robins were in town, and the two grumpy old men locked horns in a classic pitchers' duel, Alex besting the testy spitballer 1-0. The lone run was scratched out, à la the turn-of-the-century Cub teams, with a single, sacrifice (Alexander's) and two more singles with just enough snap to get the winning run home.

A Whole New Ballgame

The 1920 season marked a turning point in the game. Baseball was being shaken by the burgeoning Black Sox scandal, a constant and irritating reference point throughout the 1920 season. Then there was the tragedy of baseball's only death during a major-league game—the August 16 beaning and subsequent death of popular Cleveland shortstop Ray Chapman. The game itself was changing too. Gone were the conventions of "inside baseball"—the hit-and-run, the bunt, the base-to-base strategies, the slap hitters—replaced by a barrage of base hits, long-distance shots that awed the fans, and sluggers like Babe Ruth.

Many of baseball's great deadball-era stars were caught in various stages of their careers as the power game came into vogue, much of their game becoming obsolete. Alexander, entering his 10th major-league season, was one of them, and he had to find ways to stay ahead of the game.

In addition, the alcoholism and epilepsy were lesser demons with which to contend than the lasting effects of his service in World War I, which were a very real part of his every pitch from 1919 forward. Donald Honig in *Baseball America* brought the extent of Alexander's wartime devastation in focus:

"A dozen years later [after World War I] Alexander was sitting on the bench during spring training. 'Some kids up in the grandstand started shooting off fireworks,' teammate Bill Hallahan recalled. 'A few guys gave a little start with each burst. But Alex never budged. He just sat there stiff as a board, teeth clenched, fists doubled over so tight his knuckles were white, staring off into space like he was hypnotized. When finally someone came and chased the kids off and the noise stopped, he turned and looked at me with a sad little smile.'"

Grover Cleveland Alexander nonetheless proceeded in his effortless, inimitable way, emerging from the 1920 season as the Cubs' last pitching Triple Crown winner. He led the league in wins (27), ERA (1.91) and strikeouts (173) as well as innings pitched (363⅓) and complete games (33). He was also second in shutouts (seven to Pittsburgh's Babe Adams' eight). It was a virtuoso performance, one that surely would have been recognized with the Cy Young Award had it been part of the annual postseason honors in 1920.

GROVER ALEXANDER'S

Three Other Great Cub Seasons

	Yr	W-L	IP	GS	GC	SH	SV	PD	K/BB	OBA	OB%	ERA	PR
1.	1919	16-11	235	27	20	9	1	5	121/38	.211	.245	1.72	31
2.	1923	22-12	305	36	26	3	2	4	72/30	.259	.277	3.19	28
3.	1925	15-11	236	30	20	1	0	-2	63/29	.288	.312	3.39	23

They called him "Old Low and Away" because that's about where he put his pitches, especially when he needed a ground ball, a K, or an otherwise harmless out. Though he would not enjoy any more of those Philadelphia years that set him apart as the next Mathewson almost overnight, particularly after the devastation of World War I, there was enough left in his arm during a nine-year Chicago stay to keep on racking up a number of choice seasons. The three cited above are no match for his 1920 season, but note his K/BB ratio, his defensive numbers, and those low opponents' BA's. Those are all marks of pitching superiority. His lofty spot, No. 3 all time among the Cubs' summiteers, is no fluke. Pete earned his No. 3!

Alex's casual approach to getting ready for a ballgame bothered some of his coaches and managers. One of them, Artie Fletcher, once asked him when he was going to cut loose. Alexander looked at Fletcher and said:

"When I get out there in the middle of the diamond, that's when."

ALEXANDER: A NOTEWORTHY BOX SCORE

August 27, 1920

The Cubs push across a third-inning run against Burliegh Grimes, and the 33-year-old Alexander makes it stand up for the victory.

Brooklyn	AB	R	H	PO	A	E	Chicago	AB	R	H	P	A	E
Olson, ss	4	0	2	3	3	0	Flack, rf	4	0	3	3	1	0
Johnson, 2b	3	0	0	1	3	0	Terry, ss	3	0	1	3	5	1
Griffith, rf	4	0	1	3	0	0	Robertson, lf	4	0	0	1	0	0
Neis, pr	0	0	0	0	0	0	Merkle, 1b	3	0	0	14	0	0
Wheat, lf	4	0	1	3	0	0	Paskert, cf	3	0	1	3	0	0
Myers, cf	4	0	0	2	0	0	Deal, 3b	2	0	0	1	1	0
Koney, 1b	4	0	0	7	3	0	Herzog, 2b	3	0	1	1	6	0
Kilduff, 2b	3	0	0	3	2	0	O'Farrell, c	3	1	1	1	2	0
Miller, c	3	0	1	2	8	0	Alexander, p	2	0	0	0	3	0
Grimes, p	3	0	1	2	0	0							
							TOTALS	26	1	7	27	18	1
TOTALS	31	0	6	24	14	0							

```
Brooklyn    000  000  000  -- 0
Chicago     001  000  00*  -- 1
```

Other Baseball Highlights of 1920

- Babe Ruth plays his first season as a New York Yankee, hitting 54 homers and batting .376.

- Cleveland shortstop Ray Chapman dies on August 17, a day after being beaned by New York's Carl Mays.

- Late in the season, eight members of the White Sox are suspended for throwing the 1919 World Series.

- The spitball is abolished.

Ronald Edward Santo—1966

Chicago Cubs Summit Season
Number 4

No. 4
RON SANTO

BORN: February 25, 1940; Seatle, Washington

Chicago Cubs: 1960-1973

SEASON AT THE SUMMIT: 1966

AB-R-H	BA	OB%	2B	3B	HR	RBI	BR	FR	SB
561-93-175	.312	.417	21	8	30	94	50	29	4

How much did **RON SANTO** love playing baseball?

"If a fellow came up to me tomorrow," he said in a 1966 interview, "and said he'd give me one million dollars to quit playing baseball, I'd tell him to get lost."

A $1 million check would be a pay cut for most players today. But remember, this was 1966, when the average salary was less than $20,000.

Santo's love for the game was probably never more evident than in 1966, the best season of his career. He put up great numbers and was the clubhouse leader on a team that was the worst in the majors—achievements that 25 years later would have earned him one of those million-dollar paychecks.

Slow Start for Cubs
The Cubs opened the 1966 campaign by losing their first two games, managing just seven hits in a pair of defeats in San Francisco. Santo, hitless in the two games, got on track the next day, homering in his first at-bat and later adding a single as the Cubs gave new manager Leo Durocher his first victory, 9-4, over the Giants.

The win would be the Cubs' only one in the first week of the season as they dropped into last place at 1-5. On April 21, after they had lost their fifth in a row, the shakeups started. They sent pitchers Bob Buhl and Larry Jackson to Philadelphia for Adolfo Phillips, John Herrnstein and Fergie Jenkins. The youth movement resuscitated the Cubs only briefly. On April 24, Jenkins homered and drove in another run with a single as the Cubs beat Los Angeles, 2-0, to improve to 2-8 and move into ninth place by percentage points. But by the end of the month the Cubs had settled into last place, where they would remain.

Santo, though, was having considerably more success than his teammates: two hits off Sandy Koufax—on his way to a spectacular season—on April 22; a pair of homers against Pittsburgh on the 28th; and a 3-for-4 day against Philadelphia on May 1 that raised his average to .368.

But then came a disappointing 1-for-11 series against Houston—the Cubs lost all three games—that dropped him to .328. He began struggling at the plate, and a week later was all the way down to .286. By the end of the month, he was in the .270s, the Cubs were dead last at 13-29, and Durocher was again shaking up his ballclub.

He moved Ernie Banks from first base to third. And he made Santo his shortstop. The first three games of the experiment were losses, and Santo—never one to hide his feelings—was beside himself. "I feel so bad I don't even want to make the rest of this trip," he told reporters in Philadelphia.

The Streak
Fortunately for Santo he decided to stay. On June 4 against Cincinnati, he had two homers and a single—the Reds' Deron Johnson robbed him of another extra-base hit with a great catch—in a 6-4 Cub victory. The next day he went 2 for 3 and 1 for 5 as the Cubs and Reds split a pair. On June 18, he hit two homers in a 13-5 loss to Houston that gave him a 16-game hitting streak and moved him over .300. The next day he went 1 for 3 and 1 for 2—both hits coming in his last at-bat—in a sweep of the Astros, stretching his streak to 18 games.

"I can just imagine how it was with Joe DiMaggio when he went 56 in a row," Santo said. "I'm nowhere near anything like that, but already the pitchers are giving me less and less strikes."

Santo's hitting streak was threatened not by cautious pitchers but by a reckless one two days later. On June 21, the Giants' Juan Marichal slid into Santo on a play at third, lacerating his knee and sending him to the hospital. Despite four deep cuts, he was back in the lineup the next day, going 1 for 3 and 2 for 4 in a double-header to run his streak to 22.

Santo's next injury was considerably more serious. On June 26, he singled in the first inning against the Mets' Jack Fisher. The next time up—after the Cubs' Phillips and the Mets' Ron Hunt had been hit by pitches—Santo was struck in the face by a Fisher pitch. He spun away a split second before impact, but still took the ball on his left cheekbone. Santo's eye swelled shut almost instantly and he was taken to Wesley Memorial Hospital, where surgery was performed the next day to reduce the fracture.

True Grit
The injury, which brought an end to Santo's streak of consecutive games played at 390, would keep him out almost two weeks, doctors said. But six days after the surgery, he was taking batting practice—hitting seven balls out of Wrigley Field, according to one witness. He pronounced himself ready, and returned to the lineup the next day—in a big way.

Santo had three singles in the first game of a double-header against Pittsburgh, then provided the game-winning single in Game 2. It left him at .319, tied for fifth in the National League, and with a club record-tying 27-game hitting streak.

The next day, though, Santo's streak came to an end—even though it grew by one game. He was held hitless by the Pirates' Woody Fryman, flying out, grounding out twice and walking (after fouling off a half-dozen pitches). But instead of finishing with a 27-game streak, it went into the books as 28 games. Santo's streak had been calculated as starting in the second game of a double-header in Philadelphia on June 1. In Game 1 that day, he had walked four times and had been hit by a pitch. The league ruled, though, that streaks could not be ended by unofficial plate appearances. Because he had gone 1 for 3 the day before, that was then recognized as the start of the streak.

Santo put together another streak in 1966—hitting in 12 straight until being stopped by Atlanta's Ken Johnson on August 3. He kept his average in the low .300s the rest of the season, winding up at a Cub-best .312. But his league-leading 94 walks helped him to a .417 on-base percentage—also best in the NL. His 94 RBIs and 30 homers were also team highs. Million-dollar stats, no matter the season.

RON SANTO'S

Four Other Great Cub Seasons

	YR	GP	AB-R-H	BA	OB%	SA	K/BB	HR	RBI	SB	FR	BR
1.	1964	161	592-94-185	.313	.401	.564	96/86	30	114	3	17	50
2.	1965	164	608-88-173	.285	.379	.510	109/88	33	101	3	19	37
3.	1967	161	586-107-176	.300	.401	.512	103/96	31	98	1	31	43
4.	1968	162	577-86-142	.246	.357	.421	106/96	26	98	3	17	20

Between 1963 and 1969, Ron Santo averaged a 5.3 Total Player Rating. Those are Hall of Fame numbers. His 1964 and '67 seasons would easily rate Top 50 rankings were it not for our one-season-per-player ruling. He was not only a consistent run-producer and a constant long-ball threat, but carried his leather with distinction. Note his 31 fielding runs in 1967, indicative of his third-base prowess.

On being selected for the Cubs' team out of the Mesa, Arizona, training camp for top prospects, Santo had this to say in an interview with Peter Golenbock:

"Rogers (Hornsby, the hitting instructor) said, 'You,' meaning me, 'can hit in the big leagues right now.' And then he went through the rest of the guys, and it was back to the same old thing. It was everybody (out) but Billy (Williams) and me.

"I was thinking, These are the prospects, young kids. What does he know?

"We were the only two that made it to the big leagues."
—Peter Golenbock, *Wrigleyville*

Other Baseball Highlights of 1966

• An arthritic elbow forces Sandy Koufax to retire at the age of 30. His numbers for his final season: 27 victories, 317 strikeouts and a 1.73 ERA.

• Marvin Miller is elected president of the Major League Players Association.

• The Dodgers repeat as NL champions but are swept in four straight by the Orioles in the World Series.

SANTO: A NOTEWORTHY BOX SCORE

June 4, 1966 at Cincinnati

Santo continues his league-best 28-game hitting streak with a 3-for-4 performance against the Cincinnati Reds. Santo clubs a pair of home runs, two of 30 he'd hit in 1966.

Chicago	AB	R	H	RBI	PO	A	E	Cincinnati	AB	R	H	RBI	PO	A	E
Phillips, cf	3	2	2	0	5	0	0	Harper, rf	4	0	1	0	1	0	0
Beckert, 2b	4	0	1	0	3	3	0	Helms, 2b	4	1	1	0	1	2	0
Williams, rf	3	1	1	1	2	0	0	Pinson, cf	4	0	1	0	2	0	0
Santo, 3b	4	3	3	3	1	2	0	Perez, 1b	3	0	0	1	9	1	0
Banks, 1b	4	0	1	1	7	1	0	Rose, 2b	4	1	3	1	2	5	0
Browne, lf	2	0	0	0	3	0	0	Pavletich, c	4	0	0	0	8	0	3
Hundley, c	4	0	0	0	3	1	0	Johnson, lf	4	0	3	0	1	0	0
Kessinger, ss	4	0	0	0	2	3	0	Cardenas, ss	3	1	1	1	2	3	0
Holtzman, p	3	0	0	0	1	1	0	Ellis, p	2	0	0	0	0	0	0
Jenkins, p	0	0	0	0	0	0	0	Nottebart, p	0	0	0	0	1	0	0
Hoeft, p	0	0	0	0	0	0	0	Ruiz, ph	1	0	0	0	0	0	0
								Shamsky, ph	0	0	0	0	0	0	0
TOTALS	31	5	7	5	27	11	0	Simpson, ph	1	0	0	0	0	0	0
								TOTALS	34	3	10	3	27	11	3

```
Chicago       0 0 0   2 0 2   0 0 1  --5
Cincinnati    0 0 0   1 1 0   0 0 1  --3
```

Doubles--Harper, Williams. Home runs--Santo (2), Cardenas, Rose. Stolen bases--Phillips, Browne, Santo. Sacrifice flies--Williams, Perez. Double plays--Cincinnati 1, Chicago 1.

	IP	H	R	ER	BB	SO
Holtzman (W, 2-6)	7 1/3	8	2	2	1	2
Jenkins	1 1/3	2	1	1	0	0
Hoeft	1/3	0	0	0	0	1
Ellis (l, 2-8)	7	5	4	4	2	6
Nottebart	2	2	1	0	1	1

Attendance: 4,012. Time--2:35. Umpires: Barlick, Donatelli, Landes, Steiner

Mordecai Brown—1906

Chicago Cubs Summit Season
Number 5

No. 5
MORDECAI BROWN

BORN: October 19, 1876; Nyesville, Indiana
DIED: February 14, 1948; Terre Haute, Indiana

Chicago Colts/Cubs: 1904-1912; 1916
Hall of Fame: 1949

SEASON AT THE SUMMIT: 1906

W-L-%		IP	CG	SH	SV	K/BB	PR	DEF	ERA
26-6	.813	277.1	27	9	3	144/61	49	2	1.04

No less an authority than Ty Cobb called **Mordecai Brown**'s curveball "the most devastating pitch I ever faced."

Brown became one of baseball's greatest pitchers by accident. Literally. As a seven-year-old boy in Nyesville, Indiana, he lost his index finger in a farm accident. A few weeks later he broke his middle finger and pinkie while chasing a hog. They didn't heal properly and he was left with two gnarled, misshapen fingers on his right hand—his throwing hand.

Brown eventually discovered that the deformed hand let him do amazing things with a baseball. "That old paw served me pretty well in its time," he reminisced as an old man. "It gave me a firmer grip on the ball, so I could spin it over the hump. It gave me a greater dip."

The curve was his money pitch—Brown didn't have much of a fastball—but he had an effective change and screwball. An excellent fielder ("the greatest fielding pitcher the game ever had," said his manager, Frank Chance), he was a fitness buff who kept himself in top shape.

Brown also was a thinking man's pitcher who studied hitters and exploited their weaknesses.

Brown—"Brownie" to friends, "Miner" (he had worked in a mine earlier in his life) or "Three-Finger" in the newspapers—came to Chicago in a deal with St. Louis before the 1904 season. He blossomed into a winner in his first two years with the Cubs, winning 15 and 18 games, before he put together his memorable 1906 season.

Fast Start
The Cubs, Pittsburgh and New York jostled for first place early in the season. Brown was a big reason Chicago was in the race. He won six of his first eight decisions—despite straining his back and missing a couple of turns—including a 1-0 four-hitter against Cincinnati on April 28 and an impressive 7-2 win over the heavy-hitting Pirates on May 4.

Brown went 4-2 in June for the Cubs, who had moved into first on May 28. The first week of the month, Chicago invaded the Polo Grounds for a big four-game series with the Giants, who were only a game out when the Cubs came to town. Brown was masterful in the opener outdueling Joe McGinnity 6-0 on a three-hitter. Chicago won three of four in the series, and the month ended with the Cubs in first at 46-20, two games ahead of the Pirates and 3½ ahead of the Giants.

As the season wore on, Brown gained momentum. He was never better than the morning of July 4 when he beat the Pirates 1-0 in Pittsburgh. He allowed but one hit—a third-inning single by Pirate pitcher Lefty Leifield, who himself allowed just one hit, a ninth-inning single by Jimmy Slagle that produced the game's only run. (The two pitchers met again three days later, with Brown beating the Pirates 5-0 on a four-hitter.)

Brown rolled through July—beating Boston and New York on back-to-back seven-hitters and ending the month with a 5-0 shutout of the Braves. In the victory over the Giants he outdueled Christy Mathewson, part of a three-year stretch during which Brown beat the great Matty nine consecutive times.

Tough Customer
Brown was becoming almost impossible to score against. He blanked Philadelphia 1-0 on August 3, then stopped the Giants three days later (he allowed one unearned run). He shut out Brooklyn on August 10. He led the Dodgers 10-0 after seven innings on the 15th (Cub relievers let Brooklyn get back in the game with seven runs, but Brown still got the win). He allowed only one earned run in a 6-2 victory over the Giants on the 18th, and wrapped up August with a 4-2 win over New York on the 21st, two innings of scoreless relief against the Braves on the 25th, and an eight-hit shutout of the Reds on the 28th.

On September 1, he beat the Cardinals 8-1 with a five-hitter, the 14th straight win for the Cubs, who in one stretch won 37 of 39 to turn the National League race into a runaway.

At that point, the bigger baseball news in Chicago was across town. The White Sox had the look of an also-ran for most of the season; when August began they were entrenched in fourth place with a 50-42 record, 8½ games behind first-place Philadelphia. But manager Fielder Jones' boys—his "Hitless Wonders" who would bat a league-low .230—put together a 19-game winning streak in August to get back in the race. They battled the Yankees down the stretch before finally taking the lead for good in the last days of the season, setting the stage for baseball's first crosstown World Series.

Brown's pace slowed in September. He was roughed up by Boston in a 6-4 loss on the 18th, and took himself out of the Cubs-Giants game of the 24th, a game he still won, because of a sore arm. He still finished the season as the dominant pitcher in the NL: a 26-6 record and league-leading ERA (1.04, the second best ever recorded). He was first in shutouts (nine), and third in hits allowed per game (6.43) and opponents' batting average (.202). On paper, it seemed the Cubs—who finished 106-36 and were the NL leaders in hits, runs and batting and slugging averages—would make short work of the punchless White Sox. Such was not the case.

World Series Surprise
The World Series opened on October 9 at the Cubs' West Side Grounds with the Sox's Nick Altrock outdueling Brown 2-1. Both teams managed only four hits, but the South Siders used unearned runs in the fourth and fifth to take a 1-0 Series lead. The teams split the next two contests, and Brown took the mound on the 12th for Game 4.

He was nearly untouchable, stopping the Sox 1-0 on two hits—a sixth-inning single by Ed Hahn and an eighth-inning single by Patsy Dougherty—as the Cubs evened the Series. After the Sox came back to win Game 5 on the 13th—they exploded for eight runs and 12 hits—Chance decided to go with his ace in Game 6.

But Brown, working with just one day's rest, couldn't come through. He was knocked around in the first inning, surrendering three runs. He didn't make it through the second, leaving with the Sox ahead 5-1. They went on to win the game 8-3 and the Series in six games.

The disappointment of the 1906 World Series was just a bump in the road for Brown, a road that would take him to 122 victories over the next five seasons, 239 career wins and a deserved place in baseball's Hall of Fame.

MORDECAI BROWN'S

Four Other Great Cub Seasons

	Yr	W-L	IP	GS	GC	SH	SV	PD	K/BB	OBA	OB%	ERA	PR
1.	1907	20-6	233	27	20	6	3	4	107/40	.221	.262	1.39	28
2.	1908	29-9	312.1	31	27	9	5	-1	123/49	.195	.232	1.47	31
3.	1909	27-9	342.2	34	32	8	7	-1	172/53	.202	.239	1.31	49
4.	1910	25-14	295.1	31	27	6	7	3	143/64	.232	.277	1.86	39

The story is told about two Giants fans in Chicago for a big ballgame. They were wondering how many runs the New Yorkers were going to score, and were informed by a Cubs fan who overheard them: "You'll need more'n you're gonna get cause Miner's pitchin'!" And that's about the way things usually went with "Three Finger" Brown pitching. Those Brown-Mathewson confrontations were made in Baseball's Valhalla, bringing out the best not only in the pitchers, but in those two bitter antagonists, the New Yorks and the Chicagos, as well. Both hurlers had the HOF stamp on them right from the beginning. Brown's 1906 season belongs with the Cubs' very best single-season summiteers.

"In addition to two major league pennants and a world's championship, Chicago has produced this year a pitching wonder, greater than the great Mathewson, even at Christy's best. Mordecai Brown of the new National League champions with only three working fingers is the man..."

—Chicago Tribune on Mordecai Brown following the 1906 season

BROWN: A NOTEWORTHY BOX SCORE

July 4, 1906

Brown beats the Pirates 1-0 with a one-hitter, outdueling Lefty Leifield, who allowed just one hit himself.

Pittsburgh	R	H	PO	A	E	Chicago	R	H	PO	A	E
Beaumont, cf	0	0	4	0	0	Slagle, cf	1	1	2	0	0
Ganley, rf	0	0	1	0	0	Sheckard, lf	0	0	1	0	0
Leach, lf	0	0	4	0	0	Schulte, rf	0	0	1	0	0
Wagner, ss	0	0	1	4	1	Chance, 1b	0	0	2	0	0
Nealon, 1b	0	0	9	1	1	Steinfeldt, rf	0	0	0	4	0
Sheehan, 3b	0	0	2	2	0	Tinker, ss	0	0	3	0	0
Ritchey, 2b	0	0	2	3	1	Evers, 2b	0	0	0	4	0
Phelps, c	0	0	4	0	1	Kling, c	0	0	8	1	0
Leifield, p	0	1	0	1	0	Brown, p	0	0	0	1	0
TOTALS	0	1	27	11	4	TOTALS	1	1	27	10	0

```
Pittsburgh    000  000  000  --0
Chicago       000  000  001  --1
```

Sacrifice--Sheckard. Double play--Chicago, 1. Bases on balls--off Brown, 4. Hit by pitcher--Phelps. Struck out--by Leifield, 5; by Brown, 5. Passed ball--Phelps. Left on base--Pittsburgh, 5; Chicago, 5. Time--1:40. Umpires--O'Day, Johnstone.

Other Baseball Highlights of 1906

- The NL's Boston Beaneaters finish last, 66½ games out of first.

- The Cubs' Jack Taylor's record streak of 187 consecutive complete games ends on August 9.

- In September, the A's go 48 straight innings without scoring a run.

Ernie Banks—1959

Chicago Cubs Summit Season
Number 6

No. 6
ERNIE BANKS

BORN: January 31, 1931; Dallas, Texas

Chicago Cubs: 1953-1971
Hall of Fame: 1977

SEASON AT THE SUMMIT: 1959

AB-R-H	BA	OB%	2B	3B	HR	RBI	BR	FR	SB
589-97-179	.304	.379	25	6	45	143	46	6	2

Ernie Banks came to Wrigley Field in 1953 a shy, skinny, 22-year-old shortstop. When he left in 1971, he was Mr. Cub.

What transpired during those 19 years made Banks the most beloved—and possibly the best—player in team history. He appeared in 2,528 games in a Cub uniform, more than anyone else; he hit 512 home runs, including 12 grand slams; he drove in 1,636 runs; he was National League Most Valuable Player in 1958 and '59; and in 1977 he was elected to the Hall of Fame.

Banks was one of the few bright spots on some terrible teams in the '50s and early '60s. But no matter how badly the team was doing, fans could count on two things: Banks' consistent performance and his relentlessly sunny ("Let's play two") disposition. No wonder he was so well-liked.

Born in Dallas in 1931, Banks joined the Negro League's Kansas City Monarchs when he was 19. He later served two years in the armed forces, and when he returned home in 1953 he rejoined the Monarchs. On September 7, 1953, the Cubs purchased Banks for $20,000.

He played in 10 games for the Cubs in the last month of the 1953 season, getting 11 hits, including two homers, in 35 at-bats. In his first full season, he hit .275 with 19 homers and 79 RBIs. Toward the end of the 1954 season, he made a change that would put him in the record books.

Turning Into A Hitter

He had been using a 34-ounce bat; but he switched to a lighter (31-ounce), snappier bat that was perfect for his physical attributes (he was slightly built but had tremendously strong forearms and quick wrists). "With the heavier bat, I just couldn't get my bat around," he once explained. "The lighter one whips better, especially for a wrist hitter like me."

For proof, one had only to look at his performance in 1955: 44 home runs and 117 runs batted in. He followed that with 28- and 48-homer seasons. In his first MVP season, he had 47 homers, 129 RBIs and a .614 slugging percentage—all league-leading figures.

The 1958 season is regarded by many as the pinnacle of Banks' career. But in 1959 he combined both offense

(45 homers, 143 RBIs, .304 batting average, .596 slugging percentage) with a greatly improved defense (a league-best .985 with only 12 errors) to earn the No. 6 spot on the roster of all-time great Cub seasons.

His Best Season

Banks wasted little time playing the hero at the outset of the 1959 season. On April 14 he hit two home runs to beat San Francisco; on the 30th, another homer beat Cincinnati; after 13 games he was hitting .367. He was down to .286 but with 12 homers and 45 RBIs by the end of May.

He put together an impressive stretch of hitting from June 12 through 23. On the 12th he went 3 for 4, including his 16th homer and third in three days, to help beat the Braves. He was 2 for 4 the next day, then hit the 200th homer of his career on the 14th. He chalked up 2-for-4 and 3-for-4 games against the Pirates; a 7-for-12 series against the Phillies; and a 2-for-3 day against the Reds to conclude his 11-game hot streak, during which he hit .538 (21 for 39) to get his average over .300 again and belted four home runs, giving him 19 for the season.

Banks' 20th homer came in dramatic fashion. The Cubs and Reds were playing in Cincinnati on June 25. In the second inning, Cubs starter Bob Anderson hit the Reds' Frank Robinson with a pitch, sending him to the hospital for X-rays. When Banks came to bat in the fourth, Reds starter Bob Purkey threw behind him. The next pitch hit him. Banks got his revenge the next time up, belting Purkey's first pitch in the sixth for a long home run—the ball hit a factory behind Crosley Field's center-field wall—to snap a 1-1 tie and send the Cubs on to a 6-2 victory.

His 20 homers and 68 RBIs—and improved defense—by late June helped make Banks the overwhelming choice as the starting shortstop in the All-Star voting conducted among NL players (at the break, he was at .302 with 23 homers). In the July 7 game at Pittsburgh, he had two doubles in three trips as the NL posted a 5-4 victory. (He wasn't as lucky in the second All-Star Game of 1959, going 0 for 4 in a 5-3 NL loss on August 3.)

The Cubs found themselves in fifth place at the break at 39-41, 6 ½ games behind first-place Milwaukee. Had they had some hitting to support Banks—he had 78 RBIs at the break, one more than the entire Cub outfield combined—they would have been able to mount a challenge. As it was, they were stuck in the middle of the pack, hovering around .500 most of the year, before finally finishing tied for fifth with the Reds at 74-80.

A Hitter's Hitter

Banks continued to be the most consistent Cub through July. He tripled and homered on the 11th to help beat Pittsburgh 5-1, ending a five-game Cub losing streak; his 25th homer on the 16th helped beat Milwaukee (and complete a sweep that knocked the Braves from first to third); and another homer on the 21st helped beat St. Louis. By the end of the month he was at .310 with 29 homers and 98 RBIs.

As the Cubs continued to tread water in the NL race, all their fans could do was watch Banks' numbers climb: He got his 30th homer and 100th RBI on August 5 against Philadelphia; he hit No. 40 in the second game of a double-header sweep of the pennant-bound Dodgers on September 7; homer No. 45 came on September 25, again against the Dodgers.

The next day Banks took a Johnny Podres pitch in the calf. The leg was sore enough on the 27th to keep him out of the starting lineup for the season finale. But Banks, who had played in a Cub-record 497 consecutive games to that point, went up as a pinch-hitter in the seventh—he popped up—to keep his streak alive. (The Dodgers won the game 7-1, forcing a playoff with Milwaukee for the NL pennant.)

Banks' 143 RBIs led the majors (his closest competitor was Cincinnati's Robinson with 125). In addition, he was second in the majors in homers (45 to Milwaukee's Eddie Mathews' 46) and slugging percentage (.596 to the Braves' Hank Aaron's .636). He would never hit as many homers or drive in as many runs again, and his .304 average would be his last over .300. But over the next dozen years, Banks would firmly entrench himself in the hearts of Cub fans, earning forever the tag "Mr. Cub."

ERNIE BANKS'

Four Other Great Cub Seasons

	YR	GP	AB-R-H	BA	OB%	SA	K/BB	HR	RBI	SB	FR	BR
1.	1955	154	596-98-176	.295	.347	.596	72/45	44	117	9	5	35
2.	1958	154	617-119-193	.313	.370	.614	87/52	47	129	4	-2	48
3.	1960	156	597-94-162	.271	.353	.554	69/71	41	117	1	11	36
4.	1961	138	511-75-142	.278	.349	.507	75/54	29	80	1	13	15

Mr. Cub. 'Nuff said. Whether as player or as the Cubs' Goodwill Ambassador, he's loved by fans everywhere. His orbital years at Wrigleyville had something to do with that, of course, but so did his congeniality and effervescence. So good were his 1955, 1958, 1959 and 1960 seasons that each merit a summit ranking. We've picked his 1959 MVP year as the sixth-best Cub season, all time, a hair's breadth ahead of his 1958 or 1960 campaigns, both of which rank on about a par. The great Banks years came at the more demanding of the positions he played with consummate skill and grace, shortstop. After 1961 he moved to first base where he finished out his spectacular career. The Wrigley Field foul pole proudly wears his No. 14, the first Cub number to be retired. 'Nuff said!

"I'm a cleanup man who has nothing to clean up. Let me hit seventh—maybe someone will be on base. While I'm waiting for my turn at bat, I at least get my picture in the paper when the photographer takes a picture of Ernie crossing the plate."
—**Cub cleanup hitter Walt Moryn on what it was like hitting behind Ernie Banks in 1959**

Other Baseball Highlights of 1959

• The White Sox win the AL pennant—their first since 1919—but lose to the Dodgers in the Series in six games.

• The Red Sox become the last major-league team to cross the color line when they bring up Pumpsie Green.

• Bill Veeck buys the White Sox.

BANKS: A NOTEWORTHY BOX SCORE

April 14, 1959

Banks hits two home runs to give Bob Hillman and the Cubs a 5-2 victory over the Giants.

Chicago	AB	R	H	RBI	PO	A	E	San Francisco	AB	R	H	RBI	PO	A	E
T. Taylor	4	0	0	0	3	2	0	Davenport, 3b	4	0	2	0	1	0	0
Altman, cf	4	2	1	0	2	0	0	Brandt, lf	4	0	0	0	1	0	0
Banks, ss	3	2	2	4	3	3	0	Mays, cf	4	0	1	0	3	0	0
Moryn, lf	4	0	0	0	1	0	0	Cepeda, 1b	4	1	2	0	9	0	1
Averill, 3b	4	0	1	0	1	3	1	Alou, rf	4	1	2	2	1	0	0
Long, 1b	3	0	2	0	8	0	0	Spencer, 2b	4	0	0	0	1	4	0
Thomson, rf	3	0	0	0	4	1	0	Rodgers, ss	3	0	1	0	4	4	1
S. Taylor, c	2	1	0	0	4	1	0	Schmidt, c	4	0	1	0	8	0	0
Hillman, p	4	0	0	0	1	3	0	Sanford, p	2	0	0	0	0	3	0
Elston, p	0	0	0	0	0	0	0	Wagner, ph	1	0	0	0	0	0	0
								Worthington, p	0	0	0	0	0	0	0
TOTALS	33	5	6	4	27	13	1								
								TOTALS	34	2	9	2	27	11	2

Chicago	0 0 0	2 0 0	0 2 1	-- 5		
San Francisco	0 2 0	0 0 0	0 0 0	-- 2		

Double--Averill. Triple--Long. Home runs--Alou, Banks. Stolen base--S. Taylor. Double plays--Chicago 2, San Francisco 1. Left on base--Chicago 7, San Francisco 6.

	IP	H	R	ER	BB	SO
Sanford (L, 0-1)	8	8	4	4	4	7
Worthington	1	0	1	1	1	1
Hillman (W, 1-0)	8 1/2	8	2	2	0	2
Elston	2/3	1	0	0	0	2

Hit by pitcher--by Worthington (S. Taylor); by Elston (Rodgers). Wild pitch--Worthington. Time 2:37. Attendance: 22,489

Ryne Sandberg—1984

Chicago Cubs Summit Season
Number 7

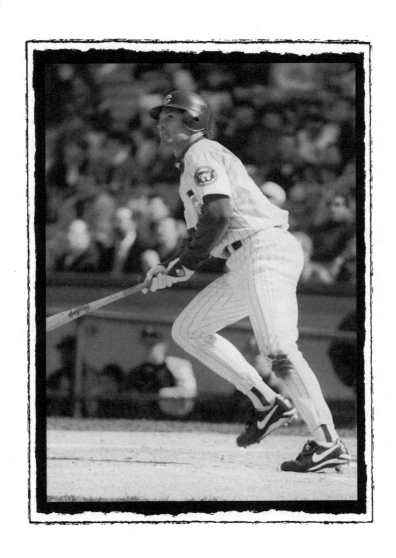

No. 7
RYNE SANDBERG

BORN: September 18, 1959; Spokane, Washington

Chicago Cubs: 1982-1994; 1996-

SEASON AT THE SUMMIT: 1984

AB-R-H	BA	OB%	2B	3B	HR	RBI	BR	FR	SB
636-114-200	.314	.369	36	19	19	84	28	23	32

He was a good player who became a legend in one astonishing day, a player whose career was defined by an incredible performance on a beautiful summer afternoon.

What **Ryne Sandberg** did on June 23, 1984 will never be forgotten by anyone who saw it. And millions of people did.

The third-place Cubs were hosting the fifth-place St. Louis Cardinals before a national television audience. For two hours, it wasn't much of a show. The Cardinals led 7-1 after two innings and 9-3 after 5½. The Cubs came back with five runs in the bottom of the sixth, highlighted by Sandberg's third hit of the day, a two-run double.

It was still 9-8 when Sandberg led off the bottom of the ninth against the Cardinals' relief ace Bruce Sutter, against whom he was 1 for 10 lifetime. Sandberg connected on one of Sutter's split-fingered fastballs and sent it into the bleachers to force extra innings.

There was little time for celebration, though, as the Cardinals pushed across two runs in the top of the 10th. In the Cub half, the first two hitters went down before Sutter walked Bob Dernier on a 3-2 count. "Then comes Baby Ruth," Cardinals manager Whitey Herzog would later say.

With a 1-1 count, Sandberg got hold of another Sutter split-finger and sent it into the left-field bleachers, tying the score at 11, setting the stage for the Cubs' winning rally in the 11th. A legend had been born.

"To go up there and think I'm going to hit a home run again is unbelievable," said Sandberg, who was 5 for 6 with seven RBIs for the day. "I'm in a state of shock."

"Sandberg is the best player I have ever seen," said Herzog.

Pressure To Produce

It's impossible to overstate what Sandberg's heroics that day meant to the future NL East champs. He electrified Wrigley Field, of course, and in front of a national audience no less. He made himself a star. And he turned the Cubs' season around.

The Cubs found themselves in a make-or-break situation in 1984. General manager Dallas Green's "new tradition" had yet to bear fruit. The roster was populated with high-priced talent, and the team was coming off a dismal fifth-place finish. They found themselves in competition for fans—and headlines—with the White Sox, who had won the AL West the year before. And after a disastrous 7-20 spring—worst in the majors—this was clearly a ballclub under the gun.

Green provided new manager Jim Frey two big pieces of the puzzle in the closing days of spring training when he obtained Gary Matthews and Dernier from Philadelphia. Dernier, especially, impacted Sandberg's season. He was a bonafide leadoff man and was installed at the top of the order by Frey, who dropped the 24-year-old Sandberg from the No. 1 spot to No. 2, where he was more at ease. And his manager encouraged him to try to pull inside pitches for home runs to boost his power stats.

Slow Start
It took a while for Sandberg, a notoriously slow starter, to get going. He finally reached .300 on May 7, going 3 for 5 against the Giants. It was the start of a 13-for-29 stretch that earned him NL Player of the Week honors and extended his hitting streak to 16 games. He hit safely in two more games, raising his average to .328, before being stopped by the Reds' Mario Soto on May 17. (Sandberg had another streak snapped six days later when he committed an error on a ground ball by Atlanta's Claudell Washington. It was his first error in 47 games. He would put together a 61-game errorless streak later in the season.)

Sandberg's June heroics weren't confined to his big day against Sutter. On June 1, he had two homers against the Phillies; he had four hits, including a homer, and four runs scored versus the Pirates on the 21st; and he contributed three hits, one a homer, in a June 27 win over the Pirates. His big month—47 hits, seven doubles, six triples, eight homers, 21 RBIs, six stolen bases and a .376 average—earned him NL Player of the Month recognition.

It also helped him get elected starting second baseman for the National League in the 55th All-Star Game. He trailed in the voting with one week left but ended up winning by a quarter-million votes. In the game itself, he had a single and a stolen base in the NL's 3-1 win.

Alternating Heroes
The Cubs got the boost that would put them over the top when they obtained pitcher Rick Sutcliffe from Cleveland in a six-player deal in June. He would go 16-1, winning 14 straight at one point. There were other heroes as well—Matthews, with timely hits and a clubhouse presence that was immeasurable; Keith Moreland, who went 15-for-30 with four homers and 11 RBIs and three game-winning hits in one eight-game stretch (included was a game-winning grand slam on August 5, using one of Sandberg's bats); iron man catcher Jody Davis; reliever Lee Smith ... the list was almost endless.

The Cubs moved into first to stay with a 5-4 victory over the Phillies on August 1. By the end of the month, the NL East title was a foregone conclusion, and they wrapped it up—the franchise's first championship of any kind in nearly 40 years—with a 4-1 victory over the Pirates on September 24, a game in which Sandberg contributed two doubles and two runs scored.

The Cubs' opponent in the NLCS was San Diego. It appeared the Cubs would make short work of the Padres as they won the first two games, in Chicago, 13-0 and 4-2. Sandberg was 2 for 4 in each game, with two runs scored in the opener and an RBI double in Game 2. But that was as far as the dream of 1984 went.

San Diego hammered Dennis Eckersley to win Game 3 7-1. Then came Game 4, when Steve Garvey's two-run homer in the ninth gave the Padres a 4-2 win and tied the series. Game 5 was even more of a nightmare as San Diego rallied for three runs in the seventh—who can forget Tim Flannery's grounder through Leon Durham, or Tony Gwynn's smash that Sandberg failed to handle?—to win 6-3 and capture the NL pennant.

It was a crushing ending to an otherwise magical year. Sandberg was voted NL MVP and Player of the Year by *The Sporting News*. He finished his season with a .314 average, 200 hits, 114 runs (best in the NL), 19 triples (also tops), 36 doubles, 19 homers and a league-high .993 fielding percentage (he made only six errors). He would have other great years—notably 1985, '90, '91 and '92—but none was, overall, comparable to 1984, the year Ryne Sandberg became a legend.

RYNE SANDBERG'S

Three Other Great Cub Seasons

YR	GP	AB-R-H	BA	OB%	SA	K/BB	HR	RBI	SB	FR	BR
1. 1985	153	609-113-186	.305	.366	.504	97/57	26	83	54	8	21
2. 1991	158	585-104-170	.291	.384	.485	89/87	26	100	22	11	30
3. 1992	158	612-100-186	.304	.374	.510	73/68	26	87	17	14	35

In 1985 Ryno became the third 25-homer, 50-steal player in major-league history. During his summit season (1984) he came within an eyelash of becoming the first in the history of the bigs to bag 200 hits, 20 doubles *and* triples, homers, and steals, all in one season, missing it by one dinger and one three-bagger. That's merely a look at the tip of 1984's iceberg of summitry—good enough to be a Top 10 selection on the Cub records that will march this fellow straight to Cooperstown and another flagpole number at the Friendly Confines. Second base at Wrigleyville is a spot only big shoes can fill. Ryno's are sized just right to carry on a magnificent tradition.

"I always tell Ryno, 'I don't want your money, I'd just like to be you for a year, to be able to play like you for a year, to know what it feels like.'"
—**Cubs coach John Vukovich during Sandberg's milestone 1984 season**

SANDBERG: A NOTEWORTHY BOX SCORE

June 23, 1984

Sandberg gets five hits, including 9th- and 10th-inning homers off relief ace Bruce Sutter, in a 12-11 victory over the Cardinals.

St. Louis	AB	R	H	RBI	E	Chicago	AB	R	H	RBI	E
LoSmith, lf	4	1	1	1	0	Dernier, cf	5	3	3	2	1
Sutter, p	1	0	0	0	0	Sandberg, 2b	6	2	5	7	0
Ramsy, ph	1	0	0	0	0	Matthews, lf	5	0	2	1	0
Rucker, p	0	0	0	0	0	Durham, lb	5	2	1	0	0
OSmith, ss	4	4	2	0	0	Moreland, rf	4	1	0	0	0
McGee, cf	6	3	4	6	0	Davis, c	3	0	0	0	1
Hendrick, rf	5	0	1	2	0	Cey, 3b	2	1	0	0	0
Green, lb	5	0	1	0	0	Stoddard, p	0	0	0	0	0
Braun, ph	1	0	0	1	0	Hassey, ph	1	0	0	0	0
Jorgenson, lb	0	0	0	0	0	Frazier, p	0	0	0	0	0
Herr, 2b	6	1	3	0	0	Woods, ph	1	0	0	0	0
Howe, 3b	3	1	0	0	0	LeSmith, p	0	0	0	0	0
Allen, p	0	0	0	0	0	Owen, ph	1	0	1	1	0
Landrum, p	1	0	0	0	0	Bowa, ss	4	1	0	0	0
Salas, lf	1	0	0	0	0	Trout, p	0	0	0	0	0
Porter, c	4	0	0	0	1	Bordi, p	1	0	0	0	0
Citarella, P	3	1	1	1	0	Johnstone, ph	1	1	1	0	0
VanSlyke, 3b	1	0	0	0	0	Noles, p	0	0	0	0	0
Lahti, p	0	0	0	0	0	Brusstar, p	0	0	0	0	0
						Hebner, 3b	3	1	1	1	0
TOTALS	46	11	13	11	1	TOTALS	42	12	14	12	2

```
St. Louis    1 6 0   0 0 2   0 0 0   2  0--11
Chicago      1 0 0   0 2 5   0 0 1   2  1--12
```

None out when winning run scored

Doubles--Matthews, Durham, Dernier, McGee. Triple--McGee. Home runs--McGee, Sandberg (2). Stolen base--Dernier, OSmith (2), LoSmith, Matthews, Van Slyke, Durham. Double play--St.Louis, 1. Left on base--St. Louis 11, Chicago 10.

	IP	H	R	ER	BB	SO		IP	H	R	ER	BB	SP
Citarella	5⅓	7	5	5	2	3	Bordi	3⅔	2	0	0	2	3
Allen	1⅓	3	3	3	2	2	Noles	⅔	3	2	2	1	0
Sutter	3⅓	3	3	3	2	0	Brusstar	⅓	0	0	0	0	1
Rucker (L, 1-1)	0	0	1	1	1	0	Stoddard	2	1	0	0	1	2
Lahti	0	1	0	0	2	0	LeSmith (W, 4-4)	2	2	2	2	1	0
Trout	1⅓	5	7	7	3	1							

Hit by pitch--by Citarella (Cey). Wild pitch--Citarella. Balk--Trout. Attendance: 38,079

Other Baseball Highlights of 1984

• Rick Sutcliffe, off to a 4-5 start with Cleveland, is traded to the Cubs and goes 16-1 to win the Cy Young Award.

• The Mets' Dwight Gooden fans 16 batters in two consecutive starts.

• Steve Garvey's 1.000 fielding average sets a major-league record for first basemen.

• Steve Carlton wins his 300th game.

Ferguson "Fergie" Jenkins—1971

Chicago Cubs Summit Season
Number 8

No. 8
FERGIE JENKINS

BORN: December 13, 1943; Chatham, Ontario, Canada

Chicago Cubs: 1966-1973; 1982-1983
Hall of Fame: 1991

SEASON AT THE SUMMIT: 1971

W-L-%		IP	CG	SH	SV	K/BB	PR	DEF	ERA
24-13	.649	325.0	30	3	0	263/37	25	2	2.77

With a little bit of luck, maybe a timely hit here or there, and a little steadier defense, **Ferguson Jenkins** could have been a 30-game winner for the Cubs in 1971.

Jenkins was as dependable and talented—he had posted four consecutive 20-win seasons—as any National League pitcher in 1971. For evidence, one has only to look at Opening Day. He faced St. Louis ace Bob Gibson, coming off a 23-7 season for the Cardinals. It was classic Ferguson Jenkins: He surrendered but three hits, struck out seven, walked none, and faced the minimum number of batters in 8 of 10 innings. And he won.

The 2-1 victory, achieved when Billy Williams homered in the 10th, was Jenkins' sixth in eight head-to-head meetings with the great Gibson. But then, Jenkins was accustomed to winning big games for the Cubs.

He had come to Chicago early in the 1966 season. In his first full year with the Cubs, Jenkins went 20-13. In '68 he was 20-15, then 21-15 the next year and 22-16 in

1970. He clearly was the ace on a team that was hoping to overcome the disappointments of second-place finishes the two previous seasons.

The 1971 season would be no different in terms of disappointment—the Cubs stumbled out of the blocks, got back in the race, but faded in August and September— or in terms of Jenkins' performance.

A Familiar Pattern

Jenkins suffered a half-dozen tough losses in 1971, perhaps none as deflating as that of April 10 against Houston. He took a four-hitter and a 1-0 lead into the ninth, but an infield single and two walks—uncharacteristic of Jenkins—filled the bases. He then balked home the tying run, and minutes later made a wild throw to third, letting the winning run score.

In his next start, delayed a day by manager Leo Durocher so his ace could go head-to-head with San Francisco's Juan Marichal, Jenkins was knocked out in 2⅓ innings, surrendering five earned runs and striking out only one Giant. Marichal, meanwhile, had a no-hitter until the ninth as the Cubs went down to a 9-0 defeat.

Soon, though, Jenkins returned to form. On April 20 he stopped Houston 3-1 on a six-hitter, facing the minimum number of batters from the third through eighth innings. The victory, thanks to Ron Santo's home run and two RBIs, got the Cubs back on track after a 3-8 road trip that had left them last in the NL East at 5-9.

Jenkins' performances generally followed a pattern: He would surrender early runs but would settle down and then be nearly untouchable. Against New York on April 25, for example, he fell behind 3-0 in the second inning, but allowed only two men as far as second base the rest of the way as the Cubs rallied to win 9-3. On May 1 against Philadelphia, he was touched early but gave up only three harmless singles after the fifth as the Cubs won 7-4. Of the first 21 runs he allowed in 1971, only five came after the third inning.

Jenkins won his next three outings—beating the Phillies 6-0 on four hits in the first game ever played at Veterans Stadium on May 10, posting his eighth complete game in nine starts and hitting a two-run homer in a 6-4 victory over San Diego May 15, and running his record to 8-2 in a 9-5 win over San Francisco four days later. He had become the NL's hottest pitcher, with seven victories in the last 29 days and only seven walks—one intentional—for the season.

His streak ended with another of those tough losses on May 23 at Wrigley Field. He had a 3-2 lead going into the ninth, but the Dodgers beat him 4-3 on Duke Sims' triple and Jim Lefebvre's home run. He also lost his next two starts—the Cubs were shut out in both—to fall to 8-5 by the end of May.

Two more wins—one a three-hitter against Atlanta for his 100th career victory—left him 10-5 before Fergie ran into more misfortune. Against the Reds on June 13, his error in the eighth led to the tying run, and Lee May's single in the 11th won it. Jenkins missed his next start because of an intestinal virus, then was beaten 2-0 on June 23 when the Cubs managed just three hits against the Giants.

No One Better In July
But he bounced back in July with his biggest month of the season. After being KO'd by Pittsburgh and losing on

July 2, he ran off six consecutive victories, and notable ones at that. He beat the NL West-leading Dodgers, then topped the Padres on a four-hitter. He worked a lackluster inning in the All-Star Game, surrendering three hits and two earned runs in a 6-4 NL loss, then got back to work where it counted with victories over the Phillies (twice), Mets and Expos. The month ended with Jenkins again the hottest pitcher in the league at 17-8 with a 2.60 ERA, 20 complete games in 23 starts and 178 strikeouts (and just 23 walks) in 211 innings.

His streak ended with another of those games he should have won, losing 2-1 on August 2 when the Cubs were two-hit by Houston's Earl Wilson—"He made a lot more good pitches than I did," Wilson said of Jenkins—but he then won three straight, including his 20th, a 3-2 victory over Houston on August 20 that brought the Cubs within 4½ games of the first-place Pirates.

Unhappy Troops
The Cubs, though, were a team in trouble. They had gone through a prolonged hitting slump in early August, and several players were having problems with Durocher, culminating in a closed-door meeting on August 24 that reportedly featured a confrontation between Santo and the manager. In support of Durocher, owner Philip K. Wrigley took out ads in the Chicago papers, ads that concluded with, "Too bad there aren't more players like Ernie Banks." Wrigley's vote of confidence for Durocher did more harm than good, as the Cubs lost 8 of 9 and 18 of 24 to fall 15 games out of first.

Jenkins, too, slumped, losing four of five decisions at one point—one on an infield single and bloop with two out in the ninth, another when the winning run scored on an error and passed ball. But he came back to win his last three decisions, finishing 24-13 with a 2.77 ERA. The 24 wins, his 30 complete games and 325 innings pitched were all league-leading stats, as was his figure of 1.02 walks per nine innings.

Jenkins had mentioned during the season that the Gibsons and Marichals had national reputations, and that he thought he deserved to be in the same class. His 1971 performance erased any doubts. The Baseball Writers Association of America agreed, voting him the NL Cy Young Award.

More players like Ernie Banks? The Cubs could have used a few more like Fergie Jenkins too.

FERGIE JENKINS'

Three Other Great Cub Seasons

YR	W-L	IP	GS	GC	SH	SV	PD	K/BB	OBA	OB%	ERA	PR
1. 1968	20-15	308	40	20	3	0	-1	260/65	.222	.266	2.63	12
2. 1969	21-15	311.1	42	23	7	1	0	273/71	.242	.290	3.21	13
3. 1970	22-16	313	39	24	3	0	-1	274/60	.224	.265	3.39	23

He was a gritty, determined competitor who made it his business to know his trade. That was Ferguson Jenkins. A professional through and through, he thrived on tough ballgames—and, of course, that's what the Cubbies specialized in during the '60s and '70s! A good hitting pitcher, he completely mastered the pitching arts and *made* you put the ball in play because he was never minded to issue any free passes. Check his whiff-to-walk ratio; it's outstanding. Fergie ran a streak of six straight 20-win seasons, the best three of which are cited above. His 1971, a 6.4 TPI masterpiece, rates top billing on the honors 50, and ranks him up there between Ryne Sandberg and another salty twirler, Jack Taylor.

"My game plan is simple. I throw strikes and make 'em hit the ball. And if they don't, I got another strikeout."

—Ferguson Jenkins on the secret of his 1971 success

JENKINS: A NOTEWORTHY BOX SCORE

September 1, 1971

Jenkins hits two home runs, drives in three runs and pitches a six-hitter to beat Montreal 5-2.

Montreal	AB	R	H	RBI	Chicago	AB	R	H	RBI
Hunt, 2b	4	0	0	0	Kessinger, ss	4	0	0	0
Day, cf	4	0	1	0	Beckert, 2b	4	0	0	0
Staub, rf	4	0	1	0	Williams, lf	4	0	1	0
Fairly, 1b	4	1	1	0	Hickman, 1b	4	1	1	0
Fairey, lf	4	0	1	0	Santo, 3b	4	0	0	0
Bailey, 3b	4	1	1	1	Davis, cf	3	0	2	1
Bateman, c	4	0	1	1	James, cf	0	0	0	0
Wine, ss	1	0	0	0	Callison, rf	3	2	1	0
Sutherland, ss	1	0	0	0	Cannizzaro, c	2	0	1	1
Stoneman, ph	2	0	0	0	Jenkins, p	3	2	2	3
Swanson, ph	1	0	0	0					
Britton, p	0	0	0	0	TOTALS	31	5	8	5
TOTALS	33	2	6	2					

Montreal	0 1 0	1 0 0	0 0 0	— 2				
Chicago	0 1 0	0 2 1	1 0 *	— 5				

Error--Beckert. Double plays--Chicago, 1. Left on base--Montreal 5, Chicago 5. Doubles--Fairey, Bateman. Triples--Cannizzaro, Hickman. Home runs--Jenkins (2). Sacrifice--Cannizzaro.

	IP	H	R	ER	BB	SO
Stoneman (L, 14-13)	6	7	4	4	1	5
Britton	2	1	1	1	0	1
Jenkins (W, 21-11)	9	6	2	1	1	6

Hit by pitcher--by Britton (Davis). Wild pitch--Jenkins. Balk--Jenkins. Time--2:12.

Other Baseball Highlights of 1971

- Bill Melton of the White Sox leads the AL in homers with 33.

- Montreal's Ron Hunt sets a modern major-league record by being hit by pitches 50 times.

- The Pirates become the first team to wear form-fitting, double-knit uniforms.

- Hall of Famers Heine Manush, Goose Goslin and Elmer Flick die.

Jack Taylor—1902

Chicago Cubs Summit Season
Number 9

No. 9
JACK TAYLOR

BORN: January, 14, 1874; Straitsville, Ohio
DIED: March 4, 1938; Columbus, Ohio

Chicago Orphans: 1898-1903; 1906-1907

SEASON AT THE SUMMIT: 1902

W-L-%		IP	CG	SH	SV	K/BB	PR	DEF	ERA
23-11	.676	324.2	33	7	1	83/43	52	3	1.33

New manager Frank Selee and his Chicago Orphans (their Colts nickname was soon to come, then to be succeeded by the present name, Cubs, in 1907) had the honor of opening Cincinnati's 1902 season at the Reds' new ballpark, called the Palace of the Fans. An overflow crowd of more than 10,000 was on hand at the April 17 inaugural, including a sizeable Chicago contingent that was delighted no end as their Orphans whipped the homestanding Reds 6-1 behind the slants of **Jack "Old Iron Arm" Taylor**. The 28-year-old got his summit season off to a roaring start, chipping in with a triple and a double, spacing seven hits and yielding no earned runs.

Four days later, in Chicago's home opener against the Cardinals, he was once again handed the ball and responded with a 4-3 victory at West Side Park. The burly right-hander, with his assortment of speeds and breaking pitches, was on his way to four straight 20-win seasons. Heading into the peak years of what turned out to be a stormy decade of major league baseball, there didn't seem, at that point, to be much standing in the way of a memorable career.

Alas, What Might Have Been...
Unfortunately, Jack Taylor's super season in 1902 turned out to be one of the few bright spots in what should have been an exceptional career. And—even as his iron man achievements piled one atop another—John Barleycorn, low-life cronies, an indulgent night life, an obsessive search for a quick buck, and a mean-spirited disposition saw to it that, in the end, organized baseball, not even in 1902's less than saintly world of professional sports, would have room for him. As rough and tumble as the Orphans were (and they were as rowdy as any team around), not even they could afford to carry Taylor and his antics on their roster indefinitely, finally bundling him off to St. Louis in a trade for no less than Mordecai "Miner" Brown, of "Three-Fingered" fame!

A Torrid April to June
Picking up from his fast start, Taylor zipped to a 9-1 mark by June 3, beating the Giants and Christy Mathewson 2-0, following that with a 12-inning, scoreless match against Cincinnati. Then he began a crucial four-game set with the Boston Braves, shutting them out on four hits. In the final game of that series he shut down the Braves and

Togie Pittinger 5-1. During that stretch from April through June he was the game's most dominating pitcher, rarely putting men on base (he walked but 43 in 324⅔ innings that super summer—that's only one per eight innings pitched, folks), and, customarily, finishing absolutely everything he started.

And Then Came June 22

The Honus Wagner-led Pirates came to the Windy City for an early showdown series opening on June 22. The legendary Deacon Phillippe opened for Pittsburgh and the Orphans countered with Old Iron Arm. And so the two had at it, the Pirates taking a 2-1 lead in the third. After that there was no scoring until the bottom of the ninth when the locals pushed one over to knot the count at 2-2. On and on they went through 12, then 15, and then 18 frames. Neither pitcher nor the score budged. Finally, in the bottom of the 19th, the Orphans squeezed one more out of the Deacon, thus winning the fourth longest game in the franchise's history. Remarkably, each hurler had gone the route, issuing but three free passes between them (Phillippe, two and Taylor, one). The effort pushed Taylor's ERA over the cliff and outta sight. At season's end, his reading stood at a sparkling 1.33 ERA, leading the league.

While a 19-inning complete game might have been extraordinary for Phillippe, or anyone else for that matter, it was just another complete game in an incredulous string of 187 straight starts and completions, including numerous extra inning games for Taylor. That finally added up to a staggering 278 completions in 286 major league starts, 97 percent, mind you, in a 10-year career!

A "Cy Young Award" Year

While he tapered off some during August and September (perhaps a few too many tall, cool lagers began taking a late-summer toll), Taylor kept his team at the edges of the first division and .500 ball with one workmanlike effort after another. Victories came over the Phillies in a 12-inning encounter, Brooklyn on August 14, 6-2, when he also tripled and walked no one, and at Philadelphia on September 1, a 6-1 victory in which he also had three hits.

Taylor, a.k.a. "Brakeman," out of his railroading background in Ohio, finished the season with a 4-2 conquest of the Cardinals, losing a shutout—it would have been his eighth, tying him for league leadership in that department—with a ninth-inning lapse. It was the 23rd notch on his 1902 victory belt in one of the more distinguished single seasons in the proud history of the franchise.

Some Noteworthy Figures and Notable Beginnings

Let's wrap up Taylor's sterling 1902 campaign with a look at more numbers. There were 33 starts, and, of course, 33 completions. That added to his skein of 187 straight which had begun in 1901 and endured into August of the 1906 season. He won 49 percent of his team's victories and was the league's leading pitcher in limiting opposing hitters to a composite .259 average. All of this, please note, with a leaky-fielding and rather weak-hitting ballclub behind him.

As for those notable beginnings: Joe Tinker, the regular shortstop that summer, catcher Frank Chance and rookie shortstop-second baseman Johnny Evers, who got into 26 games that summer, were on the same ballclub, if not yet at their Hall of Fame, Tinker-to-Evers-to-Chance positions. That was to come the next season. Batterymates Carl Lundgren and Johnny Kling were also on hand, and were to become integral parts of that famed championship dynasty.

The end of the line came for Old Iron Arm with a 1907 engagement at the Polo Grounds that followed his last victory in the bigs on June 30, beating the Pirates in 13 innings. His last start, on August 6, resulted in a 6-5 loss to the Giants. He was released by the Cubs in September over his heated complaints (it was, after all, a championship and World Series season for the team), never to appear in a major league uniform again. The final tally stood at just 13 more wins than losses, 152-139, not nearly good enough HOF numbers, but that 1902 season and that spectacular string of complete games stand as silent testimony to one of baseball's singular achievements. As they said along Tin Pan Alley: "Try that one over on your piano!"

JACK TAYLOR'S

Two Other Great Cub Seasons

	YR	W-L	IP	GS	GC	SH	SV	PD	K/BB	OBA	OB%	ERA	PR
1.	1903	21-14	312.1	33	33	1	1	1	83/57	.235	.273	2.45	28
2.	1906 CHI	12-3	147.1	16	15	2	0	0	34/39	.233	.285	1.83	13
2.	1906 TOT	20-12	302.1	33	32	3	0	0	61/86	.224	.283	1.99	21

The 1903 season and 1906's combined St. Louis-Chicago year represent a continuing pattern of hard-nosed pitching. There isn't much to choose between these two seasons, but there is a noticeable drop between the two and Taylor's 1902 banner year. Note particularly that in 1902 he amassed 52 pitching runs, a league-leading total of huge proportions. That figure alone signifies a season set apart, and marks his 1902 as a "Top 10" effort. Both 1903 and 1906 are creditable years, but lack the luster of 1902, nor would either rank among the Cubs' top 50.

"Jack Taylor was certainly no picture-perfect hurler. He was, however, as tenacious as a bulldog. He will probably never make the Halll of Fame, but his five-year complete-game streak certainly qualifies this pitcher for baseball immortality."

—Tom D'Antoni in *Baseball's .519 Iron Man*

TAYLOR: A NOTEWORTHY BOX SCORE

June 22, 1902

Taylor outduels Pittsburgh ace Deacon Phillippe over 19 innings, winning 3-2.

Pittsburgh	AB	H	PO	A		Chicago	AB	H	PO	A
Clarke, lf	8	5	1	0		Slagle, lf	8	0	3	1
Beaumont, cf	6	1	4	0		Jones, cf	5	2	5	1
Wagner, rf	8	0	3	1		Dexter, lb	8	1	25	0
Bransfield, lb	8	1	25	1		Congalton, rf	8	1	2	0
Ritchey, 2b	8	2	5	1		Kling, c	8	1	7	2
Leach, 3b	8	3	2	8		Tinker, ss	8	2	7	12
Conroy, ss	8	1	8	10		Lowe, 2b	8	3	6	8
Smith, c	8	0	8	6		Schaefer, 3b	6	2	1	3
Phillippe, p	8	1	0	1		Taylor, p	6	2	0	2
TOTALS	70	14	56	28		TOTALS	65	14	56*	29

* Two out when winning run scored

Pittsburgh	0 1 1	0 0 0	0 0 0	0 0 0	0 0 0	0 0 0	0 - - 2
Chicago	1 0 0	0 0 0	0 0 1	0 0 0	0 0 0	0 0 0	1 - - 3

Umpire: O'Day

Other Baseball Highlights of 1902

• The Pittsburgh Pirates win a then-NL record 103 games and win the pennant by 27½ games.

• Joe Tinker, Johnny Evers and Frank Chance first play together on September 15.

• Sam Mertes of the White Sox plays all nine positions during the season.

• Nig Clarke of Corsicana in the Texas League goes 8-for-8 with eight homers in one game.

• 1902-03 Baseball Peace Treaty: No mergers—and no more player raids.

Gregory Alan Maddux—1992

Chicago Cubs Summit Season
Number 10

No. 10
GREG MADDUX

BORN: April 14, 1966; San Angelo, Texas

Chicago Cubs: 1986-1992

SEASON AT THE SUMMIT: 1992

W-L-%		IP	CG	SH	SV	K/BB	PR	DEF	ERA
20-11	.645	268.0	9	4	0	199/70	39	6	2.18

There were times during the 1992 season—a seemingly endless number of times—when **Greg Maddux** could have let frustration get the best of him. Times when he could have blasted his teammates or ripped the Cubs' front office. But Maddux was and is too classy an individual for anything like that. He kept his frustrations to himself, said all the right things, ignored the distractions, and simply went out and pitched. And oh, how he pitched.

Over the winter leading to the 1992 season, Maddux and the Cubs were negotiating a long-term contract. He agreed to a multi-year deal, but Tribune Co. executives changed their minds two days later and withdrew the offer. Even though he eventually signed a one-year, $4.2 million contract, the entire process and the deal-that-wasn't left Maddux bitter.

Professional that he was, however, he didn't let his problems with management affect his performance. When the bell rang for the 1992 season, Maddux was ready. On Opening Day, April 7 in Philadelphia, he held the Phillies to six hits over seven innings—two of the hits were infield singles—as the Cubs posted a 4-3 victory. He also won his next two outings, 4-2 over St. Louis on April 12 and 8-3 against the Phillies on April 20, a game in which he hit a massive home run onto Waveland Avenue. With the season less than two weeks old, Maddux was 3-0 and looking unbeatable.

Lack Of Support
But Maddux suffered a reversal of fortune in his next outing. Against the red-hot Pittsburgh Pirates—they'd won 13 of 15—he made one mistake, a knee-high curveball to Andy Van Slyke in the sixth, and he ripped it for a run-scoring double that beat Maddux 1-0.

In his next start, the Cubs were shut out again, their fourth consecutive whitewash, and he was a 4-0 loser. Maddux struggled to an 8-4 victory over Houston on May 6, but then came a parade of frustrating outings when he'd pitch well only to come away with a no-decision or, worse, a loss. He allowed one run in nine innings against Houston on May 11 but failed to figure in the decision; he lost on the 15th when the Cubs were shut out 2-0 by

San Francisco; and he was a 2-0 loser at the hands of San Diego on May 22. He closed out his month with a 6-2 loss to the Giants on May 27, leaving him 4-5—with a 2.61 ERA.

"I'm not going to worry about it," he said after the last loss. "You're going to go through stretches like this. The main thing is you just have to concern yourself with the pitching part of the game and let the offense take care of the offense."

The problem was, the Cubs had no offense. In the May 27 loss, five of their nine starters were hitting below .200. Their team batting average of .228 was worst in the National League, and their lack of production saw them fall to sixth place (20-28) by June 1.

Maddux got some support—and a rare victory—his next time out, stopping San Diego 6-1 on a complete-game four-hitter to go 5-5. He struggled against Montreal four days later and was tagged with his sixth loss, but then posted back-to-back victories, including a four-hitter against St. Louis ("probably the best I've thrown all year") in which he had two RBI singles and lowered his ERA to 2.53.

A 4-1 loss to last-place Philadelphia ended Maddux's winning streak at two, but he was unbeatable in his next three starts—a 9-2 win over the Mets on June 25 that featured a near-brawl between Maddux and New York's Vince Coleman; a 10-strikeout, 3-1 victory over the Mets five days later that moved the Cubs into second place at 38-38; and an 8-0 blanking of Atlanta that raised his record to 10-7.

Maddux was a shutout loser in his last start before the All-Star Game—he would give up one run in 1⅓ innings of work in the American League's 13-6 romp on July 14—and reached the break at 10-8 with a 2.40 ERA.

Saying Goodbye

On July 16 Maddux made the announcement Cub fans feared: He said he had broken off negotiations on a long-term contract with the Cubs and would become a free agent after the season. "Things didn't work out," he said in a press conference in Pittsburgh, where the Cubs were playing the Pirates. "I've given them two opportunities to sign me. I really think it should have been taken care of."

As if to put an exclamation point on his announcement, Maddux went out the next night and beat the first-place Pirates 2-1, allowing six hits over eight innings, ending a five-game Cub losing streak.

Maddux's first start at home after his announcement came on July 27 against the Pirates. He had told reporters that he expected to be booed; instead, he got mild applause at the outset of the game. As the contest progressed, though, the applause grew. Finally, in the eighth, with Maddux on his way to a 3-2 win and victory No. 13, the Wrigley Field faithful gave him a standing ovation.

Over the next month, Maddux went 3-2 with two no-decisions, both losses coming when the Cubs were shut out (in his 10 losses to that point, the Cubs had been shut out seven times, and they'd managed just five runs total in the other three games). August ended with Maddux at 16-10; between the All-Star break and September 1 he was 6-2 with a 1.70 ERA.

Maddux suffered what would be his last loss of the season on September 5, falling 5-3 to San Diego. But even in that loss there were extenuating circumstances: With the score tied at 3 in the eighth, he hit the Padres' Dan Walters with a pitch, in retaliation for a pitch that almost hit teammate Ryne Sandberg in the head an inning earlier. Maddux was ejected, and the first batter reliever Jeff Robinson faced homered, hanging the loss on Maddux.

It was just a slight detour on Maddux's road to 20 wins, however. He won his last four decisions, becoming the Cubs' first 20-game winner in 15 years when he blanked the Pirates 6-0 in September 30.

Best In The NL

Maddux finished with 20 wins—tied for the league lead with Atlanta's Tom Glavine. He led the NL in innings pitched (268), was second in opponents' batting average (.210) and third in ERA (2.18) and strikeouts (199). The numbers added up to the NL Cy Young Award, the first of four in a row he would win. But the only one he would win as a Cub.

After the season, Maddux signed with the Atlanta Braves. The Cubs had made one last pitch in November, but he rejected the offer.

"Obviously, we would like to have him on board," general manager Larry Himes said after Maddux turned the Cubs down. "But if we can't, we'll go forward and find another pitcher."

The Cubs did find other pitchers, of course. But they never found another Greg Maddux.

GREG MADDUX'S

Two Other Great Cub Seasons

YR	W-L	IP	GS	GC	SH	SV	PD	K/BB	OBA	OB%	ERA	PR
1. 1989	19-12	238.1	35	7	1	0	3	135/82	.249	.317	2.95	15
2. 1990	15-15	237	35	8	2	0	8	144/71	.265	.321	3.46	9

The Texan from San Angelo, Greg Maddux, just kept improving with age. Another of those precision pitchers, he learned to live on the black with all the others who control both their pitches and their ballgames. Greg's first Cy Young Award came with his outstanding 1992 season, his last in Chicago. It's so good, in fact, that it propelled him into the No. 10 spot on our top-50 list, and deservedly so. The seasons cited above show his steady improvement as a master tradesman. His 1992 is better than Lonnie Warneke's or "Wild Bill" Hutchison's top season, but not really in the Alexander-Jenkins class. Still, it rates an A+!

"All I know is he is the best pitcher in the league right now. You look at innings pitched, opponents' average, strikeouts, durability. Heck, he hasn't missed a start in the major leagues. And every time he pitches, he just brings the ballclub to another level. He's the best. Period."

—Cubs manager Jim Lefebvre after Maddux beat the Pirates September 30, 1992 for his 20th victory of the season

Other Baseball Highlights of 1992

• Robin Yount and George Brett became the 17th and 18th players to reach 3,000 hits.

• California Angels manager Buck Rodgers is seriously injured when the team bus crashes.

• Toronto beats Atlanta in six games in the World Series—the first world champion from outside U.S. borders.

MADDUX: A NOTEWORTHY BOX SCORE

August 16, 1992

Maddux stops the Astros on four hits.

Houston	AB	R	H	RBI	E	Chicago	AB	R	H	RBI	E
Biggio, 2b	4	0	1	0	1	Dascenzo, cf	5	0	1	0	0
Finley, cf	4	0	0	0	0	Sandberg, 2b	3	1	1	0	0
Bagwell, 1b	3	0	0	0	0	Grace, 1b	3	0	2	0	0
Anthony, rf	4	0	0	0	0	Dawson, rf	2	0	1	0	0
Caminiti, 3b	4	0	1	0	0	May, lf	4	0	0	1	0
Gonzalez, lf	3	0	1	0	0	Wilkins, c	4	0	0	0	0
Candaele, ss	3	0	1	0	0	Buechele, 3b	4	0	1	0	0
Taubensee, c	2	0	0	0	0	Sanchez, ss	4	0	2	0	0
Williams, p	1	0	0	0	0	Maddux, p	1	0	0	0	0
Murphy, p	0	0	0	0	0						
Hernandez, p	0	0	0	0	0	TOTALS	30	1	8	1	0
Riles, ph	1	0	0	0	0						
Jones, p	0	0	0	0	0						
TOTALS	29	0	4	0	1						

Houston	000	000	000	-- 0
Chicago	100	000	000	-- 1

Left on base--Houston 5, Chicago 12. Stolen base--Sandberg. Sacrifice--Williams, Maddux (3).

	IP	H	R	ER	BB	SO
Williams (L, 4-4)	6	8	1	1	4	3
Murphy	2/3	0	0	0	0	2
Hernandez	1/3	0	0	0	0	1
Jones	1	0	0	0	0	0
Maddux (W, 15-9)	9	4	0	0	1	3

Hit by pitcher--by Maddux (Bagwell). Time--2:18. Attendance: 33,455.

SUMMITRY: A NOTCH BELOW THE SUMMIT

11) Lon Warneke, 1933, P
12) Fred Pfeffer, 1884, 2B
13) Bill Hutchison, 1890, P
14) Rick Reuschel, 1977, P
15) Clark Griffith, 1898, P

16) Bruce Sutter, 1977, P
17) Bill Hands, 1969, P
18) Bill Dahlen, 1896, SS
19) Billy Herman, 1935, 2B
20) Claude Passeau, 1940, P

On our listing of the greatest individual Cub seasons, those ranked between Ernie Banks in the No. 6 spot and No.18, Bill Dahlen, include 13 impressive seasons. Each, in sabermetric terms, amounts to approximately five more victories* in a given season than a league-average player might have contributed to his team's season total. Very fine lines separate these Cub stars. Consequently, the second tier of honorees from Lonnie Warneke through Claude Passeau is tightly knotted. In terms of a pitcher's won-loss record, a batting or slugging average, or even a league championship, it comes down so very often to a matter of a base hit here or there, an error or a passed ball, or a sprained muscle somewhere along the line that makes just enough difference to cost a player a higher ranking. That's simply another way of saying that these players are about on a par in overall ability and productivity; the differences in their rankings hinge on tenths and hundredths of a point in the Total Player Ratings.

Shortstop Bill Dahlen, that great Cub pivotman of the '30s, Billy Herman, and the redoubtable Freddie Pfeffer of those Cap Anson, 1880s championship teams, are the only position players in our batting order for the "second-10" summiteers. No less than seven superb hurlers from the 1890s on through the 1970s dress up this classy unit.

The Cubs' second tier of excellence features two pitchers, a starter and a reliever, from the same team (1977): Rick Reuschel (No. 14) and Bruce Sutter (No. 16). And then there is a captivating and highly gifted threesome from the 1890s, whose numbers impress enough to cause us to ask: who *are* these guys? It turns out that "Wild Bill" Hutchison, the "Old Fox," Clark Griffith, and "Bad Bill" Dahlen each climbed the heights in the same decade during those very gay '90s. Are they top 20 qualifiers? We'll see.

That leaves Bill Hands, who checks in at the No. 17 spot, with his herculean contribution to the Cubs' 1969 dash to the wire. In that first year of divisional play, one of the Cubs' better ballclubs, led by Ron Santo, Billy Williams, Ernie Banks, Fergie Jenkins, Kenny Holtzman and the ace of the staff that season, Big Bill Hands, matched the Mets stride for stride until the Shea Stadium series in August that put pennant hopes on the North Side to bed for another long, cold winter.

There you have it, 11 through 20. From Clarkson and Hornsby, in the Nos. 1 and 2 spots, on through Passeau at No. 20, the Top 20 Cub summit seasons set the pace right up there at the blue-ribbon level.

* You will recall from the Introduction that the Total Player Rating (TPR) translates from, for example, 6.2 (as in the case of Lon Warneke's 1933 TPR), to six victories. Ratings that merit six victories range from a TPR of 5.5 to 6.4.

Lon Warneke—1933

Chicago Cubs Summit Season
Number 11

No. 11
LON WARNEKE

BORN: March 26, 1909, Mount Ida, Arkansas
DIED: June 23, 1976, Hot Springs, Arkansas

Chicago Cubs: 1930-1936; 1942-1943; 1945

SEASON AT THE SUMMIT: 1933

W-L-%		IP	CG	SH	SV	K/BB	PR	DEF	ERA
18-13	.581	287.1	26	4	1	133/75	43	3	2.00

After the "new management" in the person of "Jolly Cholly" Grimm checked in at midseason to lead the Cubs' to a 1932 pennant, there was reason to believe that there would be another blue ribbon in 1933 to help along the festive spirit of Chicago's Century of Progress, its second world-class fair and exposition in the short span of 40 years. **Lonnie Warneke** had even better reason to agree, coming off a huge 1932 effort that netted a 22-6 record, accompanied by a league-leading 2.37 ERA and a second-place finish to the Phils' Chuck Klein for MVP honors. At 24, the "Arkansas Hummingbird," heading into his prime-time years, was in a zone of his own and ready to take on all comers.

An Opening Day Whitewash
On April 12, the lean right-hander opened the homestanding Cubs' 1933 season with a four-hit shutout over Dizzy Dean and the Cardinals, inaugural jitters notwithstanding. Surviving a first-inning nightmare consisting of a free pass to leadoff hitter "Sparky" Adams, a wild pitch to the second hitter, George Watkins, who was then hit by an errant Warneke offering, and a line shot by manager Frankie Frisch that fortunately found its

way into the Cubs' inner defensive network, he retired the side without further damage. Warneke got stronger as the game progressed, and brought the Cubbies home in front, 3-0. That shutout was a precursor of the kind of season-long excellence that would mark 1933 as an even better year than 1932. And that, despite a final 18-13 reading that was often marred by spotty hitting and less than adequate defense behind him.

Heatin' Up
The second of Warneke's four calciminings that summer came at the Polo Grounds where the Bruins lambasted the Giants and "Prince Hal" Schumacher 11-0 on May 2. Hall of Famers Billy Herman (4 for 4) and "Gabby" Hartnett (two round-trippers and five RBIs) figured prominently in the rout. A few days later in Boston, Lonnie celebrated a 5-2 conquest with a home run of his own as the Cubs swept two and gradually began to show signs of shaking their early season sluggishness to make a run at the first division. Warneke and his menacing curveball stood at 8-5, and in three of those losses the offense had mustered three or fewer runs. Typical of that stretch was a 2-0 shutout at the hands of the Giants' Lee Parelee on June

18. As the season's midpoint approached, the Cubs were up to a solid fourth, however, and hopes persisted that after Arch Ward's new "Game of the Century," to be unveiled at Comiskey Park on July 6, they might pull it all together and bring home a pennant for the city celebrating its World's Fair on the shores of Lake Michigan.

Something New In Baseball: An All-Star Game

Warneke, Hartnett and Woody English represented the Wrigleymen in baseball's first All-Star Game. Lithe Lonnie was clearly the star of the McGraw-led National League team. He fanned Babe Ruth, pitched superbly during a four-inning stint, and lifted a slicing triple past the Bambino along the right-field foul line, scoring subsequently on a Pepper Martin grounder for the Senior Circuit's first run in All-Star play. It was all lost, however, in the wake of one of those Ruthian inevitabilities, a two-run shot off "Wild Bill" Hallahan that proved to be enough to win the game for Connie Mack's American Leaguers.

Back To Work

Warneke started the second half of the season with a shutout to match the season opener, this time over the Giants, again at Wrigley Field, 4-0, on a 6-hitter. A few days later he lifted the Cubs to second place with a 4-1 win over the Dodgers. It was his 11th win and the Cubs' eighth straight. As things turned out, that was the apex point of the '33 campaign. When the final out had been made, the North Siders wound up a game behind the hard-hitting Pirates and six behind Bill Terry's Giants, who went on to beat Washington's Senators in the World Series.

During the Season's Dog Days

On August 14, Grimm homered to nail down Warneke's 13th—on his fifth try, which sends its own message about

no-decision pitching and a couple of losses despite continued proficiency on the firing line. And finally, on the last day of the season at St. Louis: this one was Lon's, a 7-1 win in which he helped his own cause with a pair of RBIs. The hitting, incidentally, was a steady, vital part of his play during the season. His .300 mark (30 for 100) paced all pitchers and ranks in the Cub pitchers' Top 10 since 1900.

City Series Blues

Not only did the Cubs lose still another City Series, and ignominiously, they and the baseball world lost one of the game's most respected personages, Bill Veeck Sr., the Cubs' hard-working GM. His passing held up the series, but not the White Sox's "Old Men," their 40+ pitching staff. And the greatest embarrassment was caused by 45-year-old Red Faber, who shut down the youngster Warneke and his Cub teammates in Game 2 by a 2-0 count. That was the grand old White Sox hero's last ballgame, a "something-to-remember-me-by." Two humiliations later, it was all over for the series and the season.

Big Dividends...Anyway!

In 1934 and '35 the Arkansas Hummingbird would go on to stack up a pair of 20-win seasons and a brace of brilliant World Series victories over the Tigers for Chicago's 1935 NL champs. From 1933 to 1936 he had gotten the Cubs off to four successive Opening Day victories, and ultimately wound up with 119 W's for the Cubs in two tours of duty in the Windy City. He had paid unbelievably rich dividends on the Cubs' 1930 purchase price of one solitary C-note!

LON WARNEKE'S

Three Other Great Cub Seasons

	YR	W-L	IP	GS	GC	SH	SV	PD	K/BB	OBA	OB%	ERA	PR
1.	1932	22-6	277	32	25	4	0	0	106/64	.237	.283	2.37	43
2.	1934	22-10	291.1	35	23	3	3	0	143/66	.244	.287	3.21	27
3.	1935	20-13	261.2	30	20	1	4	-1	120/50	.257	.294	3.06	28

Ranking Warneke's 1933 season over his '32 is another of those judgment calls that seems, at first glance, to be woefully out of line. Yet, with a championship team behind him, more consistent hitting, and a stronger pitching staff, his 1932 workload was easier to carry. On the other hand, it took more to post an 18-13 record with the 1933 ballclub. His ERA was down to 2.00, he went the route 26 times, saved a game, and contributed a hefty 3 on the sabermetric defensive calculation, his top career mark. All of that not only turns his 1933 season into a career year, it rates an exceptional 6.2 TPI, an important factor in his overall summit ranking at No. 11 in the midst of the Cubs' best single-season performances.

On Lon Warneke's big Ruth KO:

"Ruth took Warneke's first pitch, a fastball, for a strike. Thinking the next pitch would be a curve, Ruth swung a little late and missed...Warneke had given him another fastball."

"The Babe, now as angry as a bull, stepped out of the box, walked around in a little circle, knocked some specks of dirt out of his spikes, and moved back in. He waved his big 42-ounce bat, cocked it over his left shoulder, waited for the pitch. This time Warneke served up a sharp-breaking curve. Ruth took a wide sweeping powerful swing—and missed the ball by a foot."

—Robert Objoski, *All-Star Baseball Since 1933*

Other Baseball Highlights of 1933

•The Giants' Carl Hubbell throws 10 shutouts— more than the entire pitching staffs of seven of the eight AL teams. One whitewash was an 18-inning job vs. St. Louis on August 2.

•John McGraw ends his managerial career.

•Lou Gehrig breaks Everett Scott's record streak of 1,307 consecutive games played.

•Nick Altrock, at 57, pinch-hits in a game for the Senators.

WARNEKE: A NOTEWORTHY BOX SCORE

July 6, 1933 at Comiskey Park, Chicago

Nationals	AB	R	H	P	A	Americans	AB	R	H	P	A
Martin (STL), 3b	4	0	0	0	0	Chapman (NY), lf-rf	5	0	1	1	0
Frisch (STL), 2b	4	1	2	5	3	Gehringer (DET), 2b	3	1	0	1	3
Klein (PHL), rf	4	0	1	3	0	Ruth (NY), rf	4	1	2	1	0
P. Waner (PIT), rf	0	0	0	0	0	West (STL) cf	0	0	0	0	0
Hafey (CIN), lf	4	0	1	0	0	Gehrig (NY), lb	2	0	0	12	0
Terry (NY), lb	4	0	2	7	2	Simmons (CHI), cf-lf	4	0	1	4	0
Berger (BOS), cf	4	0	0	4	0	Dykes (CHI), 3b	3	1	2	2	4
Bartell (PHL), ss	2	0	0	0	3	Cronin (WSH), ss	3	1	1	2	4
Traynor (PIT), ph	1	0	1	0	0	R. Ferrell (BOS), c	3	0	0	4	0
Hubbell (NY), p	0	0	0	0	0	Gomez (NY), p	1	0	1	0	0
Cuccinello (BRK), ph1	0	0	0	0	0	Crowder (WSH), p	1	0	0	0	0
Wilson (STL), c	1	0	0	2	0	Averill (CLV), ph	1	0	1	0	0
O'Doul (NY), ph	1	0	0	0	0	Grove (PHL), p	1	0	0	0	0
Hartnett (CHI), c	1	0	0	2	0						
Hallahan (STL), p	1	0	0	1	0	AL TOTALS	31	4	9	27	11
Warneke (CHI), p	1	1	1	0	0						
English (CHI), ph	1	0	0	0	0						
NL TOTALS	34	2	8	24	8						

Nationals	0 0 0	0 0 2	0 0 0	2-8-0
Americans	0 1 2	0 0 1	0 0 *	4-9-1

Doubles: Traynor
Triples: Warneke
Home runs: Ruth, Frisch
RBI: Martin; Frisch; Ruth, 2; Gomez; Averill
Sac: R. Ferrell
DP: Bartell; Frisch; Terry; Dykes; and Gehrig
IP: Hallahan (L), 2; Warneke, 4; Hubbell, 2; Gomez (W), 3; Crowder, 3; Grover, 3

ER: Hallahan, 3; Warneke, 1; Crowder, 2
SO: Hallahan; Warneke, 2; Hubbell, 1; Gomez, 1; Grove, 3
Umpires: Dineen and McGowan (AL) Lem and Rigler (NL)
Attendance: 47,595
Time: 2:05

Nathaniel Frederick Pfeffer—1884

Chicago Cubs Summit Season
Number 12

No. 12
FRED PFEFFER

BORN: March 17, 1860; Louisville, Kentucky
DIED: April 10, 1932; Chicago, Illinois

Chicago White Stockings: 1883-1889; 1891; 1896-1897

SEASON AT THE SUMMIT: 1884

AB-R-H	BA	OB%	2B	3B	HR	RBI	BR	FR	SB
467-105-135	.289	.325	10	10	25	101	22	46	-

After winning the league's blue ribbon three straight times (1880-82), the White Stockings had to settle for the second rung in 1883 as the result of a disastrous late-September series in Boston, where they lost four straight and the pennant with it. Then came 1884. It was supposed to be the year the Ansonmen would bounce back to resume their championship ways. Sadly, for Chicagoans, it wasn't to be. However well they might do with their near limitless offensive weapons in the homer-friendliest ballpark of all time, they would be forced to spend the season, along with the rest of the league, in the iron grip of one of the most awesome single-season pitching efforts in the game's history. Charlie "Old Hoss" Radbourn, the Providence Hall of Famer, was the author of such a season, almost single-handedly propelling his Grays to the league championship with 60 of the team's 84 victories.

And in Chicago...

All of this, and a good deal more, was going on in a season when no less than three of the Whites were enjoying summit seasons of their own. Although Radbourn's

1884 Total Pitching Index that season ranks among the top 15 in the record books, and was clearly the rage of the year, Chicago infielders **"Unser Fritz" Pfeffer** and "Ned" Williamson, along with pitcher Larry Corcoran, logged some pretty decent numbers of their own. And they weren't that much ahead of "King" Kelly and the boss-man, Cap Anson. But it was Fritz Pfeffer whose season stood apart from the rest of the ballclub, and from most of the league, for that matter. For an opening teaser, here's a sample: In 1884 Mr. Pfeffer posted the league's front-running numbers in *every* defensive category. The extent of his defensive magic will be explored in due time.

The Second Base Aristocrat

Among the members of the Stone Wall infield, Herr Pfeffer, who made his way with the imperious bearing of a monocled German count, was the most accomplished afield. He was the second baseman non pareil of baseball's early years, establishing a tradition that extended on through Johnny Evers, Billy Herman, Glenn Beckert, and Ryne Sandberg. Mercury quick and acrobatic, an 1880's

Bill Mazeroski around the keystone sack, Fritz covered the *entire* right side of the infield as well as a man-sized chunk of outfield real estate.

The Unlevel Field of Play

Given the state of the playing fields of the day, unevenly surfaced and differing considerably from park to park around the league, as well as the primitive equipment—*especially* fielding gloves, if they may be called that—it's something of a miracle that there weren't more errors and unearned runs than regularly showed up in the scorebooks. In its September 18, 1884 edition, Chicago's *Tribune* complained about a game played on September 17 even though the Whites won it: "All played loosely in the field, but the weakest point was behind the bat...There was much fumbling and bad throwing on both sides, but Chicago kept on batting in runs and stealing bases..."

The Defensive Pacesetter

But there are always those who find a way to overcome, and Unser Fritz was one of them. His defensive play in 1884 was other-wordly. The game's fastest pivotman got to balls other players fantasized about (that also led to a league-leading total of 88 miscues), participating in 85 double plays while coming up with a record-setting 422 assists and 395 putouts in the 112-game schedule. His 7.29 chances that season stand at a lofty No. 4 spot, all time. His defensive numbers factored out at a mammoth 46 fielding runs, still another single-season mark ranking No. 7 on the all-time charts.

Lean, with the coiled strength of heavy gauge steel wire, the Whites' second sacker had surprising thump in his lumber, lofting 25 circuit smashes into the seats, second to Williamson's 27 for season honors. He topped the century mark in ribbies and his .514 slugging average ranked fifth behind Williamson, Anson and Kelly. HOF'er "Big Dan" Brouthers of Buffalo topped the league in RBIs.

The Inside Game

By 1884, the Chicago infield had what became known as the "Inside Baseball Game" down pat. Evers, who came along in 1902, would have been one to appreciate what that meant to a ballclub. Brainy keystoner that he was, he carried on the Pfeffer standard all the way to Cooperstown. Here's what he had to say about Unser Fritz and that 1880s infield in *Touching Second*, written with Hugh Fullerton:

"The Chicago team of 1880, which reached its fullest development five years later, was the pioneer of 'inside baseball,' and from that team came more original plays, now in common use, than from any other source...But it was really with the coming of Pfeffer in 1883 that the team began to play 'inside baseball' coherently, both at the bat and in the infield."

A Chicago Tradition

After his playing career, Fred Pfeffer, in the best of German traditions, ran the rather famous Pfeffer's Bar behind the McVicker's Theater in the Loop. It was one of the more popular watering holes for Chicago sportsmen during those uproarious days of Chicago's 1910s and '20s. He passed from the Chicago scene in 1932, fondly remembered as Unser Fritz, the unrivaled defensive wizard of his day.

FRED PFEFFER'S

Three Other Great Cub Seasons

	YR	GP	AB-R-H	BA	OB%	SA	K/BB	HR	RBI	SB	FR	BR
1.	1887	123	479-95-133	.278	.327	.447	20/34	16	89	57	25	-4
2.	1888	135	517-90-129	.250	.297	.377	38/32	8	57	64	38	2
3.	1891	137	498-91-123	.247	.353	.349	60/79	7	77	40	25	5

A great deal has been said about Chicago's stone wall infield, and justifiably so. Anson, Burns, Williamson, and the irrepressible Fritz Pfeffer played a tough inner defense. It was the acrobatic Pfeffer, however, who was not only the glue, but the brains that held it all together and made it work. His '87-'88 tandem seasons were bright spots both offensively and defensively. Note his 64 thefts in '88 to go along with 38 fielding runs; his '87 slugging average (89 RBIs and 16 home runs helped the cause, as well) was up there among the better numbers in the league. He was the first of the franchise's great pivotmen. Fritz was the standard bearer.

As bright as was Fred Pfeffer's career, his passing, though rather typical of sports figures during his era, was reported in more somber tones:

Harvey T. Woodruff in his "Wake of the News" column said:
"Baseball players did not receive large salaries in Pfeffer's prime. Later business ventures added no accumulation for his later years. Former friends are making the funeral arrangements. His widow, we are told, is left in destitute circumstances. This may suggest something to baseball fans of olden and present time!"

—The *Chicago Tribune*, April 12, 1932

PFEFFER: A NOTEWORTHY BOX SCORE

September 17, 1884 at West Side Park, Chicago

Whites maul Boston—"Unser Fritz" ist perfekt!

Chicago	AB	R	H	PO	A		Boston	AB	R	H	PO	A
Dalrymple, lf	6	2	3	3	1		Hornung, lf	4	1	1	4	0
Gore, cf	6	2	1	2	1		Buffinton, cf, rf	5	1	1	2	0
Kelly, rf	6	3	4	1	0		Whitney, p, 1b	2	3	1	5	4
Anson, 1b	6	4	2	14	0		Hackett, 3b	4	2	2	1	4
Pfeffer, 2b	4	4	4	0	2		Morrill, 1b, p	4	1	1	6	3
Williamson, 3b	6	3	2	0	4		Crowley, cf, rf	4	0	0	2	1
Burns, ss	6	0	0	1	7		Wise, 2b	4	0	0	1	5
Clarkson, p	5	0	2	1	8		Manning, ss	4	0	0	1	3
Flint, c	5	0	0	5	1		Hines, c	4	1	1	5	2
TOTALS	50	18	18	27	24		TOTALS	35	9	7	27	22

Boston	3 0 1	0 1 1	3 0 0 — 9
Chicago	3 0 3	5 0 1	0 3 3 — 18

Note: Chicago exercised its 9th inning option to bat.
Doubles: Williamson (2), Pfeffer, Anson, Clarkson, Morrill, Hackett; Home runs: Dalrymple, Pfeffer, Whitney, Hackett; K; Clarkson, 4; Whitney, 1; Morrill, 1; Double play: Dalrymple and Anson; Time: 2:15. Attendance: 2,100. Umpire: Ferguson.

Other Baseball Highlights of 1884

• Providence's Charles "Old Hoss" Radbourn takes advantage of a new rule allowing overhand pitching to win 60 games.

• A third major league, the Union Association, is formed, but it survives only one season.

• Providence wins the NL championship; New York finishes first in the American Association.

• The St. Louis Maroons of the new Union Association win their first 21 games and cruise to the league title.

William F. Hutchison—1890

Chicago Cubs Summit Season
Number 13

No. 13
WILLIAM HUTCHISON

BORN: December 17, 1859; New Haven, Connecticut
DIED: March 19, 1926; Kansas City, Missouri

Chicago Colts: 1889-1895

SEASON AT THE SUMMIT: 1890

W-L-%	IP	CG	SH	SV	K/BB	PR	DEF	ERA
42-25 .627	603.0	65	5	2	289/189	58	5	2.70

Leagues of their own—two for the owners and one for the players. That was the defining characteristic of baseball in the bigs, all three of them, in 1890. The turmoil in the baseball world that season had a profound effect on the game, the men upstairs, the players, and the record book. The game's upper echelon, in an unending round of meetings and conferences, had its hands full just trying to hold things together. Among the moguls and magnates, Chicago's A. G. Spalding was one of the prime forces in dealing with the enemies and demons "out there," both real and imagined. As far as his own ballclub was concerned, there were urgencies at every hand calling for sustained attention. Life was anything but boring! In their encyclopedic accounting of major league franchise history, Don Dewey and Nick Acocella explain the situation this way:

"As owner and propagandist, Spalding was never more visible than he was during the 1890 war with the Players League, the circuit set up by the Players Brotherhood to combat the most flagrant abuses of the reserve clause. As an owner, he had plenty of reason to be visible be-cause every one of his key players except Cap Anson, third baseman Tom Burns, and pitcher **Bill Hutchison** defected to the rebel league."

"Wild Bill"

It's this last named "loyalist," flame-throwing right-hander "Wild Bill" Hutchison, that draws our attention in this chapter. It happened that in 1890 Will Bill, a.k.a. "Hutch," stepped into Chicago's volatile scenario ready, willing, and more than able to register what turned out to be the franchise's 13th finest summit season on record. What he accomplished at the start of that gay, tumultuous decade of the '90s placed him among the club's top 15 summiteers, slotted in the midst of Lonnie Warneke, Fritz Pfeffer, Rick Reuschel and "The Old Fox," Clark Griffith.

Enter the Elis

Hutch had tuned up for 1890 with a 16-17 record in 1889. Nothing orbital there, mind you, but he was no worse than the 50-50 ballclub that limped home 19 games off the winning pace of New York's Giants. When it came time to throw out 1890's first ball, the Yale graduate was suddenly cast in the role of staff ace, the only veteran (entering his *second* full season) Anson had to call on, because the rest of the '89 staff had moved on to the Chicago Pirates or other Players League teams. How would he respond?

He Responded Bigtime
Let's look first at the bottom lines for 1890:

1) League leadership in five categories: most wins (42); most games pitched (71; he also saved two); most complete games (65); most innings pitched (603).
2) He was second in strikeouts (289); tied for second in allowing the fewest base hits per game (7.54); and tied for second in opposing hitters' low batting average (.221).
3) He lowered his ERA from 3.54 in 1889 to 1890's 2.70, a Top 10 figure in the league, and contributed 58 pitching runs to Chicago's cause. Hall of Famers Amos Rusie and Kid Nichols, just ahead of Hutchison, posted 63 and 62 PR's respectively.
4) He pitched in 603 of Chicago's 1,237 innings played in 1890, a barely believable .487 percent, and recorded 42 of his team's 84 wins, exactly 50 percent!

Those are Spalding-Clarkson-Corcoran kinds of numbers, and if his forerunners didn't see that as extraordinary, you can bet they certainly respected it. It's safe to say that the Ivy Leaguer had himself some kind of season.

The 1890 Season and the Colts
The National League's summer of discontent found at least one team unfazed by the acrimonious warfare all around it. That was the league's champion, the Brooklyn Bridegrooms. Proving even back then that "it was the economy, stupid," Brooklyn fielded a well-paid and consequently veteran ballclub that suffered but one defection, and came out of the opening gate at full trot, moving on to win the whole bundle in its first NL season. That's right—all that Brooklyn daffiness began with a pennant winner! Chicago, on the other hand, suffered from significant player losses, a press that hounded the team mercilessly, dwindling fan support, and a horrid start. And they wallowed in the second division right on into August.

August to October With Hutch and Pat
An inkling of what was ahead surfaced on July 25 when Hutchison picked on the front-running Brooklyns to author one of his better games of the summer, beating the Bridegrooms (whose minds might just have been elsewhere) by a 5-3 count. This is the way the *Tribune* reported on Hutch's conquest:

"Anson's Colts succeeded yesterday in stopping the Brooklyns' mad rush pennantward...They ran up against a good-sized snag in the shape of Hutchison, the Chicago pitcher, whose penchant for pulling down the averages of opposing batsmen has already been recorded in history...Hutch...sent the balls in (dirtied by play, Ed.) until the team from the City of Churches was hammering the air in all directions in a vain attempt to hit something more tangible."

Then the fun began. The Colts picked up the pace, moving from fifth to fourth, and then into third by mid-August. Along the way, the hard-throwing Hutchison bagged Nos. 20 to 25 and trained his sights on 30 plus.

Beyond Hutchison's sterling work, the season's most electrifying development was taking place. Freshman hurler Pat Luby began winning—and winning—and winning. Beginning on August 6 he won 17 straight, a "most-ever" Chicago franchise mark, before finally losing on October 3. That was a huge factor in the Colts' season and helped ease them into a second-place finish. The final Hutchison tally stood at 42 W's and Luby's at 20. During their streak the Ansonmen had registered a spiffy 21-6 in September, and another six out of their last eight in October.

And Two More
William Forrest Hutchison kept right at it in 1891 and '92, winning 44 and then 37, to add two more to as sparkling a threesome of pitching seasons as can be found in franchise annals. He was the last major-league hurler to log 600 innings pitched in a single season. Hutch retired after his baseball days to Kansas City, where he had begun his big-league career with the K. C. Unions in 1884. There are those who insist that, had he come along 10 years later, the Cubs might have won the pennant as often as those Yankee teams did in the 1950s!

Two Other Great Cub Seasons

	YR	W-L	IP	GS	GC	SH	SV	PD	K/BB	OBA	OB%	ERA	PR
1.	1891	44-19	561	58	56	4	1	-2	261/178	.232	.292	2.81	34
2.	1892	37-36	627	71	67	5	0	4	316/187	.233	.291	2.74	38

The Colts came within a season-ending series with Boston of winning the 1891 pennant. It was a strong supporting cast for Hutch. His 44 wins that summer came a good deal easier than did his near 50-50 record in 1892's NL, swollen to 12 teams (the term "big league" entered baseball's vocabulary that season), in a season that saw his team slump to a 70-76 record and seventh place. Note the difference his superior 1892 effort reflects on record, number of starts, and pitching defense (the fifth-infielder factor). His 1891 season looks glossier, but 1892 was, all things considered, a far stronger effort.

"The Brooklyn Bridegrooms ran up against a good-sized snag in the shape of Hutchison, the Chicago pitcher, whose penchant for pulling down the averages of opposing batsmen has already been recorded in history...Hutch sent balls in until the team from the City of Churches was hammering the air in all directions in a vain attempt to hit something more tangible."

—*Chicago Tribune*, July 26, 1890

HUTCHISON: A NOTEWORTHY BOX SCORE

July 25, 1890

Hutch tames the Brooklyns

Brooklyn	AB	H	PO	A	Chicago	AB	H	PO	A
Collins, 2b	4	1	0	3	Cooney, ss	3	0	2	3
Pinckney, 3b	4	2	1	0	Carroll, lf	5	0	2	0
Burns, rf	4	1	1	0	Wilmot, cf	5	1	0	0
Foutz, 1b	4	0	10	1	Anson, 1b	4	1	13	0
Terry, lf	4	0	3	0	Burns, 3b	4	1	0	1
Daly, c	3	1	8	0	Earle, rf	4	1	2	0
Smith, ss	4	1	1	4	Glenalvin, 2b	3	0	2	2
Donovan, cf	4	1	3	0	Hutchison, p	4	0	0	10
Lovett, p	4	0	0	6	Kittridge, c	4	2	6	0
TOTALS	35	7	27	13	TOTALS	36	6	27	16

```
Brooklyn   000  002  001  — 3
Chicago    100  000  031  — 5
```

Double: Burns of Brooklyn; Triple: Kittridge; Home run: Wilmot (over the center-field fence).
Umpire: McDermott. Time: 2:00; Attendance: 1,527.
Note: Chicago exercised option to bat in the bottom of the 9th.

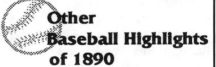

Other Baseball Highlights of 1890

- Brooklyn sweeps a triple-header from visiting Pittsburgh on September 1.

- The Players League is formed but folds after one season.

- A new rule forbids the defacing of the baseball.

- Amos Rusie surrenders 289 walks, a record that still stands.

Rick Reuschel—1977

Chicago Cubs Summit Season
Number 14

No. 14
RICK REUSCHEL

BORN: May 16, 1949; Quincy, Illinois

Chicago Cubs: 1972-1981; 1983-1984

SEASON AT THE SUMMIT: 1977

W-L-%		IP	CG	SH	SV	K/BB	PR	DEF	ERA
20-10	.667	252.0	8	4	1	166/74	31	3	2.79

When **Rick Reuschel** accomplished something on the field, he didn't lead cheers, showboat or celebrate wildly. And when things didn't go his way, he wouldn't throw tantrums, yell at his manager or kick batboys.

But it would be wrong to mistake Reuschel's lack of outward emotion for a lack of enthusiasm.

No greater competitor ever pitched for the Cubs than the even-tempered, 6-foot-3-inch, 235-pound right-hander from Camp Point, Illinois.

Signed by the Cubs out of college (Western Illinois University), Reuschel debuted with the Cubs in June 1972. Over the next 5½ seasons, he had a 62-64 record and 3.46 ERA for some mediocre ballclubs. But in 1977, he would have the best season of his 19-year career.

Flying Start

Reuschel got off on the right foot by beating New York 2-1 on April 10 at Wrigley Field. His only mistakes: gopher balls to Ed Kranepool the first two times the Met first baseman came up. "I wanted to knock him down the next time," Reuschel said, "but I figured it would be too obvious."

Reuschel, a cold-weather pitcher, quickly found his groove. After a loss to the Mets on April 16—he led 2-1 but New York had the bases loaded when he left, and the bullpen couldn't put out the fire—Reuschel put together a stretch of five consecutive victories. The streak was snapped on May 19 when he lost to Atlanta—the Cubs had won six in a row to move into second place, two games back—and he wasn't the pitcher of record in his next three starts.

But then came June, the best month of Reuschel's best season.

"Best In Baseball"

Behind the brilliant relief pitching of Bruce Sutter and Willie Hernandez and the hitting of Bill Buckner, Manny Trillo, Bobby Murcer and Ivan DeJesus, the Cubs had moved into first place on May 28, a position they would hold until August 5.

Reuschel began the month at 6-2. He wasn't the pitcher of record in his first start, on the 2nd, then won five in a row, each game more impressive than the last. On June 6, he went 6⅓ innings, allowing only three hits and retiring 17 Los Angeles Dodgers in a row on his way to a 3-1 victory. Next came back-to-back four-hit complete games against San Francisco and San Diego, leaving him with a 9-2 record and 2.53 ERA. On June 24, with July still a week away, Reuschel notched his 10th victory, beating the Mets 5-0. He ran his record to 11-2 on the 28th with a 10-inning complete-game victory over the Expos. Reuschel's numbers for June—a 5-0 record, 0.92 ERA—earned him Pitcher of the Month recognition.

After a no-decision on July 3—he had to leave in the seventh with a blister on his pitching hand—he shut out St. Louis on the 7th. At that point he had allowed only three earned runs and 36 hits in his last nine appearances, covering 58⅓ innings. He hadn't given up an earned run other than a homer since June 1. He hadn't lost since May 19, a personal-best six straight victories. He was 12-2 with a 2.03 ERA—the best pitcher in baseball whose efforts earned him a spot on the National League All-Star squad.

Reuschel had a loss and no-decision in his last two starts before the All-Star Game, where he pitched an inning, surrendering one hit in the NL's 7-5 victory. Then he picked up where he left off. On July 22, he blanked the Braves on five hits 1-0. Four days later he beat the Reds 3-0 on another five-hitter ("He's the best pitcher in either league right now," noted Johnny Bench). And for a little variety, Reuschel got the win—his 15th against only three losses—when he worked two-thirds of an inning in relief in a wild 16-15, 13-inning victory over the Reds on July 28.

Trouble On The Horizon
Manager Herman Franks brought Reuschel back two days later—his third appearance in five days. He was knocked out early in a game the Cubs would rally to win. He left his next start leading 3-1 after 6⅓ innings because of a sore arm. The Cub bullpen—minus Sutter, who had gone on the disabled list with a bad shoulder—failed to hold the lead and Reuschel missed his chance at win No. 16. He was victimized again by the lack of relief in his next outing, August 8. Reuschel led 6-5 going into the ninth, but with Sutter unavailable and his other relievers needing a break, Franks left Reuschel in, only to have Pittsburgh rally for a 7-6 victory.

Franks brought Reuschel back on three days rest to face the Phillies and he was hammered, giving up seven runs in only two innings. Clearly, this wasn't the same Reuschel who had been Pitcher of the Month in June and July. His problem was a sore arm, which first manifested itself after his brief relief appearance on July 28. "I probably should have missed a couple of turns, but you hate to miss out when you've been going so good," he later admitted.

Reuschel's fastball seemed to be back in his next start, a 4-2 complete-game victory over the Pirates on August 17, but he had no snap to his pitches on the 22nd, when he went 8⅔ innings in beating the Giants 3-2. He left his next start four days later with a sore shoulder, then gutted out a 4-1 victory over the Dodgers on August 30. His fourth win in a row, it left him 19-5 with a 2.64 ERA.

Out of Steam
But Reuschel, like the rest of the Cub pitching staff, was clearly tired. He went on to lose five of his next six decisions, notching his 20th win on September 18 by beating the Mets 6-5. Reuschel lasted only six innings before leaving with a blister, although he was around long enough to contribute two hits and three RBIs to his cause.

Despite the disappointing finish—the Cubs placed fourth, 81-81—it was a banner year for Reuschel. He led the team in victories (20), complete games (eight), shutouts (four), innings pitched (252) and strikeouts (166). His 2.79 ERA was best among starters. Quietly, as was his custom, Rick Reuschel had become one of the league's best pitchers.

RICK REUSCHEL'S

Two Other Great Cub Seasons

	YR	W-L	IP	GS	GC	SH	SV	PD	K/BB	OBA	OB%	ERA	PR
1.	1976	14-12	260	37	9	2	1	3	146/64	.265	.315	3.46	1
2.	1979	18-12	239	36	5	1	0	5	125/75	.274	.335	3.62	3

Rick Reuschel was one of the better fielding pitchers of his era. Between 1973 and 1980, he stacked up a 30 rating (almost 4 per season). Those are superior numbers. In a career of 19 years and over 3,500 innings pitched, he committed but 29 errors for a crackin' good .972 lifetime fielding average. His Gold Glove Award belied his chunky physique. "Big Daddy's" 1977 was his crowning Cub achievement, a stellar, top-20 season that ranked him above his rescuer, Bruce Sutter, whose big year for the Cubs was also 1977. He follows behind another big fellow, "Wild Bill" Hutchison of early 1890s fame. These boys could really bring it.

Bruce Sutter commenting on Rick Reuschel:

"The workhorse on the team was Rick Reuschel. Rick is a good friend of mine. Rick helped me a lot coming up. He's just so even-keeled. Rick was the same whether he won the game or if he got knocked out in the first inning. He was steady. He worked at his game all the time, worked and worked, and when the games came, he did the same thing."
—Peter Golenbock's *Wrigleyville*

REUSCHEL: A NOTEWORTHY BOX SCORE

June 10, 1977

Reuschel scatters four hits and strikes out seven to beat the Giants 3-1.

San Francisco	AB	R	H	RBI	E	Chicago	AB	R	H	RBI	E
Andrews, 2b	4	0	1	0	0	DeJesus, ss	4	2	2	0	0
Williams, p	0	0	0	0	0	Biittner, lb	4	1	2	1	0
Madlock, 3b	4	0	0	0	0	Clines, lf	2	0	0	0	0
Thomasson, cf	3	0	1	0	0	Gross, lf	0	0	0	0	0
Evans, lf	3	0	1	0	0	Murcer, rf	4	0	2	1	0
McCovey, lb	3	1	0	0	0	Morales, cf	4	0	2	1	0
Clark, rf	4	0	0	0	0	Trillo, 2b	4	0	1	0	1
Foli, ss	4	0	0	0	1	Ontiveros, 3b	4	0	0	0	0
Sadek, c	2	0	0	0	0	Mitterwald, c	3	0	1	0	0
Thomas, 2b	0	0	0	0	0	Reuschel, p	3	0	0	0	0
Knepper, p	2	0	0	0	0						
Whitfield, ph	1	0	1	1	0	TOTALS	32	3	10	3	1
Rudolph, c	0	0	0	0	0						
TOTALS	31	1	4	1	1						

```
San Francisco    0 0 0    0 0 0    1 0 0   --  1
Chicago          1 0 0    0 1 0    1 0 *   --  3
```

Double--Murcer. Stolen base--DeJesus. Double play--San Francisco, 1. Left on base--San Francisco 6, Chicago 7.

	IP	H	R	ER	BB	SO
Knepper (L, 0-1)	6	8	2	2	1	2
Williams	2	2	1	1	1	2
Reuschel (W, 8-2)	9	4	1	0	3	7

Wild pitch--Reuschel. Time--2:15. Attendance: 12,642

Other Baseball Highlights of 1977

- The American League expands to 14 teams by adding Toronto and Seattle.

- Rod Carew is the AL MVP after hitting .388.

- The Mets trade Tom Seaver to Cincinnati.

Clark Calvin Griffith—1898

Chicago Cubs Summit Season
Number 15

No. 15
CLARK GRIFFITH

BORN: November 20, 1869; Clear Creek, Missouri
DIED: October 27, 1955; Washington D.C.

Chicago White Stockings/Orphans/Colts: 1893-1900
Hall of Fame: 1946

SEASON AT THE SUMMIT: 1898

W-L-%	IP	CG	SH	SV	K/BB	PR	DEF	ERA
24-10 .706	325.2	36	4	0	97/64	63	1	1.88

Few baseball men have had as big an impact on the game as **Clark Griffith**. He was an outstanding pitcher in the National League; a pioneer in the formation of the American League; a manager for 20 years; and an owner—where he received his greatest notoriety—for more than twice that length of time.

Griffith was born in Missouri in 1869. At 18 he went into professional ball with a team in Bloomington, Indiana. From there, he spent time in Milwaukee, St. Louis and Boston of the American Association, Tacoma and Oakland of the Pacific Coast League, and Missoula, Montana, of the Rocky Mountain League. Finally, owner Jim Hart signed him for the National League's Chicago White Stockings in 1893.

A 5-foot-6½, 156-pound right-hander, Griffith was an immediate star for the Whites, winning 21, 25, 22 and 21 games in his first four full seasons. Despite the presence of stars like Cap Anson, Bill Dahlen and Fred Pfeffer, the Whites never got above fourth place in those years, and expectations weren't much higher as the 1898 sea-

son dawned. "Count us in the first three, barring accidents," Griffith told the *Chicago Tribune* on the eve of the opener. Captain Dahlen was even less bold: "I would not hesitate to predict that we will finish in one of the first four places..."

Whatever Chicago would do in 1898, it would do it without Anson, who called it quits as a player after the 1897 season, ending a 22-year National League playing career. He had also managed the White Stockings for the past 19 seasons, and had tried to purchase the franchise in the off-season, negotiations finally breaking down two days before the April 15 opener.

The White Stockings—now more often than not dubbed the Orphans, a reference to Anson's departure—began their season in St. Louis. Griffith, who would go on to his greatest season on the mound, stopped the Cardinals 2-1 on four hits. He faced just 25 men through eight innings, surrendered an unearned run in the ninth, and got out of a bases-loaded jam to record the victory.

A Pitcher's Superstition

He followed that with a two-hitter in Louisville six days later, beating the Colonels 8-2, and lost 3-2 in Cincinnati on the 26th when the Reds pushed across an unearned run in the ninth. Clearly, Griffith was the class of the National League. And he was probably even better than the numbers show.

Griffith had a superstition about shutouts—and he tried to avoid throwing one. Or so the *Tribune* explained after the Orphans' 16-2 victory over Louisville in their home opener at West Side Park on April 29.

"But for Griffith's pet superstition that it is unlucky to shut out a club, not a Colonel's name would have been engraved upon the scoreboard," the paper reported. "In the eighth, with the Colonels blanked, Griffith lobbed the ball. Even then Louisville could not score until 'Griff' called to [first baseman Bill] Everett to drop a throw. The one intentional error let in a run."

Less than two weeks later, he avoided another shutout by lobbing the ball to Cleveland hitters in the eighth inning of a game the Orphans had under control. Griffith's strategy worked: The Spiders wrapped two hits around a sacrifice to scratch out a run in Chicago's 2-1 victory, Griffith's fifth win in six decisions.

Griffith was sailing through the season—the Orphans couldn't say the same, stumbling into the second division early and staying there—and was 8-3 by the end of May. He won four of his first five decisions in June and seemed almost unbeatable. But on June 23 against Boston, he strained his back diving for a line drive in the second inning. He stayed in the game through the seventh, but by that time he had surrendered four runs and was on his way to a loss. Worse, the next morning his back was so sore he couldn't get out of bed. The injury forced him to miss two starts, and when he came back July 7 he wasn't ready, losing 7-5. A victory against lowly Washington on July 11 seemed to get him back on track, but then a case of the flu cost him another start. Griffith dropped his next two decisions, but then everything fell into place.

On A Streak

Griffith won four of his next five decisions, running his record to 17-8 with a three-hitter against Brooklyn on August 20. Four days later he beat Boston 2-1, not al-

lowing a hit after the second inning. And in his next turn, August 27, he held New York hitless for the first five innings en route to a 10-3 victory. He notched his 20th victory of the season three days later, a three-hitter against the Giants. It was part of a streak of eight straight wins for Griffith, and moved him into the NL's ERA leadership. He wound up the season at 1.88, with a 24-10 record and 36 complete games.

Griffith's career with the Orphans lasted only another three years. In 1901, he jumped to the Chicago White Sox of the fledgling American League. He went 24-7 in 1901 and 15-9 a year later and managed the team to first- and fourth-place finishes. But his biggest contributions to the new league were to come. In 1903, AL President Ban Johnson gave Griffith the task of building a successful club in New York. He founded the New York Highlanders, predecessors of the Yankees.

Griffith stayed in New York until 1908, then moved to Cincinnati, where he managed for three seasons and played for two. In 1912 he moved on to Washington, and two years later he and Philadelphia broker William D. Richardson purchased the Senators. Griffith now began concentrating on managing and ownership. He stepped down as skipper after the 1920 season—his career managerial record was 1,491-1,367—and helped build the Senators into pennant-winners in 1924 and '25.

The Old Fox

As an owner, Griffith became known for his trades and was referred to as "The Old Fox" in the press and by his peers. Other teams seldom got the better of Griffith in a trade. How tough of a dealmaker was he? In 1934 he sold shortstop-manager Joe Cronin—his son-in-law at the time—to the Red Sox.

Despite Griffith's skills as a wheeler-dealer, except for a streak in the early '30s—Washington made it to the 1933 World Series, losing to the New York Giants in five games—the Senators seldom were in contention. They finished second against wartime competition in 1945, then settled into a long stretch of ineptitude.

It was an inglorious way for Clark Griffith, a baseball pioneer, to go out. Elected to the Hall of Fame in 1946, he died on October 27, 1955 in Washington, at the age of 85.

CLARK GRIFFITH'S

Three Other Great Cub Seasons

	YR	W-L	IP	GS	GC	SH	SV	PD	K/BB	OBA	OB%	ERA	PR
1.	1895	26-14	353	41	39	0	0	1	79/91	.298	.348	3.93	34
2.	1896	23-11	317.2	35	35	0	0	1	81/70	.289	.331	3.54	29
3.	1899	22-14	319.2	38	35	0	0	6	73/65	.266	.310	2.79	38

Curious fellow, this "Old Fox." Whether playing, managing, or owning and running a ballclub from the front office, Clark Griffith did it *his* way. When it came to pitching (and he was a vastly underrated hurler), he had some quaint superstitions, and three 20-win seasons. Note further that he knew what to do with a stick in his hands (he hit .319 in 1895). His 1898 season, the best of his Orphan/Colt years, ranks a strong No. 15 along the summit line, well ahead of more readily recognizable names like Ed Reulbach and Hippo Vaughn.

"The Old Fox earned his nickname by utilizing a six-pitch arsenal, including the screwball (which he claimed to have invented), a silencing, quick-pitch delivery, and the ruse of hiding the ball in the plane of his body before delivering."

—From *The Ballplayers*, edited by Mike Shatzkin and Jim Charlton

GRIFFITH'S A NOTEWORTHY BOX SCORE

April 21, 1898

Griffith holds the heavy-hitting Louisville Colonels to two hits in an 8-2 victory.

Chicago	AB	R	H	PO	A	E	Louisville	AB	R	H	PO	A	E
Kilroy, rf	5	1	0	2	0	1	Clarke, lf	3	1	0	1	0	0
Lange, cf	5	0	1	3	0	0	Ritchey, ss	4	0	0	2	3	0
Dahlen, ss	5	1	1	1	3	0	Hoy, cf	3	0	0	7	0	1
Everett, lb	4	1	2	8	0	0	Wagner, 2b	4	1	1	1	4	0
Ryan, lf	5	1	2	4	0	1	Nance, rf	3	0	1	3	0	0
McCormick, 3b	5	1	1	1	1	0	Carey, lb	4	0	0	8	3	2
Callahan, 2b	3	0	0	1	0	1	Clingman. 3b	3	0	0	2	2	1
Donahue, c	2	2	1	6	0	0	Wilson, c	3	0	0	2	0	1
Griffith, p	4	1	1	1	3	0	Cunningham, p	3	0	0	1	4	2
TOTALS	38	8	9	27	7	3	TOTALS	30	2	2	27	16	6

Chicago	4 1 0	2 1 0	0 0 0	--	8	
Louisville	0 0 0	0 0 2	0 0 0	--	2	

Double--Dahlen. Home run--McCormick. Strikeouts--Griffith 3, Cunningham 1. Hit by pitch--by Cunningham (Donahue). Attendance--1,550 Umpires--Cushman and Haydler

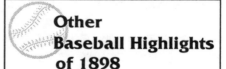

Other Baseball Highlights of 1898

- The National League introduces a 154-game schedule.

- Boston defeats Baltimore by six games for the NL pennant.

- Players in uniform are barred from sitting in the stands.

SUTTER
32

Bruce Sutter—1977

Chicago Cubs Summit Season
Number 16

No. 16
BRUCE SUTTER

BORN: January 8, 1953; Lancaster, Pennsylvania

Chicago Cubs: 1976-1980

SEASON AT THE SUMMIT: 1977

W-L-%		IP	CG	SH	SV	K/BB	PR	DEF	ERA
7-3	.700	107.1	0	0	31	129/23	31	1	1.34

How dominant was **Bruce Sutter** in 1977?

"Never saw a ball explode like his," said Cincinnati catcher Johnny Bench. "I bunted. I couldn't hit what he was throwing, so I figured I could bunt it."

"It was unhittable," said Atlanta's Dale Murphy.

"When he comes into a game, you're not going to get any more runs," said San Diego manager Alvin Dark.

The secret to Sutter's success was a split-finger fastball that made him the best pitcher in the majors during the first half of the season. The pitch started out like a fastball but would drop suddenly as it reached the plate. He learned the split-finger from minor-league instructor Fred Martin after he lost his fastball following an elbow injury in 1972. Sutter came up to the Cubs in May of 1976 and went on to become their bullpen ace with a 6-3 record, 2.71 ERA, 10 saves and 73 strikeouts in 83 innings. Excellent numbers, but nothing compared to what he did in 1977.

Untouchable

Sutter began the season unimpressively, allowing one run and three hits in 1⅔ innings of work against New York on April 7. After that, he quietly began putting together an amazing stretch—a perfect two-thirds of an inning against the Mets on April 9, one hit over 2⅔ innings against New York a day later, two scoreless innings against the Phils on the 13th, two more scoreless innings the next day against the Mets. And so it went, and by the end of April he had a streak of 9⅓ scoreless innings, and by May 7 he had lowered his ERA to 0.90. He earned his sixth save the next day with 2⅓ innings of one-hit relief, lowering his ERA to 0.86 for 22 innings of work.

Cubs manager Herman Franks had no qualms about bringing in Sutter, who seldom worked more than two innings. A typical appearance came on May 14 against Montreal. Starter Rick Reuschel tired and Sutter was called on in the ninth. He faced two batters, needing just eight pitches to retire them both and earn his eighth save. "I had it again today," he said afterward. "And I'll be ready tomorrow."

And he was. He worked one inning the next day for his ninth save of the season and third in four games. It helped him earn NL Pitcher of the Week honors.

Behind the relief work of Sutter, Willie Hernandez and Paul Reuschel and the hitting of Manny Trillo, Bill Buckner, Larry Biittner, Ivan DeJesus and Bobby Murcer (all over .300 for the first month of the season), the Cubs were immediate contenders. "This team is playing good," Franks observed after the Cubs won their sixth in a row on May 10. They eventually moved into first on May 28 with a 6-3 victory over the Pirates—Sutter working three innings—and ended the month with a one-game lead over second-place St. Louis.

Sutter's appearances were usually brief, an inning or two, sometimes just a batter or two, and usually the game was on the line, although at times he was brought in to nail down games that the Cubs had in hand (on June 7, for example, he came on in the ninth to get the last two outs in a 10-3 victory over the Dodgers, a day after working 2⅔ innings for his 16th save). But who could blame Franks for going to a pitcher who was 2-1 with a 0.86 ERA and 63 strikeouts versus only seven walks through the first third of the season?

Sutter earned his 20th save on June 27, working two scoreless innings in a 4-3 win over the Expos and lowering his ERA to 0.69. He got No. 21 a day later.

Out Of Steam
The Cubs, meanwhile, entered June with a 47-24 record and a 7½-game lead over the second-place Phillies and Cardinals. But they dropped five of six to open the month—the pitching staff was showing signs of tiring—and had their lead cut to three games.

Sutter, too, was starting to have the occasional off-game—three hits in 1⅓ innings against St. Louis, and four hits and two earned runs in 1⅔ innings against Montreal (the first time all season he was replaced in mid-inning). After he surrendered a game-winning home run to the Mets' Steve Henderson in a 4-2 loss on July 12, Sutter admitted that his shoulder was bothering him.

The soreness was first attributed to a muscle spasm, and Sutter asked to be excused from the All-Star Game ("I owe it to my team to rest the shoulder, which is all it needs, I think," he said). It wasn't difficult to see why he needed rest. Sutter had been in 45 of the Cubs' first 88 games, working 81 innings. At the break he was 5-1 with a remarkable 1.11 ERA (10 earned runs in 49 innings) and 24 saves. The Cubs were 53-35, leading the NL East by two games, largely because of Sutter, relievers Paul Reuschel (3-1, 2.33) and Hernandez (3-3, 1.92) and Rick Reuschel (12-3, 2.42). Their other starters were all at .500 (Bill Bonham at 9-9, 4.29; Mike Krukow, 7-7, 4.59; and Ray Burris, 9-9, 4.99).

Out Of The Lineup
The day after the All-Star break, the Cubs got the news they feared: There was bleeding in Sutter's shoulder. Rest was ordered, and he was sidelined until a hitless three-inning stint on July 28. He worked two-thirds of an inning on August 1 but again admitted his shoulder wasn't right. Tests two days later uncovered more damage and he was placed on the 21-day disabled list. By the time Sutter returned August 24, the Cubs were long out of first and fading.

On the 26th, Sutter came on in the eighth inning against the Giants, retired the last batter, then worked a 1-2-3 ninth for his 25th save—his first in 40 days. Sutter's stats tailed off slightly over the last month—he allowed six earned runs and 18 hits in 19⅔ innings—but he still was able to demonstrate why he was the best reliever in the league (on September 8, for example, he fanned six straight Expos in a game, including all three batters in one inning—Ellis Valentine, Gary Carter and Larry Parrish—on just nine pitches).

When the season ended, with the Cubs fourth at 81-81, Sutter had 31 saves, a 7-3 record and a 1.34 ERA, a performance that earned him a spot in the Cubs' 50 all-time greatest seasons.

BRUCE SUTTER'S

Two Other Great Cub Seasons

	YR	W-L	IP	GS	GC	SH	SV	PD	K/BB	OBA	OB%	ERA	PR
1.	1979	6-6	101.1	0	0	0	37	1	110/32	.186	.252	2.22	17
2.	1980	5-8	102.1	0	0	0	28	0	76/34	.242	.307	2.64	11

The Cub pitching staff completed only 20 games in 1979; in 1980 the count was 13. These were the years when relief pitching came on like thunder. One false move and the starters were "outta there." The Bruce Sutters of this baseball world made an early move on frontline pitching inevitable. Equipped with his devastating split-finger fastball, which just about dropped out of sight as it neared home plate, Sutter came on to nail down what few victories those inferior Cubbies could muster. He saved 37 of 80 in 1979, 28 of 64 in 1980, and 31 of 81 in 1977, his summit season at Wrigleyville. That's good enough for a top spot among Cub summiteers, just ahead of righthander "Big Bill" Hands and "Bad Bill" Dahlen!

How dominant was Bruce Sutter in 1977?

"It's just a case of being the perfect man for the perfect pitch. He has the ideal physical makeup, the perfect snap, the perfect delivery. Another pitcher with as much ability could work all year on the same pitch and not be as close to as effective. I tell you, he is the best I have ever seen."

—Cubs pitching coach Barney Schultz on Bruce Sutter

Other Baseball Highlights of 1977

• Chet Lemon of the White Sox sets an AL record for outfielders with 512 putouts.

• Nolan Ryan strikes out 341 batters and allows fewer hits (198) than walks (204).

• Baltimore's Brooks Robinson retires after 23 seasons with the same team, a major-league record.

SUTTER: A NOTEWORTHY BOX SCORE

September 8, 1977

Sutter strikes out the first six batters he faces, tying a National League mark, and picks up his sixth win in a 3-2 victory over Montreal.

Montreal	AB	R	H	RBI	E	Chicago	AB	R	H	RBI	E
Cash, 2b	4	1	1	0	0	DeJesus, ss	5	0	1	0	0
Cromartie, lf	5	0	1	0	0	Biittner, lf	5	0	0	0	0
Dawson, cf	4	0	1	0	0	Buckner, 1b	4	0	0	1	0
Perez, 1b	3	0	1	1	0	Murcer, rf	2	1	1	0	0
Valentine, rf	4	0	1	0	0	Ontiveros, 3b	4	0	0	0	0
Carter, c	3	0	0	0	1	Gross, cf	3	1	1	0	0
Parrish, 3b	3	1	0	0	1	Trillo, 2b	4	0	1	1	0
Frias, ss	4	0	2	0	0	Mitterwald, c	2	0	0	0	0
Rogers, p	2	0	0	1	0	Cardenal, ph	1	0	0	0	0
Alcala, p	1	0	0	0	0	Swisher, c	1	0	0	0	0
Kerrigan, p	0	0	0	0	0	Burris, p	1	0	0	0	0
McEnaney, p	0	0	0	0	0	Clines, ph	1	0	1	0	0
						P. Reuschel, p	0	0	0	0	0
						Morales, ph	1	0	0	0	0
TOTALS	33	2	7	2	2	Sutter, p	0	0	0	0	0
						Rosello, ph	1	1	1	0	0
						TOTALS	35	3	6	2	0

Two out when winning run scored

```
          Montreal    0 0 1   1 0 0   0 0 0   0  --2
          Chicago     0 0 0   0 0 0   2 0 0   1  --3
```

Double--Cash. Stolen base--Cromarite. Sacrifice--Kerrigan. Sacrifice fly--Buckner. Double plays--Montreal 1, Chicago 1. Left on base--Montreal 7, Chicago 7.

	IP	H	R	ER	BB	SO
Rogers	5	2	0	0	1	7
Alcala	1¹/₃	3	2	1	1	2
Kerrigan (L, 3-5)	2²/₃	1	1	0	1	0
McEnaney	²/₃	0	0	0	0	0
Burris	6	6	2	2	3	4
P. Reuschel	1	0	0	0	0	1
Sutter (W, 6-1)	3	1	0	0	1	6

Bill Hands—1969

Chicago Cubs Summit Season
Number 17

No. 17
BILL HANDS

BORN: May 6, 1940; Hackensack, New Jersey

Chicago Cubs: 1966-1972

SEASON AT THE SUMMIT: 1969

W-L-	%	IP	CG	SH	SV	K/BB	PR	DEF	ERA
20-14	.588	300.0	18	3	3	181/73	37	1	2.49

The Bleacher Bums. Willie Smith's 11th-inning pinch home run to win the season opener. Leo Durocher. Ernie Banks. Fergie Jenkins and Ken Holtzman. Ron Santo and Don Young. Those Mets.

Has any team that didn't win a pennant ever had more written about it than the 1969 Cubs?

They were the surprise of the season, Chicago's darlings, a team that jumped into the lead in the National League East and was seemingly headed for the franchise's first championship of any kind in nearly a quarter-century. It didn't happen, of course, and nearly 30 years later that team is still discussed, the season still rehashed, by Cub fans.

The heroes were many—Santo, Kessinger, Beckert and Banks, Williams, Hickman and Hundley, Jenkins, Holtzman and Hands.

Bill Hands was the No. 3 starter for Durocher. Arguably, though, he was the ace of the staff that magical summer. He had come to the Cubs from the Giants be-

fore the start of the 1966 season. He was 8-13, 7-8 and 16-10 in his first three years with Chicago.

A low-ball pitcher who was an expert at working the corners, Hands got off to a fast start in '69. He won his first outing, beating the Phillies 11-3 on April 9, striking out six and allowing just one earned run. He didn't allow an earned run in seven innings in his next appearance—he wasn't the pitcher of record—then picked up victory No. 2 on April 17 by shutting out St. Louis on three hits.

Early Slump

His luck soon changed. In his next start, Hands was shelled by the Pirates, lasting only 1⅓ innings, surrendering five runs, four earned, in a 7-5 loss. He lost four of his next five, though he performed admirably in three of the defeats—a 3-1 loss to the Phillies on April 30, in which he drove in his first run since 1967; a 3-2 loss to the Mets on May 4, during which he and Tom Seaver participated in a brushback war (he got Seaver in the ribs, Seaver hit him in the leg); and a 3-1 loss to the Dodgers on May 21.

Hands began to turn things around on May 25 when he pitched six shutout innings in a game the Cubs later won 1-0. Five days later, he showed he was back on track with a five-hit shutout of the NL West-leading Atlanta Braves that lowered his ERA for the season to 2.50—impressive for a 4-5 pitcher.

At this point, the Cubs hadn't needed much from Hands. The pitching of Jenkins, Holtzman and Dick Selma was sufficient to help them stay in first. With Hands kicking into gear, things looked even brighter.

He evened his record at 5-5 with a seven-hitter against Houston on June 3, and after being shelled by Atlanta on June 11, started making his biggest contributions to the Cubs' drive. Between June 20 and July 2, he won all four of his outings, including a five-hitter against Montreal on June 20, and a three-hitter against St. Louis on the 28th.

The Cubs saw their first-place lead cut to five games when they dropped a double-header to the Cardinals on July 6. Hands lost the opener, lasting only 3⅓ innings. Those two losses were followed by two more—both games Cub fans still talk about. After the Mets beat the Cubs on July 8, Santo ripped center-fielder Young for a misplay in the outfield; the next day, Seaver's bid for a no-hitter was broken up by Jim Qualls with one out in the ninth. The two losses left the Cubs only three games ahead of the charging Mets. Hands, though, came through in the clutch, beating New York 6-2 with a three-hitter on July 10—the second time in a month he had stopped a five-game Cub losing streak.

Building a Big Lead

Four days later, the Cub lead restored to 4½ games, the Mets came to Chicago. In the opener of the three-game series, Hands was magnificent, outdueling Seaver and winning 1-0. With Billy Williams singling home the only run he'd need in the fifth, Hands scattered six hits and struck out five before tiring. The Mets had a man on first with two out in the ninth, and Hands was behind pinch-hitter Donn Clendenon 2-0 in the count when Durocher pulled him. "He told me he couldn't throw another pitch," Durocher said. "And when Bill Hands tell you that, you'd better believe him."

The Cubs held on to win, making their lead 5½ games. But that lasted less than 24 hours as the Mets won the next two games of the series to draw within 2½. The lead was 4½ games at the All-Star break, which Hands spent at home after being snubbed by NL manager Red Schoendienst.

The rest, though, served Hands well. He won his next four outings, running his record to 15-8 and cutting his ERA to 2.43. His 4-2 complete-game victory over San Diego on August 13 gave the Cubs a seemingly comfortable 8½-game lead in the NL East race.

But Hands—and the Cubs—were running out of luck. He lost his next three outings—the first when a seventh-inning error let in two runs and sent him to a 5-3 defeat; the second 3-1 to Atlanta; and the third after he was KO'd in the ninth by the Reds, who held on to win 9-8 after the Cubs scored four runs in the bottom of the inning. He got back on track August 29, running his record to 16-11 and putting the Cubs 3½ games ahead with a six-hit 2-1 victory in Atlanta.

Fadeout

The Cubs' run, though, was over. Hands suffered two tough losses, coming out on the short end of a 2-0 decision to the Reds and Jim Maloney, who tossed a two-hitter, on September 3, and being outdueled by the Mets' Jerry Koosman, who struck out 13 Cubs on September 8. It was the fifth loss in a row for the Cubs and left them just 1½ games ahead of New York.

The Cubs lost their next three games, one to the Mets and two to the Phillies, to drop out of first. They stopped the bleeding briefly on September 12 when Hands—their stopper—seven-hit St. Louis. But it was too late. Hands would wind up with a 20-14 record, his only 20-win season of what would be an 11-year major-league career—and 2.49 ERA. And the Cubs, despite 92 victories, placed eight games back of the Mets.

"Basically, we just couldn't win at the end of the year, and they couldn't lose," Hands would later recall. "They just couldn't do anything wrong."

BILL HANDS'

Two Other Great Cub Seasons

	YR	W-L	IP	GS	GC	SH	SV	PD	K/BB	OBA	OB%	ERA	PR
1.	1968	16-10	258.2	34	11	4	0	0	148/36	.231	.264	2.89	3
2.	1970	18-15	265	38	12	2	1	1	170/76	.269	.322	3.70	10

Until muscle spasms and back miseries caught up with Bill Hands, he was a very effective pitcher for a Cubs outfit on the rise. Chess champ of the clubhouse, he was also Wrigleyville champ, especially in his big year, 1969, when manager Leo Durocher handed him the ball for the "must-have" assignments. The team's stopper in the chase to the pennant with the Miracle Mets, Hands registered his career year between two other fair-to-middlin' years in 1968 and 1970. His best was good enough to position him above fellow hurlers Dick Ellsworth and Bob Rush in the top 25. A 1972 no-hitter over the Expos was his single-game career highlight.

Cub catcher Randy Hundley, talking about Bill Hands' special niche on the '69 roster: "Nobody talks about Bill. He's kinda dropped out of sight, but he was very important to our ballclub. He had an attitude about him that was real important, too. It was a big part of it. And it rubbed off on the other pitchers. You better believe it!"

Other Baseball Highlights of 1969

•The Amazing Mets beat the Orioles in the World Series.

•To add more offense, the height of the pitcher's mound is lowered and the size of the strike zone is reduced.

•Bowie Kuhn is named commissioner.

•Twins manager Billy Martin beats up one of his own players, pitcher Dave Boswell.

HANDS: A NOTEWORTHY BOX SCORE

July 14, 1969

Hands outduels Tom Seaver and shuts out the Mets 1-0.

New York	AB	R	H	RBI	PO	A	E	Chicago	AB	R	H	RBI	PO	A	E
Agee, cf	4	0	0	0	1	0	0	Kessinger, ss	3	1	1	0	0	1	0
Boswell, 2b	4	0	1	0	1	3	0	Beckert, 2b	4	0	1	0	4	4	0
Jones, lf	4	0	1	0	5	0	0	Williams, rf-lf	3	0	2	1	2	0	0
Shamsky, rf	4	0	0	0	2	0	0	Santo, 3b	3	0	0	0	2	2	0
Garrett, 3b	3	0	1	0	2	0	0	Banks, 1b	3	0	1	0	8	0	0
Kranepool, 1b	3	0	0	0	7	0	0	Smith, lf	2	0	0	0	0	0	0
Martin, c	4	0	2	0	4	0	0	Hickman, lf-cf	1	0	0	0	0	0	0
Harrelson, pr	0	0	0	0	0	0	0	Hundley, c	3	0	0	0	5	0	0
Weis, ss	3	0	1	0	1	2	0	Qualls, cf	3	0	0	0	6	0	0
Seaver, p	1	0	0	0	1	1	0	Hands, p	3	0	0	0	0	3	0
Clendenon, ph	1	0	0	0	0	0	0	Regan, p	0	0	0	0	0	0	0
TOTALS	31	0	6	0	24	6	0	TOTALS	28	1	5	1	27	10	0

New York	000	000	000	-- 0
Chicago	000	001	00x	-- 1

Double--Martin. Sacrifice--Seaver. Double play--New York, 1. Left on base--New York 8, Chicago 4.

	IP	H	R	ER	BB	SO
Seaver (L, 14-4)	8	5	1	1	1	4
Hands (W, 11-7)	8²/₃	6	0	0	3	5
Regan	¹/₃	0	0	0	0	0

Save--Regan. Wild pitch--Hands. Umpires--Engel, Stello, Donatelli and Steiner. Time--2:25. Attendance--37,473

Bill Dahlen—1896

Chicago Cubs Summit Season
Number 18

No. 18
BILL DAHLEN

BORN: January 5, 1870; Nelliston, New York
DIED: December 5, 1950; Brooklyn, New York

Chicago Colts: 1891-98

SEASON AT THE SUMMIT: 1896

AB-R-H	BA	OB%	SA	EXBH	HR	RBI	FR	SB
474-137-167	.352	.438	.553	58	9	74	25	51

By the 1890s the only game in town was being played in the National League. After the demise of a number of leagues and associations, the ranks of organized baseball's Senior Circuit had swelled to 12 teams, and despite lingering and vexing problems, the league greeted the mid-'90s with measured optimism. Hopes were high that a good pennant race and fewer altercations on, as well as off, the field of play would prompt another upswing in league attendance, perhaps exceeding the 3 million mark.

Though Baltimore's Orioles, the dominating force in the league, were once again the team to beat, there were indications that Cleveland, Philadelphia, Boston and Cap Anson's Colts might well unseat McGraw, Kelly, Jennings, Keeler, & Co. The Colts' aspirations rested on Anson's customary formula for success: solid hitting, an alert, heady defense and enough pitching to get the job done.

The Colts and "Bad Bill"
The 1896 lineup card featured the aging but still dangerous Anson, George Decker, who ran a hitting streak of 26 games that summer, outfielder Bill "Little Eva" Lange,

who hit well all season long and swiped 84 bases to boot, and our summit hero, **Bill Dahlen**, a superbly talented but unsung short fielder who spent his best years in what many believe to be a Hall of Fame career in a Chicago uniform. Often referred to as "Bad Bill," Dahlen was a short-fused, belligerent sort who was regularly involved in scrapes and brawls. Though Anson usually had no problem with that, especially where opposing teams and umpires were concerned, he did find it necessary to put his star infielder off the train when things got out of hand one evening between Pittsburgh and New York. Among the seven games Battling Bill missed in 1896 was a series opener in New York. As always, with the Captain (Anson was never one to shy away from a line in the dirt) it was his way or the next railway. But it must also be said that Dahlen scrapped against opposing teams with the same fury (and more success) during his accomplished career, and especially during his summit season showpiece.

Off and Running in '96
The Colts opened their season on April 16 at Louisville in the company of 10,000-plus diehard Colonels fans, beat-

ing them behind pitcher Danny Friend 4-2. Dahlen contributed a triple and a couple of gems afield as the Chicagoans started out on the right foot. The next day Bad Bill homered in a 14-5 win, and the sturdy, choke-hitting shortfielder was off and winging. He had started off at a .350 clip and never strayed too far from that pace throughout the entire campaign, winding up just about as he started at the .352 mark.

By early May Anson's charges were seventh in the 12-team league and continued to spend the season in the middle of the pack—finishing with enough of a surge to place fifth, but a distant 18½ games behind the Orioles, who won their third straight National League title and the Temple Cup. Led by the irrepressible Hughie Jennings of "Eeeeeyah!" fame, this team, one of the most fabled ballclubs of all time, took a few pages out of the Chicago book with superior hitting, aggressive baserunning, deadly defense and an unrelenting attack on each and every team it played—every game. Anson's formula was simply used to better advantage by Ned Hanlon's boys. So Cleveland, Cincinnati, Boston and the Colts wound up as also-rans yet another time to the Baltimores.

The July 11 *Sporting News* lineup of hitters, fielders and pitchers listed Bad Bill at 14th (.351) in a batting race that produced more than 40 .300 hitters. That didn't change much by season's end as Lange, Bill Everett, Anson and Dahlen represented the Colts on '96's extended list of heavy hitters.

Some of Dahlen's more lustrous outings included a four-hit game on May 3, enabling Chicago to sweep a St. Louis series, numerous three-hit games, including one against Baltimore in mid-May as the Colts won, and on down into September at Pittsburgh in a tight Colt win.

There were, of course, a few games here and there when he was collared, one of which came in a Cy Young white-wash job on September 14 at the West Side Grounds as Cleveland beat the Colts 2-0. Hitless days were, however, a rarity in a season that found Dahlen sporting a .438 on-base percentage and a career-high slugging average of .553. His 19 triples were second high, his 30 doubles fourth, and his 137 runs fifth in the league.

Sums with Some Substance

Bill Dahlen's playing career (he wound up in Brooklyn and managed the team from 1910-1913) spanned 21 seasons of heady, go-get-'em shortstopping, and wound up ranking him in the top five all-time listings for career assists, assists per game, putouts, total chances per game, and at a lofty No. 3 spot with 349 fielding runs (he's headed only by No. 1 Nap Lajoie and Bill Mazeroski). During the 1896 season he logged 25 fielding runs. Swift and canny on the bases, he added 51 stolen bases to the Chicago attack.

In 1894, the season in which he hit safely in 42 straight games (the Cub record), he also posted four double-figure totals: 32 doubles; 14 triples; 15 homers; and 42 stolen bases. On the Cub all-time career charts he's listed in the top 10 among runs scored and doubles.

However volatile and contentious he might have been, there was no gainsaying his gifts, his all-out style, and his steady stickwork. Bad Bill rates a niche well above the mid-range of our summit 50. He's a solid No. 18, right in there among Cub stalwarts like Rick Reuschel (No. 14) and Bruce Sutter (No. 16), that dynamic 1977 duo, and directly ahead of Billy Herman (No.19) and Claude Passeau (No. 20). The Colt shortstop who came to play wears the No. 18 spot exceedingly well!

BILL DAHLEN'S

Four Other Great Cub Seasons

	YR	GP	AB-R-H	BA	OB%	SA	K/BB	HR	RBI	SB	FR	BR
1.	1892	143	581-114-169	.291	.347	.422	56/45	5	58	60	25	19
2.	1894	121	502-149-179	.357	.444	.566	33/76	15	107	42	32	28
3.	1897	75	276-67-80	.290	.399	.478	NA/43	6	40	15	28	11
4.	1898	142	521-96-151	.290	.385	.393	NA/58	1	79	27	26	18

In the eight seasons Bill Dahlen played in Chicago, he averaged a 3.58 Total Player Rating (TPR), representing approximately four more wins per season than the league-average player might have contributed. Had he kept up that pace through another seven or eight seasons, Dahlen would assuredly have wound up with a plaque at Cooperstown. His 1894 season was a beaut, rating a 4.8, and his last season in Chicago was rated a 4.6, just a shade less. Not too shabby!

"In 1894 Bill Dahlen collected 107 runs batted in, a total that barely placed him among the top 20 RBI men in the National League. Exactly a decade later Dahlen notched 80 RBIs, seemingly an indication that his offensive production had declined. In actuality, however, it was not Dahlen that declined but offensive production in general. By 1904, the game was so deeply in the throes of the dead-ball era that Dahlen's modest total of 80 RBIs topped the National League."
—From *Facinating Baseball Facts*

DAHLEN: A NOTEWORTHY BOX SCORE

May 3, 1896

"Bad Bill" tears up the Browns with two triples and four hits.

St. Louis	R	H	P	A		Chicago	R	H	P	A
Cooley, lf	2	2	1	0		Everett, 3b	3	2	1	6
Dowd, cf	2	1	3	0		Dahlen, ss	4	4	5	2
Douglas, c	0	1	4	0		Lange, cf	1	1	3	0
Quinn, 3b	1	1	1	4		Ryan, rf	1	0	1	1
Connor, 1b	1	2	11	1		Truby, 2b	2	3	4	2
Meyers, 2b	0	2	0	4		Anson, 1b	1	3	6	0
Parrett, rf	0	2	3	0		Flynn, lf	3	1	1	1
Cross, ss	0	0	4	2		Briggs, p	0	0	0	3
Hart, p	1	3	0	1		Donohue, c	3	2	6	2
TOTALS	7	14	27	12		TOTALS	18	16	27	16

St. Louis	012	102	010	—7
Chicago	242	004	33*	—18

Attendance: 17,200   Umpire: Waldman

Other Baseball Highlights of 1896

• The NL has two .400 hitters: Jesse Burkett of Cleveland (.410) and Baltimore's Hugh Jennings (.401).

• Philadelphia's Ed Delahanty gets four home runs July 13 at Chicago.

• The Baltimore Orioles win their third straight NL championship, then sweep Cleveland for the Temple Cup.

Billy Herman—1935

Chicago Cubs Summit Season
Number 19

No. 19
BILLY HERMAN

BORN: July 7, 1909; New Albany, Indiana
DIED: September 5, 1992; West Palm Beach, Florida

Chicago Cubs: 1931-1941
Hall of Fame: 1975

SEASON AT THE SUMMIT: 1935

AB-R-H	BA	OB%	2B	3B	HR	RBI	BR	FR	SB
666-113-227	.341	.383	57	6	7	83	26	19	6

Billy Herman's major-league debut gave no inkling of the productive 15-year playing career in his future.

It was August 28, 1931 in Wrigley Field, and the newly arrived second baseman was facing Cincinnati's Si Johnson. Herman had singled his first time up, in the second inning. Now, in the third, the Reds' right-hander delivered a high inside pitch. Herman pulled away but kept his bat close to his head; the ball hit the bat then hit Herman in the head. Down he went in a heap. "I was out cold for about 10 minutes," he would later recall.

Herman was back in the Cub lineup the next day—where he would remain for the next 10 seasons—making a favorable impression in a 4-2 loss to the Reds. "There was some consolation furnished by the deeds of Billy Herman, the new second sacker who refused to stay dizzy as the result of being hit on the head in his debut the day previous," wrote Irving Vaughan in the *Chicago Tribune.* "As a fielder, [Herman] did about everything asked of him. As a batter he walked twice, singled once to start the Cubs' first run and fouled out in the ninth...He also

showed that there is nothing slow about his running ability."

A right-handed hitter with outstanding bat control, Herman had a short, compact swing, seldom struck out and became the National League's premiere hit-and-run man. Defensively, he was as smart and sure-handed as any second baseman in baseball. And it's probably fair to say no one was more dedicated to the game. "If you gave me a bat and a ball and said, 'Hey, go play,' I played," he once said. "I gave a thousand percent every day in my playing career. Baseball was serious as hell to me. Baseball was my life."

A Season To Remember
Herman's 15-year Hall-of-Fame career also included stops with the Brooklyn Dodgers, Boston Braves and Pittsburgh Pirates. But his glory days were as a Cub—and no season was better than 1935.

He started the year quickly, hitting .327 through the first two weeks of the season, but soon went into a slump that saw him fall to .254 by June 1. As the month wore on, he slowly began building his average. Helped by games like the 4-for-5 afternoon he had against the Giants and Carl Hubbell on June 25, Herman soon got within striking distance of .300.

The Cubs, conversely, stumbled at the start of the season, losing four of their first six and slipping into sixth place, but soon righted themselves and climbed to third at 18-14 as June began.

Herman's timely hitting and dependable fielding earned him All-Star recognition—he was named to 10 All-Star teams in his career. He played the entire game, going hitless in three at-bats and handling five chances flawlessly in the NL's 4-1 loss.

The second half of the season would turn out to be among the most memorable in Chicago baseball history. The Cubs won their last four games before the break to run their record to 40-32, good for third place, when the second half started. In late July, the Cubs put together an 11-game winning streak to move within striking distance of first.

Billy's Big Bat

Much of the credit for the resurgence belonged to the pitching staff, which solidified behind Bill Lee, Charlie Root, Larry French and Lon Warneke. But Herman's hitting also deserved recognition—a pair of 2-for-4 games in a double-header against Brooklyn on July 23, 2-for-5 and 4-for-5 games the next day against the Dodgers, and a 2-for-4 performance the following day in a 4-2 victory—the Cubs' 18th in their last 21 games—that moved them into second.

Herman had another hot week in August. He went 4 for 9 in a double-header split with Philadelphia on the 18th, singled home the winning run the next day in a 2-1 victory over the Phils, then put together an 8-for-19 series as the Cubs won three of four from the first-place Giants. He had raised his average to .326 and helped the Cubs get within 3½ games of first. The deficit was 2½ games when September arrived—and the Cubs went on a stretch drive that captivated Chicago.

21 In A Row

The Streak began on September 4 when the Cubs beat the Phillies 8-2. The Cubs beat the Phils again the next day. And the next day. And the next, to move into second place. Then came Boston, and four more victories. Following was a four-game sweep of Brooklyn that put the Cubs into first and made front-page news. The Streak stretched to 21 games, with victory No. 20, September 27 against the defending NL champion Cardinals, the pennant-clincher. Two losses closed the season.

Herman was a huge factor in The Streak. When it began, he was hitting .330; when it ended he was at .340. He again was at his best against the Giants; in a series August 16-19 he went 11 for 18, including a 3-for-4 day against Hubbell.

Herman wound up at .341, including a league-leading 227 hits and 57 doubles, and he drove in 83 runs—while hitting No. 2 in the batting order. He also led NL second basemen in all four fielding categories—putouts (416), assists (520), double plays (109) and fielding percentage (.964).

With the momentum of their stretch drive and a lineup that featured Gabby Hartnett (.344), Frank Demaree (.325) and Augie Galan (.314) and a pitching staff anchored by Lee (20-6) and Warneke (20-13), the Cubs seemed to have the edge over the Detroit Tigers in the World Series.

The Cubs took the opener 3-0 on Warneke's four-hitter, but Detroit came back to win the next three games. Chicago staved off elimination in Game 5, Warneke getting the win again, but the Tigers took Game 6 and the Series 4-3 despite Herman's RBI single and two-run homer. For the Series, he finished 8 for 24 (.333) with six runs batted in, both Cub highs, and also was fined $200 by Commissioner Kenesaw Mountain Landis for using "vile and unprintable language" while taunting Detroit's Hank Greenberg. Asked by a reporter what words he used, Herman replied, "All of them."

Herman would hit .334 and .335 the next two seasons—he considered 1935, '36 and '37 the pinnacle of his career—but neither of those seasons stacked up with '35.

BILLY HERMAN'S

Three Other Great Cub Seasons

	YR	GP	AB-R-H	BA	OB%	SA	K/BB	HR	RBI	SB	FR	BR
1.	1932	154	656-102-206	.314	.358	.404	33/40	1	51	14	17	6
2.	1936	153	632-101-211	.334	.392	.470	30/59	5	93	5	15	25
3.	1937	138	564-106-189	.335	.396	.479	22/56	11	65	2	19	25

As with many of the greats and Hall of Famers, Billy Herman's record wears well over the years. His best years, as a very popular Cubbie, covered the decade of the '30s, during which he was the premier stick-handler in both leagues. To this day he ranks among the top three hit-and-run men the game has produced, so acknowledged even by that harsh and unforgiving critic of ballplayers, Leo Durocher. The 1935, 1936 and 1937 seasons presented three difficult choices for a Herman "best." His first 57-double and 227-base hit season, 1935, won out. That season he led both World Series teams with six RBIs and hit .333 as the Cubs' top player, and it was another year of All-Star play (there were 10 all told) for the chunky-appearing but deft second baseman. He's a solid top-20 pick for summit honors.

"[Cub shortstop Billy] Jurges and I did something in one year, in '35, no other second base combination has ever done. We both led the league in all four defensive categories: putouts, assists, double plays and fielding percentage. And that same year I led the league in hits and doubles and drove in 83 runs, hitting second. And I played every game on the club that won the pennant. And I didn't even come close to winning the Most Valuable Player Award."

—Billy Herman on his 1935 season

HERMAN: A NOTEWORTHY BOX SCORE

June 25, 1935
Herman gets four hits, including a first-inning homer off Carl Hubbell, against the first-place Giants.

Chicago	AB	R	H	PO	A		New York	AB	R	H	PO	A
Galan, lf	4	2	3	4	0		Moore, lf	4	2	2	2	0
Herman, 2b	5	2	4	2	3		Bartell, ss	5	1	4	0	3
Hack, 3b	1	0	0	0	0		Terry, 1b	4	0	0	9	0
English, 3b	3	0	0	1	2		Ott, rf	3	0	1	3	0
Hartnett, c	4	1	1	1	0		Leiber, cf	5	0	0	3	1
Stephenson, rf	1	1	0	1	0		Koenig, 2b	5	0	1	2	2
Cuyler, cf	4	1	1	1	0		Jackson, 3b	5	1	2	0	2
Demaree, rf	3	0	1	3	0		Danning, c	5	0	2	8	0
Klein, ph	0	0	0	0	0		Hubbell, p	3	1	1	0	0
Lindstrom, ph	0	0	0	0	0		Stout, p	0	0	0	0	1
Warneke, pr	0	0	0	0	0		Smith, p	0	0	0	0	0
Bryant, p	1	0	0	0	1		Gabler, p	0	0	0	0	0
Cavarretta, 1b	4	1	2	11	0		Fitzsimmons, p	1	0	0	0	2
Jurges, ss	4	0	0	1	6							
Charleton, p	2	0	0	0	0		TOTALS	40	5	13	27	11
Kowalik, p	0	0	0	0	0							
O'Dea, c	0	1	0	2	0							
TOTALS	37	10	12	27	12							

Chicago	1 0 1	1 0 0	1 4 2 –10
New York	0 0 2	1 0 2	0 0 0 –5

Errors–English, Galan, Bartell. Runs batted in–Herman 3, Cavarretta 2, Cuyler 2, Galan 3, Bartell 4, Terry 1. Sacrifices–Cuyler, English. Doubles–Galan, Bartell (2), Moore. Triples–Galan (2). Home runs–Herman, Cuyler, Bartell. Left on base–Chicago 5, New York 12. Struck out–by Carleton 1, by Bryant 2, by Hubbell 7. Bases on balls–by Carleton 3, by Bryant 1, by Hubbell 1, by Smith 1, by Gabler 1. Hits–off Carleton, 11 in 6 innings; off Kowalik, 0 in 1 inning; off Bryant, 2 in 2 innings; off Hubbell, 8 in 7 innings (pitched to one man in eighth); off Stout, 0 in ⅓ inning; off Smith, 1 in 0 innings (pitched to two men in eighth); off Gabler, 0 in ⅓ inning; off Fitzsimmons, 3 in 1⅓ . Winning pitcher–Kowalik. Losing pitcher–Smith.

Other Baseball Highlights of 1935

- Boston pitcher Wes Ferrell ties the major league mark for pitchers with 52 hits.

- Babe Ruth is released by the Yankees and signs with the Boston Braves. On May 25, he hits three homers in a game in Pittsburgh, then retires a few days later.

- Dizzy and Paul Dean win 47 games between them for the St. Louis Cardinals.

- The Cubs' William Wrigley is the first owner to allow his team's games to be broadcast on radio.

PASSEAU
13

Claude Passeau—1940

Chicago Cubs Summit Season
Number 20

No. 20
CLAUDE PASSEAU

BORN: April 9, 1909; Waynesboro, Louisiana

Chicago Cubs: 1939-1947

SEASON AT THE SUMMIT: 1940

W-L-%		IP	CG	SH	SV	K/BB	PR	DEF	ERA
22-13	.606	280.1	20	4	5	124/59	42	1	2.50

Claude Passeau's numbers for the 1940 season were impressive—a 21-10 record, 2.50 earned-run average, 20 complete games, and five saves for good measure.

But the stats don't tell the whole story of Passeau's most interesting—and successful—of seasons.

The tall right-hander had come to the Cubs early in the 1939 season from Philadelphia, going 13-9 and becoming a key cog in the rotation with Bill Lee and Larry French. Passeau opened his 1940 campaign in fine form, through seven innings at least. He had Cincinnati shut out until the eighth when the Reds took advantage of a hit batsman, sacrifice and two doubles to beat Passeau and the Cubs 2-1. It wouldn't be the first tough loss he would suffer.

Passeau got his first victory of the season April 26 against the Reds, winning 6-2 thanks in part to Bill Nicholson's first-inning grand slam. He had only one strikeout, but still retired 19 Reds in a row at one point.

Claude's Excellent Adventure

If there was a pattern for Passeau's performances early in the season, it was that he didn't fit any pattern. He might be masterful, as he was against the Reds that day; or he might be shelled, as he was on April 22 against Pittsburgh (six runs in five innings) or April 30 against Boston (seven runs and eight hits in 3⅔ innings). He could be great, as he was May 7 against Philadelphia, when he allowed just five hits in eight innings. But that didn't translate into a victory—the Phils beat him 1-0 when a run scored on a dropped third strike. Clearly, Passeau wasn't catching the breaks and he and his teammates weren't in sync.

By the end of May he was at 3-5 and the Cubs had fallen to fourth place at 18-19. Passeau suffered two more tough losses in early June—he was beaten by Brooklyn 3-2 on Dolf Camilli's homer on the 3rd, then suffered a 3-1 loss on the 11th to the New York Giants, who scored their first two runs thanks to Cub errors.

Passeau and the Cubs soon found themselves on the same page as he was able to even his record at 7-7. He five-hit Boston 9-1 on May 16, thanks to an eight-run sixth inning; a seven-run sixth on the 22nd lifted him to a 10-2 victory over the Phils; and he got a win with four hitless innings of relief on the 25th when the Cubs scored five times in the 13th to beat the Dodgers 8-3.

His next outing resulted in another tough loss as he held the Reds to five hits on June 29 and still lost 4-1. But Passeau rebounded by winning his next three decisions, thanks largely to some timely hitting by his teammates.

He struggled all day against Pittsburgh on July 3 and was rewarded with a 7-5 victory when Bobby Mattick singled with the bases loaded in the eighth. A week later Passeau beat the Reds 8-2, striking out seven and losing his shutout in the ninth on two Cub errors. And on July 14 he worked six innings of five-hit relief against the Giants, getting the win—his 10th in 18 decisions—when Nicholson homered in the 13th inning.

Fun at the Old Ballpark

Passeau's mates came to his aid in another way on July 19. The Cubs were facing the Dodgers in Wrigley Field, and led 8-3 after seven innings thanks to two, four-run outbursts. Passeau was cruising to his 11th victory when he stepped to the plate against Brooklyn right-hander Hugh Casey in the eighth.

Casey had started the inning as the third Brooklyn pitcher. Jim Gleeson greeted him with a double, which was followed by a home run by Nicholson. Four batters later, Passeau stepped in. Casey's first pitch was wild, sending a third run across the plate. The next pitch was a passed ball. The third hit Passeau squarely in the middle of the back.

He responded by throwing his bat at the Dodger pitcher, causing both benches to empty. Casey tried to get Passeau but Brooklyn backup outfielder Joe "Muscles"

Gallagher got there first, wrestling Passeau to the ground. At that point, Cub manager Gabby Hartnett stepped in, grabbed Gallagher and pulled him off his pitcher. And Cub third baseman Stan Hack delivered a haymaker to Gallagher's nose.

After police and ushers restored order, Passeau was ejected—he was later fined $75—but he did have his fourth straight win.

Claude To the Rescue

That was about as entertaining as the Cubs got in the summer of 1940. July ended with them at 49-49, well out of the NL pennant race. Still, Passeau was able to provide a few thrills—as a relief pitcher.

He came on against Brooklyn in the ninth inning on August 2 to strike out Pete Reiser and Pee Wee Reese to nail down a 4-3 victory. In another relief appearance five days later against Cincinnati, he came on in the 10th with the bases loaded and one out. He turned Frank McCormick's smash to the mound into a force at the plate, then retired Bill Baker on a fly to get the save.

Passeau then put together his best stretch of pitching of the season, winning five games in less than two weeks—a 1-0 five-hitter against the Reds on August 15, in which he didn't allow a runner past first after the first inning; four innings of relief that got him a win on the 17th; a three-hit shutout of the Phillies on the 20th; five innings of four-hit relief on the 23rd that resulted in his 16th victory; and a seven-hit 3-1 decision over New York on the 27th.

Passeau lost two of his next three decisions before winding up his season with two victories. No. 20 came on September 23 against the Cardinals as he scattered four hits in front of an intimate crowd of 1,843 at Wrigley Field. He also homered—a fitting exclamation point on a successful season.

CLAUDE PASSEAU'S

Three Other Great Cub Seasons

	YR	W-L	IP	GS	GC	SH	SV	PD	K/BB	OBA	OB%	ERA	PR
1.	1939	13-9	221	27	13	1	3	1	108/48	.254	.297	3.05	21
2.	1942	19-14	278.1	34	24	3	0	1	89/74	.260	.309	2.68	20
3.	1945	17-9	227	27	19	5	1	3	98/59	.238	.289	2.46	34

Square-jawed Claude Passeau, a Mississippian, was a tough-minded sort who asked no quarter and, sure as shrimp creole, gave none. Further, he looked one of baseball's favorite no-nos in the eye, that old hex—No. 13, and said: "That's jes' right for me!" And he stared down many a hitter, then claimed the inside corner with one of his dusters. All told, it made for a fightin' package of baseball grit. In Game 3 of the 1945 World Series, which followed a league-leading season in shutouts and total pitching index, he brought it all together with a one-hit whitewash job on the Tigers. His 1940 season rounds out our Top 20, following the distinguished company of Hall of Famer Billy Herman at No. 19.

Commenting on Claude Passeau and No. 13, Art Ahrens, a Cub authority, had this to say:
"He [Passeau] once said: 'That's [13] my lucky number. My auto tag is 13. The serial on my rifle is 13. The last two digits on my life insurance are 13, and my address is 113 London Street.' He also spent 13 years in the majors, and his name is 13 letters long."

PASSEAU: A NOTEWORTHY BOX SCORE

August 15, 1940

Passeau holds the Reds to five hits in a 1-0 victory.

Cincinnati	AB	R	H	RBI	PO	A	E	Chicago	AB	R	H	RBI	PO	A	E
Werber, 3b	4	0	1	0	2	4	0	Hack, 3b	3	0	0	0	2	4	0
M. McCormick, lf	4	0	2	0	1	0	0	Herman, 2b	3	1	2	0	4	3	0
Frey, 2b	2	0	0	0	3	5	0	Gleeson, lf	2	0	0	0	3	1	0
F. McCormick, 1b	4	0	1	0	9	0	0	Nicholson, rf	3	0	1	0	1	0	0
Lombardi, c	3	0	0	0	4	0	0	Leiber, cf	3	0	1	1	1	0	0
Craft, cf	3	0	0	0	3	0	0	Bonura, 1b	2	0	1	0	10	0	0
Gamble, rf	3	0	0	0	1	0	0	Todd, c	3	0	0	0	5	0	0
Joost, ss	3	0	1	0	1	1	0	Warstler, ss	3	0	0	0	1	2	0
Derringer, p	3	0	0	0	0	1	0	Passeau, p	3	0	0	0	0	3	0
TOTALS	29	0	5	0	24	11	0	TOTALS	25	1	5	1	27	13	0

```
Cincinnati    000  000  000  -- 0
Chicago       000  100  00*  -- 1
```

Triple--Herman. Sacrifice--Gleeson. Double plays--Chicago 3, Cincinnati 2. Left on base--Cincinnati 4, Chicago 2. Bases on balls--Derringer 2, Passeau 2. Strikeouts--Derringer 4, Passeau 3. Time –1:35. Attendance--6,944. Strikeouts--Kilinger 2, Passeau 1, MacFayden 1. Bases on balls--Klinger 3, MacFayden 1, Mooty 2, Root 1, Page 1, Raffensberger 1. Hits--Mooty 6 in 3²/₃ innings, Root 4 in 3¹/₃, Page 1 in 1²/₃, Klinger 9 in 7²/₃, Brown 2 in 2²/₃, Raffensberger none in ¹/₃, Passeau 3 in 4; MacFayden 4 in 4¹/₃. Hit by pitcher--by Klinger (Gleeson), by MacFayden (Hack). Wild pitch--Brown. Winning pitcher--Passeau. Losing pitcher--MacFayden. Umpires--Pinelli, Reardon and Goetz. Time–3:18. Attendance--6,603.

Other Baseball Highlights of 1940

• After the season, Detroit's Hank Greenburg becomes the first major-leaguer to enlist in the service in anticipation of World War II.

• City of losers: The Philadelphia Phillies and Athletics both lose 100 or more games and finish last.

• In his first full season, Cleveland shortstop Lou Boudreau has 101 RBIs and leads the AL in fielding.

• The Cubs finish below .500 for the first time in 15 years.

• Reds' catcher Willard Hershberger commits suicide.

AT MIDPOINT

21) Dick Ellsworth, 1963, P
22) Heine Zimmerman, 1912, 3B
23) Orval Overall, 1909, P
24) Bob Rush, 1952, P
25) Hack Wilson, 1930, CF

26) Lee Smith, 1983, P
27) Gabby Hartnett, 1935, C
28) Bill Nicholson, 1943, RF
29) Joe Tinker, 1908, SS
30) Ed Reulbach, 1905, P

Three of Cooperstown's permanent residents, emblazoned with those "immortalizing" plaques, grace the middle range of the Cub franchise's top 50 seasons. They are Hack Wilson, the stubby, record-setting slug-meister; 1935's MVP, "Gabby" Hartnett, beloved catcher and manager under Bill Wrigley and his son Phil; and Joe Tinker, savvy shortstop of the early 1900s champs. Along with Heine Zimmerman and Bill "Swish" Nicholson, they halve this grouping of five position players and five pitchers.

Dick Ellsworth, who seems to have packed all his career goodies into one season, 1963, in a frequently troubled and frustrating string of Cub years, stands at the head of this class of 10 "middle of the pack" summiteers with a fistful of career pitching bests. Zimmerman (No. 22), arrived on the Chicago scene as Orvie Overall (No. 23) was about to leave it. These two occupy the next two spots. Heine's summit season and Overall's 1909, an even more valuable effort than his not-inconsiderable contributions to three straight pennant-winners (1906-'08), rate just about even with a slight nod in Zimmerman's direction on the basis of his overpowering career year.

Starter Bob Rush (No. 24) and reliever Lee Smith (No. 26), along with Wilson, wind up in the middle of the middle. Both Rush, in 1952, and Smith, three decades later, kept similarly shoddy Cub teams out of the basement with superlative individual seasons.

Another of the Cubs' stable of accomplished hurlers during their early 1900s championship years, Big Ed Reulbach, completes the list of 10 in this 21-30 range of the Cubs' top 50. Reulbach was one of three 18-game winners who helped the Colts to a third-place finish in 1905, posting a miniscule 1.42 ERA, the 22nd lowest in the game's history, as he logged one of the finest rookie seasons in the franchise's annals.

In the calculus of sabermetric ratings, these 10 summit seasons average out at Total Player Ratings of 4.94, or a solid five in the Cubs' win column (i.e: a contribution of five more victories in a given season than the league-average player was able to make). Let's not forget: that's contributing at Hall of Fame levels—at least for one season. The Cubbies who follow in the rankings from 31 to 40 on this honors list drop to a 4.45 TPR, and the 11 to 20 group, directly ahead of these middle-of-the-roaders, weighs in at a hefty 5.73. Consider, then, that our top 10, at a 6.89 TPR average, puts these averages into sharply meaningful perspective, lending credence to the "middler" status of the Ellsworth to Reulbach group, or 21-30 range, and the regal superiority of the single seasons logged by the likes of the Clarksons, Alexanders and Sandbergs.

Dick Ellsworth—1963

Chicago Cubs Summit Season
Number 21

No. 21
DICK ELLSWORTH

BORN: March 22, 1940; Lusk, Wyoming

Chicago Cubs: 1958-1966

SEASON AT THE SUMMIT: 1963

W-L-%		IP	CG	SH	SV	K/BB	PR	DEF	ERA
22-10	.688	290.2	19	4	0	185/75	38	2	2.11

I n his first four seasons with the Cubs, **Dick Ellsworth** had never won as many games as he had lost. Ellsworth, who made his major-league debut in June, 1958 fresh out of high school—he gave up four hits and walked three in 2⅓ innings in a loss to Cincinnati—came into the 1963 season with a 26-45 career record and 4.30 earned-run average. In 1962, he had gone 9-20 with a 5.09 ERA. By the end of the 1963 campaign, though, Ellsworth was being mentioned in the same breath as Sandy Koufax, Juan Marichal and Jim Maloney.

The 23-year-old left-hander set the tone for his season in his first start, blanking the Los Angeles Dodgers—who would go on to win the National League pennant by six games—on a three-hitter on April 11. Unfortunately for Ellsworth, the Cubs also set the tone for their season in that game by scratching out just one run.

Runs were a luxury for the Cubs in 1963, particularly when Ellsworth was pitching. He lost his second start of the season on the 17th 1-0 to the Dodgers on Bill Skowron's 10th-inning single. Four days later the Cubs erupted for four runs on Ellsworth's behalf as he beat the

Giants 4-1. But they managed just two runs against New York on April 25 and Ellsworth was saddled with another loss. A month into the season, Ellsworth had a flashy 1.09 earned-run average with 19 strikeouts and only 22 hits allowed over 33 innings, but only a 2-2 record to show for his efforts.

Shutting the Door

Ellsworth made up for a lack of support by simply shutting the opposition down. On May 9, he beat Pittsburgh 3-1 on a two-hitter that moved the surprising Cubs— they'd lost 103 games the year before–into second place at 16-11. The only hits were singles by Donn Clendenon in the second and Dick Schofield in the ninth. In his next start he held Cincinnati to five hits in eight innings and won 2-1 thanks to Ken Hubbs' eighth-inning home run. And on May 19 he scattered eight hits and beat Milwaukee 3-2—he lost his shutout on Hank Aaron's two-run homer in the eighth. But a pitcher can do only so much. In his next start he suffered his second 1-0 loss of the season, this time to St. Louis, despite allowing just four hits in seven innings. It left him with a mediocre 5-3 record and sparkling 1.09 ERA.

The secret for Ellsworth was a revived pitch repertoire. His slider had been ineffective after an arm injury earlier in his career, but Cubs roving instructor Fred Martin and teammates Bob Buhl and Larry Jackson had worked with Ellsworth on his delivery and brought the pitch back to life. He was also having great success with his sinker. In the May 9 victory, for example, the Pirates were beating the ball into the ground and keeping the infielders busy all day—first baseman Ernie Banks set a major-league record with 23 chances, 22 of them putouts at first.

Ellsworth's best effort of the year came on May 31 in Philadelphia when he stopped the Phillies on one hit in a 2-0 Cub victory. And the only hit off Ellsworth, who had lost five of six career decisions to the Phils, was a cheap one: free-swinging Wes Covington's fifth-inning bunt. On the play, Ellsworth charged off the mound in pursuit, and Banks retreated to first to take the throw. But Ellsworth couldn't catch up with the ball and by then it was too late for Banks to come off the bag to make the play. "Had I yelled right away to Ernie to take the ball, we would have had time for the putout with me covering first," Ellsworth said afterward. Nothing came of Covington's hit, and Ellsworth had only one other serious jam, that in the sixth when two Cub errors and a walk filled the bases. But Ellsworth struck out Covington— one of just four strikeouts he registered—to end the threat.

A Strong July

With Ellsworth (now 7-3), Jackson and Buhl (both of whom had won their last two starts) getting into a groove, the Cubs were in the thick of the NL race. After they swept a double-header from the first-place San Francisco Giants on June 5—Ellsworth won the opener 9-5—they were within a game of first.

But Ellsworth and the Cubs hit a dry spell. He was shelled in his next outing—six earned runs in 5⅔ innings—and lost 11-8 to the Dodgers; in his next start he allowed the Giants just four hits, but two were homers and he lost 2-1. Five days later he beat Houston 3-1 thanks to Banks' two-run homer, but on June 22 was again a victim of the Cubs' lack of hitting, losing 3-0 to the Phillies to fall to 9-6. The Cubs, too, had slipped to fifth place by that time, and though they'd rally slightly in July, they were done challenging for first.

Ellsworth strung together some outstanding performances in July—he beat the Reds 7-0 in 11 innings on July 11; on the 16th he ran his record to 13-6 by beating the Cardinals 2-0; he stopped the Reds 2-1 with a four-hitter, his 10th complete game, on the 24th; and on the 28th he struck out 10, including Stan Musial three times, in a 5-1 win over the Cardinals. And the Cubs started getting him some runs—he was on the winning end of 8-1 and 10-1 scores in early August.

Good Finish

Ellsworth needed plenty of help when he got victory No. 20 on Labor Day. He beat the Giants 7-5 despite giving up eight hits, four walks and four earned runs in six-plus innings. He lost his next three outings—again largely because of non-support as the Cubs scored just two runs in the three games—to drop to 20-10. But Ellsworth closed out his career season with two typical performances, a 1-0 three-hit victory over the Braves on September 20, and a 4-1 five-hit win over Milwaukee on the 28th.

Ellsworth finished 22-10—only Marichal, Koufax, Warren Spahn and Maloney won more in the National League—and with a 2.11 ERA, second only to Koufax in the majors. For his efforts, he was honored as Chicago's Major League Player of the Year by the Baseball Writers Association of America, and was voted NL Comeback Player of the Year by the Associated Press.

"I didn't have any specific goal," Ellsworth would later say in summarizing his season, "other than to help our club win ballgames."

No team could ask for more; and no pitcher could have done more than Dick Ellsworth in 1963.

DICK ELLSWORTH'S

2wo Other Great Cub Seasons

	Yr	W-L	IP	GS	GC	SH	SV	PD	K/BB	OBA	OB%	ERA	PR
1.	1961	10-11	186.2	31	7	1	0	3	91/48	.292	.338	3.86	4
2.	1965	14-15	222.1	34	8	0	1	2	130/57	.265	.313	3.81	-7

A big, strapping Wyoming lefty, Dick Ellsworth spent eight seasons with the Cubs, most of which were in the National League's lower regions. There was one exception, 1963, when they ventured as high as seventh in that season's 10-team arrangement. Getting up into that rarified air was due largely to Ellsworth's own effort, a huge 22-10 season that landed him the No. 21 spot among summiteers Zimmerman, Orrie Overall and Claude Passeau. One look at the rest of his career assures students of the game that it *is* possible to get things right at least once. A couple of seasons later Dick tied the record for the most Cub losses in a season. Oh well, there was always 1963!

"The additions of Bob Buhl and Larry Jackson to our staff in 1963 brought a higher level of intensity. We spent hours discussing hitters' weaknesses and the role that the catcher and the middle defense positions played. The approach was much more positive and professional than I had experienced previously. I gained a high level of confidence in myself and my abilities."
—**Dick Ellsworth on his 1963 season**

Other Baseball Highlights of 1963

• The Dodgers sweep the Yankees in the World Series—the first time New York has been swept since 1922.

• Sandy Koufax wins the NL MVP and Cy Young awards.

• Early Wynn, 43, wins his 300th game.

• The Mets' Roger Craig loses 18 consecutive games.

ELLSWORTH: A NOTEWORTHY BOX SCORE

June 1, 1963

Ellsworth allows just one hit—Wes Covington's bunt in the fifth—to run his record to 7-3 and lower his ERA to 1.08.

Chicago	AB	R	H	RBI	E	Philadelphia	AB	R	H	RBI	E
Brock, rf	4	0	2	0	0	Taylor, 2b	4	0	0	0	0
Hubbs, 2b	4	0	0	0	1	Gonzalez, rf	4	0	0	0	0
Williams, lf	4	0	0	0	0	Demeter, cf	4	0	0	0	0
Santo, 3b	4	1	1	0	0	Sievers, 1b	3	0	0	0	0
Banks, 1b	4	0	1	1	0	Covington, lf	3	0	1	0	1
Rodgers, ss	2	1	1	1	2	Hoak, 3b	3	0	0	0	0
Matthews, cf	3	0	0	0	0	Averill, c	3	0	0	0	0
Bertell, c	3	0	0	0	0	Rojas, pr	0	0	0	0	0
Ellsworth, p	2	0	0	0	0	Dalrymple, c	0	0	0	0	0
TOTALS	30	2	5	2	3	Wine, ss	3	0	0	0	0
						Boozer, p	2	0	0	0	0
						Lemon, ph	1	0	0	0	0
						Baldschun, p	0	0	0	0	0
						TOTALS	30	0	1	0	1

Chicago	000	010	001	--2	
Philadelphia	000	000	00*	--0	

Double plays--Cubs, 1. Left on base--Cubs 3, Philadelphia 4. Double--Banks. Triple--Santo. Home run--Rodgers.

	IP	H	R	ER	BB	SO
Ellsworth (W, 7-3)	9	1	0	0	2	4
Boozer (L, 0-1)	7	3	1	1	2	8
Baldschun	2	2	1	1	0	3

HBP--by Ellsworth (Covington). Time--2:14. Attendance--3,902.

Heine Zimmerman—1912

Chicago Cubs Summit Season
Number 22

No. 22
HEINE ZIMMERMAN

BORN: February 9, 1887; New York
DIED: March 14, 1969; New York

Chicago Cubs: 1907-1916

SEASON AT THE SUMMIT: 1912

AB-R-H	BA	OB%	2B	3B	HR	RBI	BR	FR	SB
557-95-207	.372	.418	41	14	14	99	50	2	23

On May 12, 1912, a game between the Cubs and New York Giants was rained out. Afterward, Cub President Charles Murphy was asked what he thought about infielder **Heine Zimmerman**, who was having—even at that point—a phenomenal season. Murphy minced no words: "I think Heine Zimmerman will lead the National League in batting this year," he predicted. "He is now second with an average around .450. I think he is right where Hans Wagner was 10 years ago."

A bold prediction from Murphy, but only partly accurate. Zimmerman did go on to lead the National League in hitting that season. But what Murphy couldn't foresee was that in 10 years, instead of being lauded as one of baseball's greats, as Wagner was, Zimmerman would be out of the majors, banned for helping fix games.

Henry Zimmerman was born on February 9, 1887 in New York City. He broke in with the Cubs in 1907 and for his first four seasons was no more than a capable utilityman for manager Frank Chance, who played him at second, short, third and in the outfield. He became a regular in 1911, hitting .307 in 143 games. When the 1912 season arrived, though, he was ticketed again to be a utilityman. But then fate intervened and the feisty Zimmerman became, arguably, the National League's biggest star. For one season, at least.

Zim's Lucky Break

Numerous beanings over the course of his 15-year career had left Chance subject to severe headaches. He had to take himself out of the lineup for a time during the 1911 season, but after a winter of rest—and no headaches—he thought the problem had cleared up. But after an exhibition game on a particularly warm spring day in Nashville, the headaches returned. And when the Cubs opened the season in Cincinnati—again, in unseasonably warm weather—the headaches persisted, and Chance announced he was through as a player.

He didn't have to look far for someone to take his place at first base. Zimmerman had played a handful of games there the year before, and Chance was happy to get his bat in the lineup. (Soon, though, Chance moved him to third base, where he would play 121 games in 1912.)

With the Cubs off to an 0-2 start, Zimmerman—he liked to be referred to as "The Great Zim"—took over for Chance on April 14. Once he got in the lineup, it would be impossible to get him out.

He hit safely in his first 23 games as a regular, raising his average to over .450 and providing Cub fans with plenty to cheer—a 6-for-10 series against St. Louis; a tremendous home run to beat Pittsburgh at Forbes Field; two triples, one with the bases loaded, in a victory over the Pirates in Chicago; an 8-for-17 series against Boston, including a double, triple and homer in one game. His streak came to an end May 17 in Chicago, when he went hitless in five at-bats—with three strikeouts—in a 7-5 loss to the Phillies.

Zimmerman bounced back the next day with a homer and two singles in a 5-4 victory over Brooklyn. For most of the summer, he was a one-man wrecking crew—a homer, two singles and a steal of home May 22 against Brooklyn, raising his average over .435; a 3-for-4 afternoon, including a homer, against Brooklyn on June 8; two home runs in a 9-8 win over the first-place New York Giants on June 10; a single, two doubles and a triple, with five RBIs, in a 10-2 thrashing of St. Louis on June 22; a 12-game hitting streak between July 7 and 18 during which he hit .367 (18 for 49).

Umpire Troubles

At times it seemed that the only person who could stop Heine Zimmerman was Heine Zimmerman. He was never known as a smart ballplayer. And his temper often got the best of him. An argument with an umpire on June 11 earned him an ejection and a three-game suspension; another run-in with an ump on July 6 got him ejected and brought a $50 fine, later doubled to $100 by the league; still another beef with an umpire on August 10 cost him another $50.

Zimmerman's average began tailing off in July. An 0-for-3 afternoon against Brooklyn on the 23rd dropped him

below .400. He reached .400 once more, August 1 after getting two hits in a win over Brooklyn, but went hitless in his next two games as part of a 1-for-19 slump and dropped below .400 for good. In mid-August he briefly lost the league batting lead to Boston's Bill Sweeney, but regained it by going 18 for 39 over the last 10 games of the month.

Zimmerman coasted home with the National League's batting crown—as Murphy had predicted—finishing at .372. He also led the league in home runs (14), slugging percentage (.571), hits (207) and total bases (318). For years he had been credited with a league-best 103 runs batted in, but a re-analysis of game accounts showed he finished with only 99, thus costing him a Triple Crown. As for the Cubs, they ran third behind the Giants and Pirates, 11½ games off the pace.

Zimmerman had three more seasons with Chicago, each less productive than the previous one. During the 1916 campaign he was sent to the Giants, where his career ended in scandal. In September of 1919, he was suspended by manager John McGraw. The reason wasn't announced, but McGraw had learned that Zimmerman had offered teammate Rube Benton $800 to throw a game. Zimmerman always denied that he had thrown games, but in a 1921 affidavit admitted that he had acted as a go-between.

End Of The Line

Zimmerman's career as a ballplayer was over, but not his days as a controversial figure. In 1935, his name surfaced in a tax evasion case against racketeer and bootlegger Dutch Schultz, with whom Zimmerman had been a partner in a speakeasy.

Zimmerman, for one season the greatest slugger in baseball, lived out his years in New York, dying on March 14, 1969 at the age of 82.

HEINE ZIMMERMAN'S

Two Other Great Cub Seasons

	Yr	GP	AB-R-H	BA	OB%	SA	K/BB	HR	RBI	SB	FR	BR
1.	1911	143	535-80-164	.307	.343	.462	50/25	9	85	23	-1	14
2.	1913	127	447-69-140	.313	.379	.490	40/41	9	95	18	5	26

The 1912 voting for the National League's MVP award featured a tight race between Larry Doyle, a .330 hitting outfielder with the pennant-winning Giants, and perennial standout Hans Wagner. Doyle won it, but the question is, whatever happened to "Zim?" He was buried in sixth place behind teammate Joe Tinker, et al. Check his 1912 season once more. He *WAS* the Chicago offense that season. It seems the voting sportswriters had their eyes elsewhere. It wouldn't be the last time that kind of monkey business would louse up the prestigious award. Zim's 1912 season was such a solid effort that it perched him on the 22nd summit rung. By the end of the New York Giants phase of his career, by the way, he no doubt wished he could have stayed in the Windy City, where McGraw and World Series footraces to home plate would no longer be able to bother him.

"In the eight years Heine served with the Cubs, he was under five different managers and had trouble with every one of them."
—**James Crusinberry in the *Chicago Tribune* on August 29, 1916, after Zimmerman's trade to New York.**

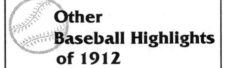

ZIMMERMAN: A NOTEWORTHY BOX SCORE

May 8, 1912

Zimmerman homers, doubles and triples to lead a 9-8 victory over Boston.

Chicago	AB	R	R	BB	PO	A	E	Boston	AB	R	H	BB	PO	A	E
Sheckard, lf	4	2	3	1	3	0	0	Sweeney, 2b	4	1	3	1	3	3	0
Schulte, rf	4	1	0	1	1	0	0	Campbell, cf	5	0	1	0	0	0	0
Tinker, ss	4	0	0	0	1	3	1	R. Miller, rf	5	0	0	0	1	0	0
Hofman, cf	4	2	2	0	1	1	1	Kirke, lf	5	2	2	0	2	0	1
Zimmerman, 1b	5	2	3	0	11	0	0	Devlin, ss	3	2	2	1	3	3	0
Evers, 2b	4	1	2	0	2	5	0	Houser, 1b	4	1	2	0	13	3	0
Lennox, 3b	2	1	0	2	1	0	0	McDonald, 3b	3	2	1	1	1	0	0
Archer, c	4	0	0	0	6	2	1	Kling, c	2	0	0	1	2	1	0
Cole, p	0	0	0	0	0	0	0	Hogg, p	0	0	0	0	0	1	0
Reulbach, p	0	0	0	1	1	1	0	Tyler, p	3	0	0	0	0	2	0
Toney, p	1	0	0	1	0	1	0	Dickson, p	1	0	0	0	1	3	0
W. Miller, ph	0	0	0	1	0	0	0								
Richie, p	0	0	0	0	0	0	0	TOTALS	35	8	11	4	26	16	1
TOTALS	33	9	10	7	27	12	3								

Chicago	5 0 0	1 0 0	1 0 2	—	9
Boston	3 0 0	3 0 0	1 1 0	—	8

Doubles--Sweeney, Zimmerman. Triple--Zimmerman. Home run--Zimmerman. Strikeouts--by Reulbach, 1; by Toney, 1; by Tyler, 1. Bases on balls--by Cole, 1; by Hogg, 1; by Reulbach, 2; by Tyler, 5; by Toney, 1; by Dickerson, 1. Double play--Chicago 1. Hits--off Hogg, 2 in ⅓ inning; off Cole, 4 in 1 inning; off Reulbach, 3 in 8 innings; off Tyler, 3 in 5 innings; off Toney, 4 in 5 innings. Wild pitch--Toney. Passed ball--Kling. Time 3:12. Umpires--Johnstone and Eason.

Other Baseball Highlights of 1912

- The Giants' Rube Marquard wins 19 straight games.

- Twice in an 11-day period, Eddie Collins steals six bases in a game.

- The Pirates' Chief Wilson sets an all-time record with 36 triples.

- At age 37, Honus Wagner leads the NL with 102 RBIs and bats .324.

Orval Overall—1909

Chicago Cubs Summit Season
Number 23

No. 23
ORVAL OVERALL

BORN: February 2, 1881; Farmersville, California
DIED: July 14, 1947; Fresno, California

Chicago Colts/Cubs: 1906-1910; 1913

SEASON AT THE SUMMIT: 1909

W-L-%	IP	CG	SH	SV	K/BB	PR	DEF	ERA
20-11 .645	285.0	23	9	3	205/80	37	0	1.42

Frank Chance knew that **Orval "Jeff" Overall** would make a great major-league pitcher. Trouble was, the huge right-hander was with the wrong major-league ballclub. But since the Peerless Leader was in a position to do something about that, he did. By the end of July, 1906, a little more than a year into Overall's career in the bigs, Chance, who by then was the Cubs' manager, saw to it that his former teammate in California was on the way to Chicago in a trade that sent Bob Wicker and cash to Cincinnati.

That deal turned Overall's career around in a hurry, and he celebrated with a 12-3 contribution to the first Cub pennant in 20 years. He kept right on celebrating. In 1907 he put together a glittering 23-7 season with a superb 1.68 ERA and eight shutouts, which led the league. Although the husky twirler dropped off some from his stratospheric start as a Cub, he managed 15 wins in 1908 plus a big 6-1 World Series victory over the Tigers.

Great - But No Bunting

On April 14, 1909, Overall opened the Cub season at West Side Park with a three-hitter, beating St. Louis 3-1. The next day's *Chicago Tribune* summed up his big day like this:

"The Californian demonstrated he was right with an accent on all five letters, and used his fast, sharp drop, which proved so killing in the World Series last Fall, with deadly effect on the Cardinal kids."

Though Overall would move on to a 20-11 record, leading the league in shutouts (nine), strikeouts (205) and the NL's lowest opponents batting average (.198), it wasn't quite good enough to help pull off a fourth straight pennant. In 1909, both the Giants and Chicago's defending pacesetters, who gave chase to the Wagner-led Pirates, found that Pittsburgh's ballclub just wasn't to be denied. Winning 110 times, six more than the Cubs, they turned back every challenge and finally whipped Detroit in the storied Wagner-Cobb World Series. It marked the 10th straight season (and, there were still four more to follow) that the three National League titans were locked in feverish pursuit of the league's blue ribbon.

The Staff Supreme

One of the reasons Chance's Cubs were in the thick of things was the continuing brilliance of his hurling corps. Overall was a key part of one of the very best pitching staffs ever assembled. And in order to match Mathewson, McGinnity and Wiltse of New York, or Phillippe, Camnitz and Willis of Pittsburgh, it had to be. (For a further check on that extraordinary Cub pitching machine of the early 1900s see Appendix C.)

As the spring wore on, Overall's win total mounted, and after his May 25 conquest of Boston, a 2-0, four-hitter, his record stood at 8-2, right up there among the league's leaders. The *Tribune's* report card on the big fellow's shutout read straight A, right on down to the last strikeout that finished the game. That one, along with a 3-0 blanking of the Phillies on July 12, were two of his best during the campaign.

Then Came the Bad News

The Overall log for 1909 shows three saves and a number of relief appearances to round out his 285-inning season. That was a few innings too many, as Chance no doubt knew. It was Chance, after all, who cut back on Jeff's (he was also known as "Orrie") work load when he joined the club from Cincinnati. That was because he knew Overall's heater and specialty pitches, like his roundhouse curve and drop ball, known today as a sinker, took plenty out of his arm. Chance had reasoned, correctly, that less meant more.

The 1909 pennant race was a dogfight a good piece of the way. That meant fellows like Miner Brown, Ed Reulbach and Overall were needed for extra innings. In Overall's case the extra strain caught up with him at just about the time he was beginning to look invincible. In fact the May 26, 1909 *Tribune* put it this way:

"The way Overall is going at present, the betting should be even he will not lose more than one or two more games this season."

Right. Then the sore arm, accompanied by a mid season slump, set in. By the end of June his 8-2 record stood at 8-6, and both manager and pitcher decided to ease up

some, not only in the number of appearances, but in the use of those baffling breaking pitches, as well. It simply wouldn't have worked had not Overall had such great control and placement—a Chicago pitching trademark, by the way. Somehow, they got into August without too much serious damage.

Back "In the Zone"

From July on through the season's end, Orrie notched 12 more wins to run his final record to 20-11, a 12-5 tally despite persistent aches and assorted pains. Remarkably, he threw nine shutouts during the season, almost half his win total, which lowered his ERA to a basement-level 1.42. The staff that season *averaged* a league-leading 1.75 ERA, the second lowest figure in baseball history. The lowest? Brown, Reulbach, Overall & Co., set the record at 1.73 in 1907. Even for an era infamous for its dead ball, those are incredible numbers!

No World Series
But A Championship, Anyway!

For almost a half-century there was always unfinished baseball business in Chicago until the City Series was played. And 1909 was no exception. While there was no World Series in the Windy City, there was, nonetheless, a championship on the line. For the Cubs that meant a golden opportunity to avenge an embarrassing humiliation administered in the 1906 World Series by those low-lifes on the South Side known as the White Sox (so regarded, at least by the true-believing Cub faithful). Orv Overall had been a part of the Cubs' final two losses in Games 5 and 6. He had a score of his own to settle.

Two Big Ones In the City Series

The big fellow didn't waste any time. When handed the ball for the series opener on October 9, he whitewashed the South Siders at West Side Park on a cold, raw day, giving up but four hits. Two first-inning runs were all he needed to best Ed Walsh, the Sox titan.

By the time Game 4 was due to be played, the Cubs had forged a 2-1 series lead. That meant another Walsh-Overall clash, and once again Jeff turned back the Sox, this time by a 2-1 score. In 18 innings he had given up one run. That was vengeance enough, and it was enough to forecast an ultimate Cub victory in the series. That came in the next game. Overall's 1909 had ended on a victorious note, after all!

ORVAL OVERALL'S

Two Other Great Cub Seasons

	Yr	W-L	IP	GS	GC	SH	SV	PD	K/BB	OBA	OB%	ERA	PR
1.	1907	23-7	268.1	30	26	8	3	2	141/69	.208	.268	1.68	24
2.	1908	15-11	225.0	27	16	4	4	-1	167/78	.208	.280	1.92	11

When fellows like Mordecai Brown and Big Ed Reulbach are on a pitching staff, there isn't too much ink left over to spread around on other pitchers like Carl Lundgren, Jack Pfiester, or Jeff Overall. That doesn't mean they weren't worthy. Overall's pitching, in fact, was so good that he found his way into the upper half of the summit 50. His 5.1 TPI for 1909 is a good enough indication that he merits ranking ahead of Hack Wilson and Gabby Harnett, a pretty decent pair of Cubs Hall of Famers.

"Overall emerged as Chicago's top pitcher in 1907, going 23-7... and tying Christy Mathewson for the league lead with eight shutouts. In World Series competition, he beat the Tigers once in 1907 and twice in 1908—including a Series-clinching shutout in Game 5 in which he struck out four men in an inning (the first inning), the only man to do so in WS history."

—Mike Shatzkin (Editor), *The Ball Players*

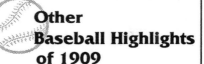

OVERALL'S A NOTEWORTHY BOX SCORE

May 25, 1909

Overall's four-hitter in Boston runs his record to 8-2.

Chicago	AB	R	H	P	A		Boston	AB	R	H	P	A
Evers, 2b	4	1	0	0	1		Bates, lf	3	0	0	0	1
Sheckard, lf	3	1	1	2	0		Becker, rf	4	0	0	2	0
Schulte, rf	5	0	2	2	0		Sweeney, 3b	4	0	1	1	2
Hofman, cf	5	2	2	3	0		Beaumont, cf	4	0	0	1	0
Steinfeldt, 3b	4	0	2	0	0		Starr, 2b	3	0	0	0	4
Howard, 1b	4	1	2	10	0		Dahlen, ss	1	0	1	4	3
Zimmerman, ss	5	1	0	3	4		Beck, 1b	3	0	0	13	1
Moran, c	4	1	2	7	3		Bowerman, c	3	0	0	3	0
Overall, p	4	0	1	0	2		Mattern, p	3	0	0	3	3
TOTALS	38	7	12	27	10		TOTALS	28	0	2	27	14

Chicago	1 0 0	0 0 3	0 1 2	— 7
Boston	0 0 0	0 0 0	0 0 0	— 0

Double: Sheckard; Triple: Moran; Home run: Moran; Strikeouts: by Overall, 8; by Mattern, 5; Bases on balls: Overall, 5; Mattern, 3; Umpires: Klem and Kane.

Other Baseball Highlights of 1909

- Pirate rookie Babe Adams wins three World Series games.

- On July 9, Cleveland shortstop Neal Ball pulls off the first unassisted triple play in the majors.

- The Cardinals commit 17 errors in a July 3 double-header.

- Ty Cobb wins the Triple Crown with a .377 average, 9 homers and 107 RBIs.

RUSH
17

Bob Rush—1952

Chicago Cubs Summit Season
Number 24

No. 24
BOB RUSH

BORN: December 21, 1925; Battle Creek, Michigan

Chicago Cubs: 1948-1957

SEASON AT THE SUMMIT: 1952

W-L-	%	IP	CG	SH	SV	K/BB	PR	DEF	ERA
17-13	.567	250.1	17	4	0	157/81	29	2	2.70

Some guys just *look* like major-league ballplayers. Take **Bob Rush**.

At 6-foot-5, 200 pounds, he fit the profile. And when he unleashed his fastball, it was obvious why the Cubs signed him out of Riley High School in South Bend. But in Rush's first four years in the majors, he never won more than he lost, and in fact led the league in losses in 1950 with 20.

It wasn't until the 1952 season that Rush developed into a complete pitcher. He didn't just look like a ballplayer, he performed like one.

Not much was expected of the Cubs that season—they had finished last in three of the four previous years—but it became obvious from the outset that this wasn't a last-place team. And much of the credit had to go to Rush and to the Cubs pitching staff.

Under the tutelage of pitching coach Charlie Root, starters Rush, Warren Hacker and Paul Minner would all have

the best seasons of their careers, and 43-year-old reliever Dutch Leonard would put Father Time on hold. None of the starting pitchers showed as dramatic an improvement as Rush.

His first four outings were unimpressive—he left the first trailing 4-1 after eight innings (a game the Cubs rallied to win); he picked up his first victory on April 22, scattering nine hits in an 11-2 win over Pittsburgh; he lost the next time out, working a third of an inning in relief April 26 in a 4-3 loss to St. Louis; and he lasted just five innings April 29, losing to Philadelphia 8-2. That left him at 1-2 with a 4.43 ERA. Hardly an auspicious start. But then things fell into place.

In the Groove
On May 3, Rush beat Brooklyn 3-2 in 10 innings, allowing only one earned run on eight hits, striking out seven. He was even more impressive a week later, beating Pittsburgh 3-1 with a four-hitter on May 10. And on May 16, he beat first-place New York 3-2—knocking the Giants out of the lead—by scattering five hits, striking out three and walking four. Rush's 4-2 record and shrinking ERA

put him in the spotlight. How had he turned things around?

Root helped Rush by repositioning him on the pitching rubber and by having him speed up his delivery. And Rush helped himself by developing an effective curveball.

Rush showed how commanding he could be during the last two weeks of May and the first week of June. During that stretch he won four straight games, throwing 32 consecutive shutout innings at one point.

His streak started in the May 16 victory over New York. He added to it with a four-hit shutout of Boston on May 22, a six-hit whitewash of St. Louis four days later, and a two-hit victory over Cincinnati on the 30th. The last of those shutouts may have been the most impressive. Rush didn't allow a hit until the seventh, he struck out 10 and didn't walk a batter. The victory ran his shutout streak to 29 innings, during which his earned-run average dropped to 1.34.

End Of The Streak

The Giants ended Rush's streak at 32 innings when they scored twice—only one of the runs was earned—in the fourth inning against him on June 4. Rush still had the satisfaction of winning 6-2 with a six-hitter, running his record to 8-2 and taking over the league strikeout lead.

Rush's performance earned him a spot on the National League All-Star roster. The game, at Shibe Park in Philadelphia, was shortened by rain to five innings, a first. Rush came on in the fourth inning with the National League ahead 1-0. He surrendered two runs on a double, walk and two singles, but was taken off the hook in the bottom of the inning when Cub teammate Hank Sauer hit a two-run homer off Bob Lemon. The rains came an inning later, and Rush had himself a 3-2 All-Star victory.

Second-Half Fade

Behind the pitching of Rush and Hacker (on his way to a 15-9, 2.59 season) and the hitting of Sauer (a league-leading .352 average and 18 homers through the first third of the season), the Cubs found themselves in the unaccustomed position of contender. In mid-June, they were 32-19, in third place, just four games out of first.

But the second half of June and July turned out to be disappointing months for Rush and the Cubs. He lost his last two decisions in June and his first in July to drop to 9-6 at the All-Star break. He was routed in his first outing after the break, giving up three runs, two earned, on three hits in just a third of an inning against Brooklyn on July 10. Although he caught a break when the Cubs rallied to win, it was his fifth failed attempt to win No. 10. Rush finally earned it on July 23 against Boston in his eighth try—his first victory since June 13 in a streak that saw him lose four, suffer two no-decisions, and have another start rained out.

Rush lost four of his next five outings—including 1-0 defeats at the hands of Pittsburgh and St. Louis on August 8 and 12, respectively. Those two losses left him at 11-11, but with a sparkling 2.67 ERA.

On the morning of September 1, the Cubs were anchored in fifth place at 65-67, 21½ games out of first. And Rush, who had been 9-3 on June 13, was at 13-12. He closed out the season winning four of his last five decisions for a 17-13 record while the Cubs faded to a 77-77 finish.

Rush's record may not have been dazzling, but his other stats—a 2.70 ERA, an opponents' batting average of just .216—help rank his 1952 season among Cub pitchers' best.

BOB RUSH'S

Two Other Great Cub Seasons

	Yr	W-L	IP	GS	GC	SH	SV	PD	K/BB	OBA	OB%	ERA	PR
1.	1954	13-15	236.1	32	11	0	0	3	124/103	.243	.326	3.77	8
2.	1955	13-11	234.0	33	14	3	0	1	130/73	.234	.295	3.50	14

Just how big Bob Rush's summit season, 1952, turned out to be was reflected in a seven-game winning streak and three shutouts during that 17-13 campaign. Further, he was the National League pitcher of record in its 3-2, rain-shortened All-Star victory over the American League, courtesy of Cub teammate Hank Sauer's two-run blast. How about the sportswriters? When it came time to select the NL's MVP, he garnered nary a vote; shucks, even teammates Warren Hacker and Toby Atwell gathered a couple—can you imagine that?! The hurler from "Kellogg-town," USA (that's Battle Creek, Michigan, folks) was a *very* talented pitcher, richly deserving of his No. 24 spot at midpoint along the honors list.

"He finally has arrived as a pitcher. He has confidence and poise out there now. Nothing rattles him. He's the boss out there."

—Cubs manager Phil Cavarretta on Bob Rush's 1952 season

RUSH: A NOTEWORTHY BOX SCORE

May 30, 1952

Rush stops the Reds on a two-hitter, running his consecutive scoreless inning streak to 29 straight innings.

Cincinnati	AB	R	H	RBI	PO	A	E	Chicago	AB	R	H	RBI	PO	A	E
Borkowski, rf	4	0	0	0	1	0	0	Miksis, ss	5	0	1	0	2	4	0
Adams, 3b	3	0	0	0	1	2	0	Ramazzotti, 2b	5	4	3	0	0	4	0
Hatton, 2b	3	0	1	0	3	0	0	Hermanski, rf	2	0	1	0	0	0	0
Temple, 2b	0	0	0	0	1	1	0	Addis, rf	3	0	1	0	1	0	0
Post, lf	3	0	0	0	3	0	0	Sauer, lf	2	2	2	2	2	0	0
Westlake, cf	3	0	0	0	3	1	0	Serena, 3b	4	1	1	2	1	2	0
Pellagrini, 1b	3	0	1	0	7	0	0	Fondy, 1b	5	2	2	3	9	0	0
Howell, c	3	0	0	0	5	0	0	Edwards, c	4	1	2	2	11	0	0
McMillan, ss	3	0	0	0	0	6	0	Jeffcoat, cf	3	1	1	1	1	0	0
Byerly, p	0	0	0	0	0	1	0	Rush, p	4	0	1	1	0	1	0
Nuxhall, p	3	0	0	0	0	2	1								
TOTALS	28	0	2	0	24	13	1	TOTALS	37	11	15	11	25	11	0

Cincinnati	0 0 0	0 0 0	0 0 0	—0
Chicago	5 1 0	1 1 2	1 0 *	—11

Doubles--Ramazzotti, Fondy, Jeffcoat, Serena, Hatton. Triple–Fondy. Stolen bases–Ramazzotti, Sauer. Double plays--Chicago 1, Cincinnati 1. Left on bases–Cincinnati 1, Chicago 7. Struck out--by Byerly, 2; by Nuxhall, 3. Hits–Byerly: 7 in 2 innings; Nuxhall, 8 in 6 innings. Runs and earned runs–Byerly, 6-6; Nuxhall, 5-5. Wild pitch--Nuxhall. Winning pitcher--Rush (7-2). Losing pitcher--Byerly (0-1). Time 2:01. Attendance--35,999. Umpires--Conlan, Stewart, Guglielmo, Gore.

Other Baseball Highlights of 1952

- The Yankees win their fourth straight World Series.

- Ted Williams goes into the Air Force; without him, the Red Sox tumble to sixth.

- Detroit's Virgil Trucks throws two no-hitters—versus Washington on May 15 and against the Yankees on August 25.

- At 47, the Browns' Satchel Paige shuts out Detroit 1-0 in 12 innings on August 6.

- The Braves draw only 281,278 in their last year in Boston.

Lewis "Hack" Wilson—1930

Chicago Cubs Summit Season
Number 25

No. 25
HACK WILSON

BORN: April 26, 1900; Elmwood City, Pennsylvania
DIED: November 23, 1948; Baltimore, Maryland

Chicago Cubs: 1926-1931
Hall of Fame: 1979

SEASON AT THE SUMMIT: 1930

AB-R-H	BA	OB%	2B	3B	HR	RBI	BR	FR	SB
585-146-208	.356	.454	35	6	56	190	74	-7	3

Hack Wilson and Chicago were a perfect match. In six seasons with the Cubs, he hit 190 home runs. He hit at least twice as many speakeasies. Wilson's drinking escapades were legendary. And so was his hitting.

Wilson came to the Cubs in 1926. In his first four seasons, he hit 21, 30, 31 and 39 homers and batted a composite .325. His slugging averages for those years were .539, .579, .588 and .618. His 159 RBIs in the pennant-winning 1929 season led the majors.

But he was just warming up for 1930.

The Year Of The Hitter

Thanks to a juiced-up ball, hitters dominated the game as never before in 1930. The National League team batting average was a remarkable .303. Nine major-league teams and 71 individuals hit over .300. As author William Curran pointed out in "Big Sticks" (Harper Perennial), the experience of Brooklyn's Babe Herman illustrates what it was like trying to establish oneself as a hitter in the

National League in 1930. Herman hit .393, had 241 hits—including 48 doubles, 11 triples and 35 home runs—scored 143 runs and drove in 130 more. Yet he failed to lead the league in any offensive category. Pitchers were pummeled with regularity—the NL earned-run average was 4.97; in the AL it was 4.65—and only one NL pitcher, Brooklyn's Dazzy Vance, had an ERA under 3.75 (2.61).

Less than a week into the season, Wilson gave fans an idea of what to expect. On April 21 in Cincinnati, the 5-foot-6-inch, 200-pound center-fielder hit a massive home run in a 9-1 victory over the Reds. The ball, traveling an estimated 425 feet, cleared the center-field wall at Crosley Field. Only Herman, Ethan Allen and Babe Ruth, in an exhibition game, had ever hit a ball as far at Crosley.

Wilson's first really big day came on April 25, when he singled, doubled and homered in five at-bats. His average through April hovered around .260, and he had only four homers. But as the weather warmed up, so did Wilson. On May 6, he slammed a tremendous two-run first-inning homer off Vance—an old nemesis who had struck him out six consecutive times the season before—the ball bouncing off Wrigley Field's center-field scoreboard. The next day Wilson had an RBI single and a three-run double in a 9-5 win over the Dodgers. The following afternoon he homered in another victory. By June 1, he had 14 homers, and his average was well above .300. Wilson was on his way.

Just Warming Up
He would go on remarkable hitting binges—he hit .448 (13 for 29) in the last week of June, including a 5-for-6 afternoon against Philadelphia on the 24th. That got his average up to .348 and helped the Cubs move into first place.

The Cubs soon slipped into second behind Brooklyn, but Wilson continued to terrorize NL pitching. On July 26, he hit three home runs in a 19-2 win in Philadelphia, Nos. 30, 31 and 32, making him only the third Cub to hit three in one game.

August, however, turned out to be Wilson's month. Multi-hit games were the rule—2 for 5 against Pittsburgh on the 2nd, 2 for 4 the next day, a pair of 2-for-4 efforts (including three homers) in a double-header sweep of Boston on the 10th, 2 for 3 against Brooklyn on the 14th, 4 for 5 on the 18th against Philadelphia, 3 for 4, two of the hits homers, against St. Louis on the 30th.

And the home runs kept coming. He started the month with 33, 10 behind Chuck Klein's NL record. Wilson tied the mark on August 19 in a loss to the Phillies. It took him a week to hit No. 44, and he did it in dramatic fashion.

In the seventh inning against the Pirates, Wilson fell down while chasing a fly ball by Lloyd Waner, and Little Poison circled the bases for an inside-the-park home run. When he got back to the dugout, Wilson told Cub pitcher "Sheriff" Blake that he'd get the run back. And he did, his next time up. Hack blasted the home run that gave him the NL record as well as four RBIs for the day.

Wilson closed out his big month on the 30th with two home runs—Nos. 45 and 46—and five runs scored against St. Louis (the Cardinals smartened up the next day, walking Wilson three times). Wilson's August numbers were prodigious: a .385 batting average, 13 home runs and a team-record 53 runs batted in.

Cubs Come Up Short
The Cubs, meanwhile, had moved into first on August 13. It had been a tumultuous season for them—starting pitcher Harold Carlson had been stricken with internal bleeding and died on May 28. Two days later, Cubs hopes were jolted again when second baseman Rogers Hornsby broke his ankle, ending his season. Still, the Cubs were in the race all season, a season that saw first place change hands 22 times. They finally fell out of first on September 12, passed by the Cardinals, who went on to win the pennant by two games over Chicago.

Wilson wound up his remarkable season with a big September—he broke his own NL record for RBIs (159) when he drove in four runs in a 19-14 romp over Pittsburgh on the 6th. And he hit .383 over the last month of the season. He finished with 190 RBIs and 56 homers—NL records that still stand. His .723 slugging average, 105 walks and 84 strikeouts also led the league. His final batting average was .356.

The big numbers—and his fun-loving personality—made Wilson the toast of baseball. Endorsements and a vaudeville act followed. He got caught up in his fame, and that, along with his drinking, did him in. Quickly.

In 1931 he hit only .261 with 13 homers. In September, Wilson was suspended for the rest of the season after a confrontation with Hornsby, then the Cub manager. Following the season, he was traded to Brooklyn. After a lackluster year and a half there, he was sent to the Phillies, where he finished out his career in 1934, his days as the NL's premiere slugger just a dim memory. At 34, Wilson was finished.

HACK WILSON'S

Three Other Great Cub Seasons

	Yr	GP	AB-R-H	BA	OB%	SA	K/BB	HR	RBI	SB	FR	BR
1.	1926	142	529-97-170	.321	.406	.539	61/69	21	109	10	2	38
2.	1927	146	551-119-175	.318	.401	.579	70/71	30	129	13	-1	45
3.	1929	150	574-135-198	.345	.425	.618	83/78	39	159	3	-3	49

Mr. Lewis Robert Wilson flattened baseballs much like he drained bottles of Jim Beam—completely. And by 1931 he had completely drained himself. But up to that point he was nothing but a relentless pain to NL pitchers. Within a span of five seasons, he had launched 177 bleacher shots and brought home 707 Cub runs, right at 141 per season. And in the 1929 World Series, he hit a sizzling .471 to lead all Series hitters, his riotous fielding notwithstanding. No wonder manager Joe McCarthy somehow found a way to keep him in the lineup.

"Our trainer, Andy Lotshaw, had Hack in one of those big, high old tubs, sobering him up. In the tub with Hack was a 50-pound cake of ice. Well, what would you do if a 50-pound cake of ice jumped into your bathtub with you? You'd try to jump out, right? That was precisely what Hack was trying to do. Every time Hack's head would bob up, Andy would shove it back down under the water and the cake of ice would come bobbing up. It was a fascinating sight, watching them bob in perfect rhythm, first Hack's head, then the ice, then Hack's head, then the ice...(but) that afternoon Hack hit three home runs for the first and only time in his life!"

—**Bill Veeck with Ed Linn, in *Veeck as in Wreck***

WILSON: A NOTEWORTHY BOX SCORE

June 24, 1930

Wilson hits for the cycle as the Cubs defeat the Phillies 21-8.

Philadelphia	AB	R	H	PO	A
Sothern, cf	5	1	2	2	0
Sherlock, lb	5	0	0	8	1
O'Doul, lf	4	0	3	1	0
Klein, rf	5	1	2	0	0
Whitney, 3b	3	1	1	1	2
Friberg, 2b	4	2	1	2	5
Thompson, 2b	0	0	0	0	0
Thevenow, ss	3	1	1	4	4
Davis, c	4	2	2	6	0
Willoughby, p	1	0	0	0	0
Speece, p	3	0	0	0	0
Williams, ph	0	0	0	0	0
TOTALS	37	8	12	24	12

Chicago	AB	R	H	PO	A
Blair, 2b	6	2	2	3	5
English, 3b	5	1	1	1	1
Bell, 3b	0	0	0	0	0
Cuyler, rf	6	4	3	0	0
Wilson, cf	6	5	5	2	0
Stephenson, lf	6	2	4	0	0
Grimm, lb	6	2	2	14	1
Hartnett, c	4	2	2	4	1
Beck, ss	3	2	2	1	10
Bush, p	5	1	3	2	1
TOTALS	47	21	24	27	19

```
Philadelphia    0 3 0   0 0 4   1 0 0   —8
Chicago         4 0 0   5 1 5   5 1 *   —21
```

Runs batted in--Cuyler 2, Wilson 4, Bush 3, Blair 3, Stephenson 3, Hartnett 1, Grimm 1. Davis 3, Friberg 2, O'Doul 1. Doubles--Harnett, Whitney, Friberg, Sothern, Wilson. Triples--Bush, Wilson. Home runs--Wilson, Davis (2). Bases on balls---off Willoughby, 3; off Bush, 2. off Speece, 1. Strikeouts--by Willoughby, 1; by Bush, 3; by Speece, 3. Hits--off Bush, 12 in 9 innings; off Willoughby, 12 in 4 1/3 innings; off Speece, 12 in 3 2/3 innings. HBP--by Bush (O'Doul). PB--Hartnett. Losing pitcher--Willoughby.

Other Baseball Highlights of 1930

• On October 2, Cardinal George Watkins becomes the first NL player to homer in his first World Series at-bat.

• After a long holdout, Babe Ruth signs for $80,000, a major-league record.

• The Athletics' Lefty Grove leads the AL in wins (28-5), winning percentage, games, strikeouts and saves.

• On May 6, Gene Rye of Waco in the Texas League hits three homers in one inning.

Lee Arthur Smith—1983

Chicago Cubs Summit Season
Number 26

No. 26
LEE SMITH

BORN: December 4, 1957; Shreveport, Louisiana

Chicago Cubs: 1980-1987

SEASON AT THE SUMMIT: 1983

W-L-%		IP	CG	SH	SV	K/BB	PR	DEF	ERA
4-10	.286	103.1	0	0	29	91/41	23	-1	1.65

A batter didn't have to do much guessing when he stepped in against **Lee Smith**. He knew what was coming. No knuckler, no big curves, no split-finger fastballs. Nothing cute. Just heat. Major heat.

"I don't run from anybody," the Dodgers' Dusty Baker said during Smith's breakthrough 1983 season. "But the general opinion around the National League is that you're in no real hurry to get to him."

A finesse pitcher Lee Smith was not. His stock-in-trade was a fastball that made the 6-foot-6-inch right-hander one of the most effective relievers in the 1980s and '90s.

His 1983 Cub season stands out as classic Lee Smith, not because of his won-lost record—he was just 4-10—but because of his league-high 29 saves, his 1.65 ERA and an opponents' batting average of .194.

Through the first 10 days of the season, Smith was of little use to the Cubs. They lost their first six games, and manager Lee Elia had no opportunity to use Smith as his closer. He got an inning of work on April 9 in an 8-4 loss

to Cincinnati, and another inning two days later in another defeat at the hands of the Reds. Finally on April 12, he got to perform under a little pressure. With the Cubs leading Montreal 5-0, Smith came in with two on and one out in the ninth. He got Terry Francona to hit into a game-ending double play to save the win for Steve Trout.

"Let's Get It On"

Elia finally got to use Smith like he wanted to on April 16 in Pittsburgh. The Cubs led 6-5 going into the bottom of the ninth—only the second time all season they had had a lead past the fifth inning. When the Pirates' Johnny Ray led off with a single against Bill Campbell, Elia brought in his big gun.

Tony Pena was able to bunt Ray to second. But then Smith struck out Dale Berra and Richie Hebner for save No. 2. "There's no doubt in my mind he's the hardest thrower in the game," said Cubs catcher Jody Davis. "Just bring your bats up there and let's get it on."

But the ineptitude of the Cubs—they lost 13 of their first 18—gave Smith little opportunity to be a hero. He got a chance on April 29, but his failure resulted in one of the darker episodes in team history.

Smith came on in the eighth of a 3-3 game after the Dodgers' Ken Landreaux had doubled and was sacrificed to third. He unleashed a wild pitch that brought Landreaux home and cost the Cubs the game. Afterward, a frustrated Elia launched into his famous profanity-filled tirade about Cubs fans. He later apologized, but his diatribe would be a major contributing factor in his losing his job before the end of the season.

Smith made the most of his next chance. On May 6, the Cubs led San Diego 3-2 when he came on in the eighth. With one out, Alan Wiggins singled and Juan Bonilla walked, and both advanced on Steve Garvey's fly to the wall. An intentional walk filled the bases, but Smith got out of the jam when Sixto Lezcano flied out. He then worked a 1-2-3 ninth for his third save.

Uneasy Sailing

Three days later Smith was tagged with his first loss, giving up three hits and a run—the first charged to him all season—in a 4-3 loss in Los Angeles. The next day he earned his fourth save with three innings of work, but it was hardly vintage Lee Smith: six of the nine outs were fly balls, including two to the wall. A 10th-inning error by Larry Bowa on the 15th against Philadelphia led to two Phillies runs and Smith's second loss in a week. Worse, after the game he suffered back spasms that landed him in Northwestern Memorial Hospital for three days.

He returned on the 21st with an uneventful inning of work in an easy win over the Reds, but in two of his next three outings was roughed up. He was KO'd by Houston after surrendering two runs in two innings of work on the 24th, and on the 31st he gave up two runs in $1\frac{2}{3}$ innings against the Astros. After the second loss, Smith watched some films of himself and noticed a flaw in his delivery. The adjustment he made worked—he earned three saves and a win over the next eight days. His most impressive save came on June 5 when he struck out four of the five Pirates he faced to preserve a 3-1 win. And his victory over the Mets on June 8, the Cubs' seventh win in a row, achieved on Keith Moreland's ninth-inning single, was Smith's first since July 19, 1982.

Smith finished the first half of the season with a 3-4 record, 1.30 ERA and 10 saves, earning him All-Star honors. Even more impressive were his stats since he was moved to the bullpen in July of '82. Over the subsequent 66 games, he had allowed one earned run seven times, and two earned runs on two occasions. In the other 57 appearances, he was unscored-upon.

His showing in the July 6 All-Star Game, though, was less than stellar ("I got kind of goose-pimply when I went out there. I wasn't sharp," he said) as he gave up two runs, one earned, and two hits in an inning of work during the American League's 13-3 win.

In A Groove

Despite their stumbling start and overall lackluster play, the Cubs were still in the race at the break. Only 38-41 and in fourth place, they were just four games out of first.

The rest of July was good for Smith—two impressive innings against the Giants on the 9th for his 11th save; $3\frac{1}{3}$ sharp innings on the 15th vs. the Dodgers for No. 12; saves on the 21st, 24th and 30th. By August 1, he was 4-6 with a 1.25 ERA and 15 saves.

A sore knee and sore toe affected Smith through much of August, limiting his ability to blow people away. Instead, he often found himself getting out of jams he created. On the 9th against St. Louis, for example, he gave up a double and single in the ninth, putting the tying runs on base. But he fanned the next two hitters to earn save No. 18. He would pick up four more saves and see his ERA climb to 1.58 before the end of August, a month that also saw the firing of Elia on the 22nd after the Cubs had fallen to fifth at 55-69.

September was much the same for Smith. He picked up seven more saves and suffered three losses (two coming during a mid-month series against St. Louis, when Willie McGee beat him with ninth- and 10th-inning RBI singles). He got his 29th and last save of the season on September 27, fanning two and walking one in one inning of work, preserving a 3-0 victory over the Phillies.

Smith would have four more solid seasons for the Cubs—he had 133 more saves in those years—before going to Boston in 1988, taking that wicked fastball with him.

LEE SMITH'S

Three Other Great Cub Seasons

	Yr	W-L	IP	GS	GC	SH	SV	PD	K/BB	OBA	OB%	ERA	PR
1.	1985	7-4	97.2	0	0	0	33	-1	112/32	.242	.305	3.04	6
2.	1986	9-9	90.1	0	0	0	31	0	93/42	.215	.306	3.09	6
3.	1987	4-10	83.2	0	0	0	36	-1	96/32	.259	.326	3.12	9

Jumbo-sized Lee Smith, with his 95 MPH blazer, intimidated and then tamed most opponent attacks leveled at the Cubs in the late innings between 1981 and 1987. In 1983, his summit season, the Cubs won 71 times and he saved 29 (41 percent); in '85 (above), it was 33/77 (43 percent); '86: 31/70 (44 percent); and 36/76 (47 percent). That's not only the kind of consistency ballclubs and managers appreciate—it's very, very good. With a fifth- or sixth-place ballclub, it's awesome. His other seasonal numbers are equally consistent, all of which make for the dependable, steady late-inning guardian he was—in both leagues and with many teams. That's what earns him summit honors, at No. 26, indicative of his team value and personal contribution to the meager success the Cubs enjoyed during the years cited above.

"It was scary. Very scary."
—**Third-string Cub catcher Keith Moreland after catching for Lee Smith for the first time during the 1983 season.**

Other Baseball Highlights of 1983

- The White Sox run away with the AL West title, only to lose to Baltimore in the ALCS.

- Boston's Wade Boggs wins his first batting title (.361).

- George Brett hits his famous "pine tar" homer vs. New York on July 24.

- Cubs second baseman Ryne Sandberg wins his first Gold Glove.

- LaMarr Hoyt wins 13 games in a row for the White Sox.

SMITH: A NOTEWORTHY BOX SCORE

June 5, 1983

Smith strikes out four of the five Pittsburgh batters he faces to earn his eighth save.

Pittsburgh	AB	R	H	RBI	E	Chicago	AB	R	H	RBI	E
Lacy, lf	4	0	2	0	0	Hall, cf	4	0	2	1	0
Mazzilli, cf	2	0	0	0	1	Sandberg, 2b	2	0	1	0	0
Madlock, 3b	4	0	0	0	0	Buckner, 1b	4	0	0	0	0
Thompson, 1b	2	1	1	0	0	Cey, 3b	3	0	0	0	0
Morrison, ss	4	0	1	0	0	Johnstone, lf	3	1	1	1	0
Parker, rf	4	0	0	0	0	Moreland, rf	3	0	0	0	0
Pena, c	4	0	2	1	0	Davis, c	0	0	0	0	0
Ray, 2b	3	0	0	0	0	Lake, c	3	1	1	0	0
Tunnell, p	2	0	0	0	0	Bowa, ss	3	1	1	0	0
Harper, ph	1	0	0	0	0	Lefferts, p	3	0	0	0	0
Scurry, p	0	0	0	0	0	Smith, p	0	0	0	0	0
Hebner, ph	1	0	0	0	0						
TOTALS	31	1	6	1	1	TOTALS	28	3	6	2	0

```
Pittsburgh    0 0 0    1 0 0   0 0 0  —1
Chicago       0 0 0    0 3 0   0 0 *  —3
```

Double--Sandberg. Home run--Johnstone. Stolen base--Lacy (2). Sacrifice--Mazzilli. Double plays--Pittsburgh 1, Chicago 1.

	IP	H	R	ER	BB	SO
Tunnell (L, 1-3)	6	6	3	2	2	4
Scurry	2	0	0	0	0	2
Lefferts (W, 1-3)	7⅓	6	1	1	4	2
Smith (S, 8)	1⅔	0	0	0	0	4

Time--2:26. Attendance--22,649

Charles Leo "Gabby" Hartnett—1935

Chicago Cubs Summit Season
Number 27

No. 27
GABBY HARTNETT

BORN: December 20, 1900; Woonsocket, Rhode Island
DIED: December 20, 1972; Park Ridge, Illinois

Chicago Cubs: 1922-1940
Hall of Fame 1955

SEASON AT THE SUMMIT: 1935

AB-R-H	BA	OB%	2B	3B	HR	RBI	BR	FR	SB
413-67-142	.344	.404	21	1	22	91	30	15	1

Gabby Hartnett was there behind the plate when Babe Ruth hit his "called shot" home run in the 1932 World Series.

In his major-league debut in 1922, he caught the great Grover Cleveland Alexander.

He was also on the catching end when National League pitcher Carl Hubbell fanned Ruth, Lou Gehrig, Jimmie Foxx, Al Simmons and Joe Cronin in succession in the 1934 All-Star Game.

And Hartnett hit the most famous home run in Cub history—the "homer in the gloamin'," "the greatest thrill in my life," he once recalled—that carried the Cubs to the 1938 pennant.

But memories and historical moments aside, none of those events outshines Hartnett's 1935 campaign.

A Baby And An All-Star Berth
Hartnett started this most memorable of seasons in dramatic fashion on April 16, hitting a home run and driv-

ing in the eventual winning run with an eighth-inning double as the Cubs beat the defending National League champion St. Louis Cardinals 4-3.

There was little extraordinary for the Cubs in the first half of the season; they settled into third place and remained within striking distance of first-place New York and second-place St. Louis. Hartnett quickly got his average over the .300 mark while doing his usual skillful work behind the plate.

Hartnett had a lot to celebrate in late June. He became a father on June 28—he welcomed his new daughter by going 4 for 4 against Pittsburgh that day, raising his average to .330. And he was named to the NL All-Star team, the third time he was so honored in the four-year history of the game. (His contribution in the contest, played July 8 in Cleveland, was modest: He caught the last two innings of the NL's 4-1 loss.)

The second half of the season started with Hartnett at .329 and the Cubs in third place, 9½ games behind the first-place Giants. Two July winning streaks—one of nine games, the other of 11—marked the Cubs as serious contenders.

Hartnett was hitting over .340 by late July, but was knocked out of the lineup on July 31 when he injured an ankle in a 4-2 victory over the Pirates. He tried to score from second on a hit to right by Chuck Klein; Hartnett was not only thrown out by Paul Waner, but was hurt on the play. It was at first diagnosed as a fracture, but doctors later decided it was just a severe sprain. Hartnett came back quickly—maybe too quickly—and was back in the lineup on August 11, pinch-hitting for Walter "Tarzan" Stephenson and then catching two innings in a 3-2 victory over the second-place Cardinals.

He stayed in the lineup for the next two weeks—going 4 for 4 with three runs batted in one victory over the Phils, going 2 for 4 with a homer and three RBIs in another game, then going 3 for 8 in the first two games of a crucial series against first-place New York on August 22 and 23. But the ankle was still sore, and Hartnett—with his .344 average—had to come out of the lineup for nearly a week.

He returned in dramatic fashion—his 12th home run and two singles helped beat Boston August 29 and brought the Cubs within two games of first—and just in time for the Cubs' drive to the pennant.

Simply Unbeatable

From September 4 through 27, the Cubs won 21 straight games. Their remarkable charge began with a four-game sweep of the Phils. Hartnett missed three of the four games because of his still-tender ankle, but came back with a 5-for-11 series against the Braves and a 7-for-15 series against the Dodgers, during which the Cubs moved into first place. By now they were front-page news, and when they swept four from the Giants—Hartnett going 6 for 15 to raise his season mark to .351—the race was all but over.

The clincher came on September 27, a 6-2 victory over the Cardinals and the Cubs' 20th straight victory. They also won Game 2 of that day's double-header in what would be the final victory of their streak.

The Cubs' drive to the pennant was a great story, but there was no happy ending in the World Series.

One of the more interesting matchups of the Series figured to be between the two catchers, Hartnett and Detroit's Mickey Cochrane, regarded as the game's top two players at the position. They played to a draw—both were 7 for 24—and neither was much of a factor in the Series, which the Tigers won in six games. The Cubs won the opener 3-0, but Detroit took the next three before the Cubs came to life to win Game 5. The Tigers wrapped it up in Game 6, pushing across a run in the bottom of the ninth to beat Larry French 4-3.

Hartnett finished third in the NL with his .344 batting average; his .545 slugging average was fifth. Defensively, his .984 fielding average was tops among NL catchers, as was his figure of 77 assists. After the season he was voted league MVP by the Baseball Writers Association of America.

Hartnett became Cubs manager midway through the 1938 season and guided the team to the NL Championship—his legendary home run on September 28 of that year propelling the team to the pennant. But the Cubs slipped to fourth in 1939 and fifth in 1940, and he was let go. He spent his last season as a player-coach with the Giants in 1941.

Hartnett retired as a player after the 1941 season, managed a number of minor-league teams in subsequent years, and was elected to the Hall of Fame in 1955. He died on December 20, 1972, his 72nd birthday.

GABBY HARNETT'S

Four Other Great Cub Seasons

	Yr	GP	AB-R-H	BA	OB%	SA	K/BB	HR	RBI	SB	FR	BR
1.	1928	120	388-61-117	.302	.404	.523	32/65	14	57	3	9	25
2.	1930	141	508-84-172	.339	.404	.630	62/55	37	122	0	3	35
3.	1934	130	438-58-131	.299	.358	.502	46/37	22	90	0	14	18
4.	1937	110	356-47-126	.354	.424	.548	19/43	12	82	0	1	28

Nineteen years a Cub, and the franchise's all-time No. 1 catcher—that's "Gabby," the Massachusetts Mauler. He capped a Hall of Fame career with a 1935 season that delivered a pennant to the North Side. It was a 5-star year that earned the No. 27 spot, just past the midpoint of the summit honors list. The 1935 season was part of a four-year streak of league-leading fielding honors (1934-37), and his all-around brilliance that season led to his MVP award. With Bill Dickey and Mickey Cochrane, he introduced baseball to the hard-hitting catcher, an additional strong stick in the lineup. That was relatively unknown before the terrific trio showed up.

"If I had that guy to pitch to all the time, I'd never lose a game."

—Dizzy Dean on what it was like to have Gabby Hartnett as his catcher

HARTNETT'S A NOTEWORTHY BOX SCORE

June 29, 1935

Hartnett goes 4 for 4 with the game-winning RBI to move the Cubs into second place.

Pittsburgh	AB	R	H	RBI	PO	A	E	Chicago	AB	R	H	RBI	PO	A	E
L. Waner, cf	4	0	1	0	0	0	0	Galan, lf	4	0	1	0	1	0	0
Jensen, lf	4	0	1	0	1	1	0	Hermanski, 2b	3	1	1	0	1	5	0
P. Waner, rf	4	0	1	0	4	1	0	Cavarretta, lb	4	0	1	0	12	0	0
Vaughan, ss	4	1	2	0	1	5	0	Hartnett, c	4	0	4	1	2	0	0
Young, 2b	4	0	2	1	7	1	0	Lindstrom, cf	4	0	1	0	3	0	0
Suhr, lb	4	0	0	0	6	0	0	Klein, rf	4	1	1	1	3	0	0
Thevenow, 3b	3	0	1	0	1	2	0	English, 3b	4	0	1	0	1	2	0
Grace, c	3	0	0	0	4	0	0	Jurges, ss	3	0	0	0	4	7	0
Lucas, p	3	0	1	0	0	3	0	Warneke, p	1	0	0	0	0	1	0
TOTALS	33	1	9	1	24	11	0	TOTALS	31	2	10	2	27	15	0

```
Pittsburgh    000  100  000  — 1
Chicago       011  000  00*  — 2
```

Doubles--Thevenow, English, Herman, Hartnett. Home run--Klein. Sacrifice--Jurges. Left on base--Pittsburgh 4, Chicago 9. Double plays--Pittsburgh 2, Chicago 2. Struck out--Lucas, 2; Warneke 1. Bases on balls--Lucas, 3. Wild pitch--Warneke. Time--2:01. Umpires--Moran, Magerkurth, and Quigley.

Other Baseball Highlights of 1935

- On July 10, the Reds' Babe Herman hits the first homer in a night game.

- The Braves go 38-115, suffering the most losses ever by an NL team over a 154-game schedule.

- Cincinnati beats the Phils in baseball's first night game on May 24, 2-1.

William "Bill" Beck Nicholson—1943

Chicago Cubs Summit Season
Number 28

No. 28
WILLIAM NICHOLSON

BORN: December 11, 1914; Chestertown, Maryland
DIED: March 8, 1996

Chicago Cubs: 1939-1948

SEASON AT THE SUMMIT: 1943

AB-R-H	BA	OB%	2B	3B	HR	RBI	BR	FR	SB
608-95-188	.309	.386	30	9	29	128	50	6	4

Bill **Nicholson**, the brawny slugger Cub fans affectionately called "Swish," was the proud possessor of a Naval Academy appointment in 1932, but, unfortunately, never matriculated at Annapolis because the Navy medics found him to be color blind. Eventually, that kept him out of the Armed Services—and in a baseball uniform—during World War II. During the 1944 season he was, further, diagnosed as a diabetic after having reported increasing episodes of a lack of energy and weariness. That helped to explain why his already robust slugging wasn't even more imposing during the 1942 and '43 seasons, particularly 1943.

A Wartime Summit Season
A number of great ballplayers enjoyed summit-type seasons between 1942 and '45; Spud Chandler, Dizzy Trout, Hal Newhouser, Mort Cooper and Rip Sewell, among the pitchers, and Luke Appling, Stan Musial, Dixie Walker and Phil Cavarretta, among the hitters, rush to mind. Bill Nicholson was another. His 1943 season, which came at the very depths of WW II, with all that that meant from national, industrial, entertainment and professional sports

perspectives, was the midpoint of an awesome trio of Wrigleyville years. Between 1942 and '44 Swish averaged 28 four-baggers, 109 RBIs, a .297 batting average, and 3+ fielding runs per season. Those fielding runs give an insight into his fine defensive work, another of those well-kept baseball secrets, by the way. His RBI and home run totals were the class of the National League during the war years, those lopsided, dead and balata-centered balls notwithstanding. It was his 1943 effort, however, that, despite everything said about wartime baseball—and his physical problems—was a standout effort worthy of summit classification. It ranks a solid No. 28 on our honors list and marks the rugged run-producer, who is but one of six Cub players to clout more than 200 career home runs, as a bright spot during an otherwise dull stretch of years in Chicago between the 1938 and 1945 pennants.

Struggling To See Daylight
The Cubbies drew only 9,044 to their home opener against Pittsburgh's Rip Sewell, who would beat them six times during the 1943 season. Manager "Jimmie" Wilson's boys wound up on the short end of a 6-0, 3-hitter. It

sent them immediately into the second division where they remained submerged the rest of the season, though by season's end they did rise to a fifth-place finish, albeit 5½ games out of the National League's upper echelons. Without Nicholson, it would have been a far leaner harvest. He, with Cub captain Stan Hack, provided the only consistently potent hitting the Wrigleymen fielded on a day-to-day basis. Big Nick was the bellwether.

The Long Way Up

It took the Cubs a while to find the main action in 1943 and by the time they did, around mid-May, they had settled into a losing mode, winning but seven of their first 23 games. Nicholson, who was to play in every Cub game that summer, also got off to a slow start, hovering near the .250 mark after a 3 for 23 slump that made the merry month of May miserable.

During June, however, Nicholson jumped from the .250s to the .270s, increasing the voltage in his offensive attack to get into the home run and RBI race with ex-Cub favorite Billy Herman, now pacing the Dodgers, Pirates' third-sacker Bob Elliott, and another of the DiMaggios, Vince. To close out the month, his eighth circuit smash beat the Braves in a War Relief Game and raised his batting average to .293, with 40 RBIs. Lo and behold, the Cubs had moved up with Swish to the seventh rung, by now sporting a 23-38 record. Perhaps a line in the dirt had been drawn?

Heatin' Up

When mid-July rolled around, the Cubs returned from an extended road trip that raised a little dust and a few hopes with a 13-6 log, and the North Siders found themselves in the unfamiliar surroundings of fifth place, though still eight games under .500. The remainder of the month Nicholson claimed as his own, pushing his homer total up to double digits and his RBIs beyond the 70 mark. Within another couple of weeks he had made his way into the ranks of the .300 hitters.

As the season turned toward the Labor Day milestone, Big Bill had already jacked more than 20 into the cheap seats, with more than 100 runs driven home. Though the Chicago press and Cub fans were frustrated, realizing their team was not a first-division-caliber ballclub, there *was* one ray of bright light: the National League's All-Star right-fielder. For him, it was "hats-off" time. Here's what Ed Burns, the witty and whimsical Chicago sportswriter had to say in the September 23, 1943 *Sporting News* after a scintillating Nicholson performance at St. Louis:

"The day we're talking about, Sunday, September 19, was especially joyful for Bill Nicholson, the man who usually carries the Cubs on his back whenever they move in the right direction. For three weeks prior to September 19, Nick had busted only three homers and had fattened his runs-batted-in total by only five runs. On the big emancipation Sabbath he busted his twenty-third and twenty-fourth homers and drove in six runs. Harry Lowery, who made four doubles , scored the four RBI's that Nick didn't register himself. In addition to his pair of homers, one in each game, Nicholson smacked two doubles and two singles."

The Numbers At Season's End

Nicholson wound up his banner year with a 4-for-5 day in a double-header split with the Braves. He singled twice, walked thrice, doubled, and cracked his 29th dinger of the season, driving home his 127th and 128th runs before just under 10,000 at the Friendly Confines. He was the league's leader in HRs and RBIs, finished second to Stan Musial in total bases (323), and slugging average (.531), and third in runs scored (95).

MVP? Not quite. He finished third in the voting behind winner Musial and Walker Cooper. In 1944 he was to come much closer, missing the award by a single vote to yet another Cardinal, Marty Marion. En route Swish Nicholson had learned how to control his health problems—without a whimper—to emerge as one of the Windy City's favorites.

BILL NICHOLSON'S

Three Other Great Cub Seasons

	Yr	GP	AB-R-H	BA	OB%	SA	K/BB	HR	RBI	SB	FR	BR
1.	1940	135	491-78-146	.297	.366	.534	67/50	25	98	2	-2	31
2.	1942	152	588-83-173	.294	.382	.476	80/76	21	78	8	11	42
3.	1944	156	582-116-167	.287	.391	.545	71/93	33	122	3	2	48

Many baseball observers rate Bill Nicholson's 1944 season his greatest. We're suggesting that his 1943 season was even better, a more valuable contribution to the Cubs cause than the '44 campaign. During '43 he carried the club from the basement to a more respectable fifth-place finish, and he did it just about by himself. In 1944, the ranks of the top-flight players were even thinner, and there was bettter balance throughout the Cubs lineup to help along. That doesn't diminish a fine '44 effort one bit. Big Nick played great ball during the war years and that is reflected in our respect for his ability and productivity with the No. 28 ranking on the honors list, just ahead of Joe Tinker, Ed Reulbach and Ned Williamson. That's the kind of distinguished company he deserves.

"Nicholson...was asked about sharing a place in baseball lore with Babe Ruth. Without hesitation, he said, 'Babe was a great ballplayer...I was just so-so. I'm not in the same class.' Indeed, Bill Nicholson is in a class by himself."

—Bob Mayer in *The National Pastime: A Review of Baseball History*

NICHOLSON: A NOTEWORTHY BOX SCORE

September 19, 1943

Nicholson enjoys a big day in St. Louis

Chicago	AB	H	P	A	E		St. Louis	AB	H	P	A	E
Hack, 3b	4	0	1	0	0		Klein, 2b	4	0	5	1	0
Stanky, 2b	4	1	2	2	1		Garms, rf	4	0	1	0	0
Lowrey, ss	5	3	0	4	0		Musial, cf	4	4	2	0	0
Nicholson, rf	5	4	3	0	0		O'Dea, c	3	0	7	1	0
Cavarretta, 1b	4	0	12	1	0		Kurowski, 3b	4	1	2	2	0
E. Sauer, lf	4	1	1	0	0		Demaree, lf	3	0	3	0	0
Platt, cf	4	1	1	0	0		W. Cooper, ph	1	0	0	0	0
McCullough, c	3	1	6	0	0		Hopp, 1b	3	0	5	1	0
Wyse, p	3	1	1	4	0		Sanders, ph-1b	1	0	0	0	0
							Marion, ss	4	2	2	2	1
TOTALS	36	12	27	11	1		Gumbert, p	0	0	0	0	0
							Munger, p	2	0	0	0	0
							Walker, ph	1	0	0	0	0
							Dickson, p	0	0	0	1	0
							Litwhiler, ph	1	0	0	0	0
							TOTALS	35	7	27	8	1

```
Chicago       3 0 0   0 0 0   2 0 1  — 6
St. Louis     0 0 0   0 0 0   0 0 0  — 0
```

Doubles: Musial 2, Lowrey 3, Nicholson 2, Sauer, Platt; Home run: Nicholson; Double play: Marion, Klein and Hopp; Bases on balls: Wyse, 1; Gumbert, 1; Munger, 3; Strikeouts: Wyse, 3; Munger, 6; Dickson, 1. Losing pitcher: Gumbert.

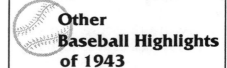

Other Baseball Highlights of 1943

- The Yankees win their seventh pennant in eight years, then beat the Cardinals in the World Series in five games.

- The bankrupt Philadelphia Phillies franchise is sold to the NL for $50,000; Bill Cox becomes the owner.

- Commissioner Landis bans Phils' owner Cox for life for betting on his own team.

Joseph Bert Tinker—1908

Chicago Cubs Summit Season
Number 29

No. 29
JOE TINKER

BORN: July 27, 1880; Muscotah, Kansas
DIED: July 27, 1948; Orlando, Florida

Chicago Colts/Cubs: 1902-1912; 1916
Hall of Fame: 1946

SEASON AT THE SUMMIT: 1908

AB-R-H	BA	OB%	2B	3B	HR	RBI	BR	FR	SB
548-67-146	.266	.307	22	14	6	68	8	30	30

People are often judged by the company they keep. Look at **Joe Tinker**. A lifetime .263 hitter, he's in baseball's Hall of Fame largely because of the teams—the Cubs' world champions of 1907 and '08—and the players—specifically Johnny Evers and Frank Chance—that he was associated with.

Tinker started his minor-league career with Denver in the Western League in 1900 and came to the Cubs two years later. Chicago's first baseman at the time was Chance, and two years later they were joined by Evers, forming the legendary Tinker-to-Evers-to-Chance double play combination later immortalized in verse by a New York sportswriter, Franklin P. Adams.

Although not in the same class as other Hall-of-Fame shortstops—Wagner, Appling, Aparicio, Boudreau, Maranville—there's no arguing Tinker had talent. He was a smooth fielder, a daring and intelligent baserunner, and a slightly above-average hitter, and he was blessed with baseball smarts. That's not all: He played a key role in those Cub world championships, particularly the 1908 season.

The Cubs were runaway National League champions in 1906 and '07, winning by 20 and 17 games, respectively. And they were heavy favorites to repeat in 1908. But the 1908 season would turn out to be the closest and most exciting in NL history—with Tinker in the thick of it.

Picking Up The Slack
The Cubs jumped to a quick lead, sweeping the Reds in a season-opening series in Cincinnati. But by April 23, Pittsburgh and New York had also spent time in first place. On that date, the Cubs took over the lead and would hold it for more than two months while the Pirates, Giants and, briefly, the Reds, battled for second.

Chicago was beset by injuries—Chance, Evers, left-fielder Jimmy Sheckard, third baseman Harry Steinfeldt, catcher Johnny Kling and utilityman Heine Zimmerman were all disabled at one time or another—and the Cubs pitching staff struggled early in the season. About the only player performing consistently was Tinker.

He wasn't hitting particularly well—he was below .200 for the first month of the season—but his hits were timely. On May 17, for example, he went 2 for 4 and scored three runs in Mordecai Brown's one-hit victory over Brooklyn. A week later, he singled home the winning run in the 10th inning of a game against the Giants. And on May 30, he went 4 for 9 in a double-header sweep of St. Louis.

But the multiple-hit games were rare. It would be early July before he got over the .200 mark to stay. Still, Tinker was a key factor in the Cubs' success. His fielding, for example, was sparkling. He made several outstanding plays in a June series against the Giants, and went from June 1 to June 29 without making an error.

Down The Stretch
But the injuries and the strong challenges from Pittsburgh and New York finally caught up with the Cubs, and the Pirates grabbed the lead on June 30. The Cubs went back into first on July 4, but Pittsburgh moved back on top the next day. That lasted only until July 8, when Chicago regained the lead, but a week later the Pirates were back on top, where they would stay until late August.

Tinker was doing his part for the Cubs, coming up with key hits—he tripled and scored in the 11th to beat Philadelphia on July 10, he homered to beat the Giants' Christy Mathewson 1-0 on July 17, and on July 18 his two-run double in the ninth beat New York 5-4—and putting together an 11-game hitting streak as he got his average over .250.

The Giants moved into first on August 20, the Pirates wrested the lead away the next day, but three days later New York regained it and held first place until September 29. What proved to be the turning point of the season came on September 23 in New York in a game between the Giants and Cubs. In the ninth inning with two out, the score tied and Giants on first and third, Al Bridwell singled, ostensibly scoring Moose McCormick with the winning run. But Fred Merkle, the runner on first, never got as far as second, leaving the basepaths and heading to the clubhouse after Bridwell's hit. Cubs

second baseman Evers called for the ball, touched second, and appealed to the umpires, claiming a force on Merkle. Because of darkness and a mob of fans on the field, the game could not continue. The league declared the game a tie, and when the Cubs and Giants finished the season with identical 98-55 records, a one-game playoff was set for October 8 in New York.

The Giants sent Mathewson—in the midst of a 37-11, 1.43 ERA season—against the Cubs. One of the few players Matty didn't dominate in 1908—opponents hit just .200 against him—was Tinker. The Cub shortstop hit .467 (7 for 15) with two homers versus the Giants ace. And Mathewson was aware of that when Tinker came to bat in the third inning. He waved to center-fielder Cy Seymour to play deeper. Seymour refused to move. Matty took off his glove and waved it. Seymour waved back, almost in mockery. Mathewson turned back to Tinker. On the next pitch, he lashed a triple over Seymour's head, and minutes later scored on Kling's hit, tying the score 1-1. The Cubs went on to a 3-2 victory that put them in the World Series against Detroit.

Bring On The Tigers
After the exciting pennant race, the Series was almost anticlimactic, as the Cubs beat the Tigers in five games. There were plenty of heroes for Chicago—Chance hit .421, Schulte .389 and Evers .350. Orval Overall won two games, striking out 15. But again Joe Tinker provided key hits and the spark. He drove in two runs and scored another in the ninth inning of Game 1, when the Cubs scored five runs for a 10-6 victory; he homered in Game 2, another Cubs victory. For the Series, he hit .263 and handled 27 chances in the field flawlessly.

There would be one more World Series for Tinker as a Cub, in 1910. He became manager of the Reds in 1913, jumped to the Federal League in 1914, and came back to the Cubs in 1916 to close out a 15-year career marked by consistency and dependability. Tinker and his two cohorts, Evers and Chance, were to share the spotlight one more time. In 1946, all three were elected to the Hall of Fame.

Three Other Great Cub Seasons

	Yr	GP	AB-R-H	BA	OB%	SA	K/BB	HR	RBI	SB	FR	BR
1.	1910	134	473-48-136	.288	.322	.397	35/24	3	69	20	16	3
2.	1911	144	536-61-149	.278	.327	.390	31/39	4	69	30	23	-2
3.	1912	142	550-80-155	.282	.331	.351	21/38	0	75	25	25	-11

Joe Tinker's 1908 season ranks at No. 29 along the summit trail. That season he registered a career-high 30 fielding runs, hit a World Series homer in the Cubs' conquest of Detroit in Game 2, hit reasonably well and especially in the clutch during the season, and turned in his accustomed stellar performance afield. Of the fabled infield trio, he was just as velvety smooth at short, if not a cut above, as Frank Chance was at first base, and just as cerebral about infield play as the keystone partner with whom he rarely spoke, Johnny Evers. All three wound up in the Hall of Fame, and each of the three, though linked through their years together and in the baseball poetry of the day, belong in baseball's pantheon on merit. Each went on to manage the Cubs and each enriched Cub tradition.

"These are the saddest of possible words...Tinker to Evers to Chance. Trio of Bearcubs and fleeter than birds. Tinker to Evers to Chance. Thoughtlessly pricking our gonfalon bubble, making a Giant hit into a double. Words that are weighty with nothing but trouble: Tinker to Evers to Chance."
—*Baseball's Sad Lexicon* by Franklin P. Adams

TINKER'S A NOTEWORTHY BOX SCORE

July 17, 1908

Tinker's fifth-inning home run beats Christy Mathewson and the New York Giants 1-0.

New York	AB	R	H	RBI	PO	A	E	Chicago	AB	R	H	RBI	P	A	E
Tenney, 1b	4	0	0	0	8	1	0	Slagle, cf	4	0	1	0	7	0	0
Doyle, 2b	4	0	1	0	2	3	0	Sheckard, lf	4	0	1	0	4	0	0
Bresnahan, c	3	0	0	0	5	3	0	Howard, rf	3	0	1	0	1	0	0
Donlin, rf	4	0	1	0	0	0	0	Chance, 1b	3	0	1	0	8	2	0
Seymour, cf	4	0	1	0	1	0	0	Hofman, 3b	3	0	0	0	1	1	0
Devlin, 3b	4	0	2	0	2	2	0	Evers, 2b	3	0	1	0	1	1	0
McCormick, lf	3	0	0	0	3	0	0	Moran, c	3	0	0	0	3	1	0
Bridwell, ss	3	0	1	0	3	0	1	Tinker, ss	3	1	2	1	0	5	0
Mathewson, p	3	0	0	0	0	4	0	Brown, p	3	0	0	0	2	2	0
TOTALS	32	0	6	0	24	13	1	TOTALS	29	1	7	1	27	12	0

New York	000	000	000	— 0
Chicago	000	010	00*	— 1

Double--Devlin. Triple--Evers. Home run--Tinker. Strikeouts--Mathewson, 4; Brown, 1. Bases on balls--Off Brown, 1. Double plays--New York 1, Chicago 1. Wild pitch--Brown. Time--1:26. Umpires--O'Day and Johnstone.

Other Baseball Highlights of 1908

•The White Sox's Ed Walsh wins 40 games.

•The song "Take Me Out to the Ball Game" is first introduced to the public.

•Washington's Walter Johnson throws three shutouts in a four-day period versus New York.

•The Cubs' Ed Reulbach twirls a double-header shutout against Brooklyn on September 26, winning by 5-0 and 3-0 scores.

Edward Marvin Reulbach—1905

Chicago Cubs Summit Season
Number 30

No. 30
EDWARD REULBACH

BORN: December 1, 1882; Detroit, Michigan
DIED: July 17, 1961; Great Falls, New York

Chicago Colts/Cubs: 1905-1913

SEASON AT THE SUMMIT: 1905

W-L-%	IP	CG	SH	SV	K/BB	PR	DEF	ERA
18-14 .563	291.2	28	5	1	152/73	51	-1	1.42

Edward "Big Ed" Reulbach gave the Chicago Colts' No. 1 bird-dog, George Huff, fits. Having seen the strapping youngster pitch at Notre Dame, and having determined to bring his dazzling array of breaking pitches to the West Side Grounds, Huff set about the task of hunting the big guy down. It wasn't easy. Collegians operated on admittedly different wavelengths, but Reulbach, an engineering major who later passed his bar exam cum laude, was especially difficult to track down. After trips here and there, extending all the way from Missouri to Vermont, the determined sleuth nailed his man and brought him into the Colts' fold. As soon as the semester ended for Reulbach (those were different days, of course; if you were fortunate enough to go to college, you *finished* what you started), he packed his duds and spikes, took the train to Chicago and began one of the more distinguished, yet vastly underestimated, pitching careers in the franchise's history.

A Losing Start

It would be nice to be able to say that Ed Reulbach's career opener, against the nasty New Yorkers, no less, was an unqualified success. Sorry, it wasn't. The Giants nailed him for a 3-spot at the Polo Grounds in his May 16 debut and went on to beat him 4-0 behind Red Ames' two-hitter. It was a tough way to start out, but it *was* a start. And it just so happened that it was the start of the best year he ever had, a Rookie of the Year kind of season if ever there was one.

It Didn't Take Long

Only 2,900 were on hand at Baker Bowl in Philadelphia to witness Big Ed's next outing. They saw him come to the Colts' rescue, after Carl Lundgren was pummeled early on, with a brilliant shutout blanking that beat the Phillies 9-4. It nailed down his first win and he was on his way.

Before you could say "Fightin' Irish," Reulbach had put together an imposing string of shutout and low-scoring games that led to an early June showdown series with McGraw & Co., in Chicago. On June 11 a Sunday crowd of more than 20,000 turned out to see the college phenom mix it up with the veteran Joe McGinnity. He didn't let the West Siders down, firing a six-hit white-washing at the Giants. His 4-0 conquest was aided in no small way by several twin killings, two of which Ed initiated himself. There was consensus: "Joe College" had arrived—and in a hurry! (Two days later on June 13, another bright young lad, Christy Mathewson by name, beat Chicago's "Miner" Brown 1-0 in the ninth on a no-hitter. It was New York's only win in the four-game, "White-wash Series," a harbinger of sorts of the three Mathewson shutouts in the Giants-Athletics 1905 World Series.)

Eight Straight
Victories over Brooklyn and Philadelphia ran his streak to eight before he faltered. Then came a St. Louis assignment on June 24 that turned out to be one of 1905's more stunning exhibitions. A crowd of 7,200 was on hand at Robison Field to watch Jack Taylor, now in "exile" with the Cardinals, and the fellow who only weeks before had been cramming for exams. In the bottom of the ninth St. Louis evened the score at 1 on a run-scoring double by Josh Clarke, subbing in right field. After that it was all Taylor and Reulbach and the two toiled through 18 innings, when right-fielder Billy Maloney's long sacrifice fly scored "Wild-fire" Schulte, who had tripled. That was all Ed needed to win—and to set a major-league record.

There were more improbabilities ahead. Fast forwarding to August 24, we find the rugged Michigander hooked up with Tully Sparks, veteran Phils' hurler, in yet another of those marathons. Unbelievably, this one was even longer— no less than 20 frames, and for another record, as well as another 2-1 victory for Reulbach. Both twirlers had, once again, gone the distance.

But There Were Troubling Times In Chicago
It seemed that in 1905, Chicago's baseball fortunes, despite a pitching staff that was rapidly evolving into the 20th Century's finest, was forever doomed to second rate status behind New York's haughty but superior Giants. Injuries that shelved key players and growing concern for the health of one of baseball's most respected managers, Frank Selee, who had rebuilt the team into a legitimate pennant contender, combined to cripple Chicago's hopes—at least for 1905. At midseason, Frank Chance took over the reins when complications from pneumonia forced Selee's resignation. For Reulbach, who liked and respected the Peerless Leader, Selee's father-like presence was missed and though he pitched well, it *did* make a difference. The net result at season's end was another Giant pennant and a third-place finish for the Colts.

One for the Book
Between mid-July and September Reulbach ran a string of nine ballgames in which he gave up no more than three runs in a game, shut out McGinnity (again) in New York by another 4-zip margin, and Phillies ace Togie Pittinger 7-0. He also lost a couple of heart-breakers, one to Matty in the ninth, 1-0, and still another ninth-inning loss, this time to Brooklyn, 2-1. He closed out the season at Pittsburgh with his 18th victory, a 2-1 squeaker over another fine rookie, Lefty Leifield. The final totals stacked up to a league-leading opponents' batting average of a miserly .201, the best ERA of his career, 1.42, and 28 completions in 29 starts, another career high.

Three other 1905 figures are worth noting. His hits per game tally at 6.42 ranks as the 49th lowest ever registered in the game's history. Other high all-time rankings include: 5.3 pitching wins (No. 88), and his .201 opponents' batting average (No. 94-[T]). Ah yes, Big Ed Reulbach's 1905 did leave its mark.

ED REULBACH'S

Two Other Great Cub Seasons

	Yr	W-L	IP	GS	GC	SH	SV	PD	K/BB	OBA	OB%	ERA	PR
1.	1906	19-4	218.0	24	20	6	3	3	94/92	.175	.278	1.655	24
2.	1908	24-7	297.2	35	25	7	1	-1	133/106	.24	.292	2.03	11

Reulbach's winning percentage topped the league three straight years, 1906-'08. At first blush his 1906 and '08 seasons look better than his summit season in 1905. Look at the numbers closely, noting the difference in pitching runs, ERA, and completion ratio. In 1909 Ed came back with a 19 and 10, and once again dipped below two at a snappy 1.78 ERA for his last super season, and it ranks better than the other two, though still off the 1905 pace. Reulbach ranks at #30 on our top 50 list, a strong position near the super season midpoint, among "Swish" Nicholson, Joe Tinker, "Ned" Williamson and Al Spalding.

"The masterpiece (June 24) which Reulbach inflicted on the Cardinals was a great piece of work, and after the game the mob poured on the field and gave the young pitcher a wonderful ovation...The oldest men on the team say that there never was such a youngster—a boy who stepped right into the National League and, without bench work, substitute stunts, or preliminary tryouts, proceeded to show himself the equal of the oldest pitchers in the game!"

—Billy Phelon, syndicated writer, in the June 24, 1905 issue of _Sporting Life_

REULBACH: A NOTEWORTHY BOX SCORE

June 24, 1905

Reulbach outduels St. Louis' Jack Taylor in 18 innings.

St. Louis	AB	R	H	P	A		Chicago	AB	R	H	P	A
Shay, ss	7	0	1	0	5		Slagle, cf	7	0	0	4	0
Shannon, lf	8	0	2	8	0		Schulte, lf	8	1	2	2	1
Arndt, 2b	8	0	1	5	5		Maloney, rf	8	1	1	2	0
Beckley, 1b	8	0	2	18	0		Chance, 1b	7	0	4	27	2
Brain, cf	7	0	1	4	1		Tinker, ss	8	0	1	4	11
Clarke, rf	4	1	2	5	0		Evers, 2b	6	0	1	4	9
Burke, 3b	7	0	3	4	3		Casey, 3b	6	0	0	2	4
Warner, c	6	0	2	10	1		Kling, c	7	0	2	9	2
Taylor, p	7	0	1	0	4		Reulbach, p	7	0	0	0	2
TOTALS	62	1	15	54	19		TOTALS	64	2	11	54	31

```
Chicago     000  100  000  000  000  001  — 2
St. Louis   000  000  001  000  000  000  — 1

Attendance: 7,200        Umpires: Bauswine and O'Day
```

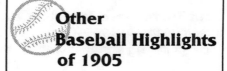

Other Baseball Highlights of 1905

- The deadball era is in full swing: Only three AL hitters bat over .300, and Boston's Cy Young is 17-19 despite a 1.82 ERA.

- Christy Mathewson pitches three shutout World Series wins versus Philadelphia.

- The Cubs' Frank Chance is hit by pitchers a record five times in a Decoration Day double-header.

ROUNDING OUT THE TOP 40

31) Ned Williamson, 1884, UT
32) Al Spalding, 1876, P
33) Johnny Schmitz, 1948, P
34) Larry Corcoran, 1884, P
35) Stan Hack, 1940, 3B

36) Mike Kelly, 1886, UT
37) Jim Vaughn, 1918, P
38) Billy Williams, 1972, RF
39) Andy Pafko, 1948, 3B
40) Hank Sauer, 1952, LF

This is an amazingly versatile group of summiteers. Their number includes two 19th-Century hurlers, right-handers Al Spalding and Larry Corcoran; two southpaws, Jim "Hippo" Vaughn and Johnny Schmitz; two, in Ned Williamson and Mike "King" Kelly, who played every position at one time or another, and are, therefore, listed as utility players; and two outfielders, Billy Williams and Hank Sauer. Two third basemen complete this unique listing of pairs, Stan Hack, the genial Cub hero of the '30s and '40s, and Andy Pafko, shifted by manager Charlie Grimm to the hot corner for the 1948 season, where he responded with league-leading figures in putouts, assists and fielding runs.

From Williamson (No. 31) to Sauer (No. 40) there is, once again, heated contention for each slot along the list of rankings. A mere sixth-tenths of one point separates these 10 Chicago greats in terms of Total Player Ratings. Spalding, Schmitz and Corcoran bunch together in the 32-34 spots with only slight differences even in the more telling numbers like pitching runs and pitcher defense. The Grandpapa of Cubs baseball, Spalding, had a fine 1.75 ERA in 1876, but he pitched for a better ballclub than did either Schmitz, fated to contribute his finest season (Pafko met with the same misfortune) with a tailender, or Corcoran, whose 1884 teammates should have finished higher than a tie for fourth, but didn't. That kind of thing makes for differences in a player's productivity.

Hack, Kelly and Vaughn presented similar ranking difficulties in and near the number No. 35 position. A paper-thin margin separates them from Spalding, Schmitz and Corcoran. Hack's 1940 season is about on a par with Kelly's 1886, despite "the King's" league-leading .386 average. "Smilin' Stan" has all the better of it afield, leading the league in putouts, double plays, assists, and fielding runs, as well as offering sterling offensive credentials. Vaughn, the greatest of the Cubs' southpaws, led them to a 1918 pennant with league leadership in wins, shutouts, innings pitched, ERA, pitching runs, and the lowest opponents' batting average. That levels off this accomplished trio, but it isn't good enough to position the Total Player Ratings of one significantly higher than another.

Williams finished second to Johnny Bench for 1972 MVP honors, winning the batting crown that year. He's included with yet another threesome that also has Pafko and Sauer. These three hold down the bottom of the order in the 31-40 grouping. They are, as those above them, presented in their Cub career years, though it must be said, at least in Williams' case, that his 1965 season is as good, if not a tad better, than his batting championship year of 1972.

And here's a final interesting tidbit: These 10 players have enough versatility to field a team consisting of Mike Kelly (C), Al Spalding (1B), Larry Corcoran (2B), Ned Williamson (SS), Stan Hack (3B), Hank Sauer, Billy Williams and Andy Pafko (OF), with a pitching staff of lefties Hippo Vaughn and Johnny Schmitz. Although some are out of position in this lineup, each did play a number of games at the positions cited. Anyway, it would make for a whale of a team nucleus, right?

Edward "Ned" Nagle Williamson—1884

Chicago Cubs Summit Season
Number 31

No. 31
NED WILLIAMSON

BORN: October 24, 1857; Philadelphia, Pennsylvania
DIED: March 3, 1894; Willow Springs, Arkansas

Chicago White Stockings: 1879-1889

SEASON AT THE SUMMIT: 1884

AB-R-H	BA	OB%	2B	3B	HR	RBI	BR	FR	SB
417-84-116	.278	.344	18	8	27	84	28	24	-

Edward "Ned" Williamson was to the 19th Century what Ernie Banks was to the 20th. He was not only the most popular star in Chicago, he was among the best loved ballplayers in any of the major leagues—quite possibly until the Babe's time. That covers a lot of territory, about as much as Williamson actually covered on the diamond. A versatile and multi-gifted athlete, he was stationed about anywhere Cap Anson happened to need him and did everything, absolutely everything, with a deft, smooth touch that left the fans gasping. Yes sir, he was worth the price of admission just about by himself!

Time for the Youngsters - and the Ladies

Here was a ballplayer who took time to be with the game's next generation, drawing huge crowds of young wannabes like steel filings to a magnet. And when evening came, why, there he was, dressed in his finery and mesmerizing the fair damsels. The three B's of the day (it wasn't Bach-Beethoven-Brahms by a long shot) definitely applied to the tall young man with the flawless physique: baseball, booze and broads. All three in huge

doses. He could have qualified as the Babe's roomie hands down!

1884: Ned's Career Year

The 1884 season, as we have seen, was less than satisfying for the White Stockings, a year that was clearly not up to their expectations—or standards, for that matter. Not so for Williamson. Among his 13 seasons under the Big Tent, 1884 stood out as his career year. It was the year he set the major-league record for homers in a single game, enjoyed a career-high .554 slugging average, contributed 24 fielding runs and otherwise had the time of his life as the toast of the town. That only covers the upper layer of his piece of cake. Usually a third baseman that summer, Williamson was also stationed behind the plate for a number of games; in fact, he caught the day he hit three homers, a part of the record 27 he hit that took some 35 years to better. And who broke it? The Babe—naturally!

Superstitious Ballplayers

The big fellow was another of those superstitious ballplayers who, when he felt the game was going against him, would take a small stone or pebble from around third base and put it under the outside part of the base on the foul line. Was it mere coincidence that one of his more sparkling fielding plays would follow soon after? If that can't be explained, here's one that can: Ned made one of the most remarkable plays of his career that summer. It was a catch in foul territory that he had no business getting to in the first place, only to still have to jump, extending his arm over a barbed wire fence to catch the ball bare-handed. C. G. Perkins, a Chicago sportswriter, called it the doggonedest catch he had ever seen in watching big-league ball over 40 seasons! That's right—it happened after one of those "pebble placements"—no less!

League Leader and Anson's Handyman
In the summer of 1884 Williamson led the league's third basemen in assists, double plays and fielding runs, caught 10 games, and, as usual, made a few appearances on the mound (he got around to that each season from 1881-1887). He was a top five hitter in total bases, RBIs, walks, slugging average, and batting runs (linear weights measure of runs contributed beyond that of a league-average player whose average is 0).

Ned Williamson didn't leave many stones unturned (as we've seen) during his dozen years around Chicago's big-time baseball scene. And while he spent the wee hours carousing, much to Anson's disgust, the Chicago captain gave his star a wide berth in the sure knowledge that when he stepped on the diamond, Williamson could be counted on for another four-star ballgame. Through the years the Windy City's premier third sacker gave Anson no reason to think otherwise.

They Knew They Had Seen Something Special
Though the career numbers aren't quite there, Ned's Chicago years come within shouting distance of Cooperstown consideration, an oft-repeated sentiment among baseball observers of the past. Here's what sportswriter Perkins had to say in the *Chicago Tribune* on March 5, 1894, on the occasion of Williamson's passing:

"He could do more with a baseball than anybody I ever saw and I have seen them all. Even after he had been here a few years and got fat he was the quickest man ever seen at short after a hard ball. He would gather it up slowly and gracefully and wait until the runner had almost reached first base, and Anson would be dancing around in rage, and then slam the ball over so hard that it would almost knock Anson off the base, getting it there just about a foot ahead of the runner...He is credited with the longest hit on the West Side Grounds ever made there.

"He would make the most daring base steals of anybody who played in those days except Mike Kelly, having a feet-foremost slide that would get his feet on the base and his body out of the way of the ball."

Williamson's season of 1884 was full of the derring-do and just plain great baseball that marked his West Side Park career. His rank, at the No. 31 position in our summit 50, is near the midpoint, right among several Cub greats including Ed Reulbach, Joe Tinker and Johnny Schmitz. That's pretty classy company—and old Ned adds a distinctive glitter to their ranks.

NED WILLIAMSON'S

Two Other Great Cub Seasons

	Yr	GP	AB-R-H	BA	OB%	SA	K/BB	HR	RBI	SB	FR	BR
1.	1879	80	320-66-94	.294	.343	.447	31/24	1	36	-	17	16
2.	1882	83	348-66-98	.282	.333	.408	21/27	3	60	-	16	11

By modern standards, 80-85 games looks like half a season, which would hardly compare with the 130-160 games represented in most of our summit seasons. But when those games are played on the diamonds of the 1880s and 1890s those same 80-90 games, played under the travel and playing conditions of that time, no doubt made demands as exacting as our elongated contemporary seasonal grind. Consequently, we'll take Williamson's numbers on a par with our latter day heroes—without a qualm. Big Ned's productivity in three key seasons, 1879, '82 and '84, his summit campaign, average out at a nifty 3.5 TPR with superior fielding run ratings (22 in 1881 and 24 in 1884) to garnish his timely and productive stickwork. That's good enough to hoist his summit rating into the midst of the Tinker-Reulbach-Hack and Vaughn grouping at No. 31.

The *New York Sun's* Joe Villa, who had seen them all in his time, picked the popular Williamson for his pre-1900 All-Star team, as did others, including Cap Anson, interviewed by Harold Kaese, who included this Anson assessment in his book *The Boston Braves*:

"Ned was, in my opinion, the greatest all-around ballplayer the country ever saw...Taking him all in all, I question if we shall ever see his like on a ballfield again."

WILLIAMSON: A NOTEWORTHY BOX SCORE

May 30, 1884

Record-setting Williamson blasts three home runs.

Detroit	AB	R	H	PO	A	Chicago	AB	R	H	PO	A
Wood, lf	5	1	2	1	0	Dalrymple, lf	5	2	3	1	0
Farrell, 3b	5	1	2	1	1	Gore, cf	3	1	0	3	0
Hanlon, cf	4	0	1	2	0	Kelly, rf	4	2	2	1	0
Bennett, c	4	0	1	2	0	Anson, lb	5	1	3	15	0
Geiss, 2b	4	0	0	2	5	Kinzie, 3b	5	0	0	1	3
Scott, lb	4	0	2	16	0	Williamson, c	5	4	4	2	0
Weldman, p, ss	4	0	0	0	4	Pfeffer, 2b	5	1	2	3	4
Weber, rf	4	0	0	0	0	Goldsmith, p	4	1	0	0	4
Meinke, ss, p	4	0	0	0	6	Burns, ss	3	0	0	1	4
TOTALS	38	2	8	24	16	TOTALS	39	12	14	27	15

```
Detroit     1 0 1   0 0 0   0 0 0  — 2
Chicago     1 1 4   0 1 0   3 2 *  —12
```

Doubles: Anson, Williamson, Farrell, Scott; Triples: Dalrymple, Wood. Home Runs: Williamson 3; Double plays: Geiss, Scott, Meinke (2). Strikeouts: Goldsmith, 1; Meinke, 2; Bases on balls: Weldman, 1; Meinke, 3; Goldsmith, 0. Time: 2 :00. Attendance: 5,000. Umpire: Decker.

Other Baseball Highlights of 1884

- Buffalo's Pud Galvin no-hits Detroit 18-0 on August 4.

- The American Association becomes the first league to award a batter first base for being hit by a pitch.

- The NL changes from nine to six the number of balls needed for a walk.

- The Providence Grays defeat the American Association's New York Metropolitans in their postseason championship series.

Albert G. Spalding—1876

Chicago Cubs Summit Season
Number 32

No. 32
AL SPALDING

BORN: September 2, 1850; Byron, Illinois
DIED: September 9, 1915; San Diego, California

Chicago White Stockings: 1876-77
Hall of Fame: 1939

SEASON AT THE SUMMIT: 1876

W-L-%	IP	CG	SH	SV	K/BB	PR	DEF	ERA
47-12 .797	528.2	53	8	0	39/26	33	4	1.75

The Cubs as well as the National League itself are indebted to the vision, persistence and organizational genius of **Albert Goodwill Spalding**. Better known as Al, or "A.G.," the native Illinoisian launched a new season, a new team, and, in fact, a new professional baseball league during America's Centennial Exposition Year, 1876. And that was not all. In February of that same year the broad-shouldered young pitcher (he was only 26 at the time) also opened a sporting goods store on Randolph Street that would soon capture a vast sporting goods market.

By April 22, the day on which the budding National League opened its first championship season, Chicago, which had more than tripled in size from its Civil War population of about 109,000, was abuzz with excitement over its "new and improved" White Stockings and their chances of overtaking the powerful Bostons, the team that Spalding and three of his more gifted teammates had left. The Windy City denizens needn't have wondered, much less have worried about it. Not with Spalding on the scene. He had seen to it that little if anything had been left to chance, right on down to the baseballs, uniforms and most of the other equipment the Whites, as they were commonly called, used on the field of play. Big Al took care of *everything* —in spades.

And when it came time to open Chicago's season, Spalding dealt Louisville a 4-0 whitewashing, the NL's first shutout, on April 25. A couple of weeks later, when the White Stockings opened at home with some 3,000 plus on hand at the 23rd Street Grounds, a smallish, wooden-fenced, partially enclosed diamond, he fashioned another shutout, this one over Cincinnati's Red Stockings, for the second of his total of eight during the 1876 campaign. By the time October rolled around Chicago's new heroes had logged a pennant-winning 52 victories and Spalding's name was written into the space provided for the winning pitcher no less than 47 times! That represents a whopping 90.3 percent of his team's victory total, and the 47 is topped only by John Clarkson's titanic 53, the franchise's single-season record. Absolutely awesome!

Double Duty

When he wasn't pitching, Spalding's name was written into the lineup as an outfielder. All told, he played in every Chicago engagement that summer, hit .312 with but three strikeouts in 292 at-bats, logged a staggering 53 complete games, and ran up in excess of 500 innings of pitching while the pennant-winners won out over St. Louis and Hartford, Connecticut tied at second place six games out, and over archrival Boston, in fourth place 15 games out of the running.

The ballclub that president William Hulbert and manager Spalding put together for that epoch-making season hit a ton—and in a day and age when pitching was a dominating factor in the game. Their .337 team batting average established a major-league record unbroken to this day, as they averaged 14 hits a game. Around the infield, first baseman Cal McVey, who was credited with the "other" five pitching wins, hit a starchy .347; third baseman Anson (he was to move over to first base a little later), hit .356 in the first of his 22 seasons in Chicago; shortstop Johnny Peters, .351; the senior circuit's first batting champion, second baseman Ross Barnes, one of Spalding's closest friends and teammates at Boston along with McVey and Deacon White, hit a lusty .429. White, whose mark of distinction was an immense, drooping, walrus mustache, made the most of his only Chicago season with a rousing .343 average while doing the catching from a position close behind the hitter, a new development in the game back then. A swift and steady outfield of Bob Addy, Paul Hines, John Glenn, Oscar Bielaski and the aforementioned McVey rounded out this stellar cast of champions.

A Star In Any Era

But none was more sensational either on that team or in the league itself than the White Stocking ace, Spalding. Had there been one, a Cy Young-type award would surely have been accorded the fellow with the cricket-like, straight-armed, underhanded delivery. To be sure, the game was in many respects far different than the game we know today. But three outs, nine innings, base hits, errors, and rooting for the home team remain staples that Spalding & Co. shared in common with all of us, and if the supreme measure of greatness is towering superiority over one's peers, then Big Al did everything that could be expected—and then some.

Ranking among the league's top five in 12 of pitching's major categories and leading in wins and winning percentage, he staked Chicago's White Stockings, later to be known as the Cubs, to a lofty position among professional baseball teams, a distinction they held at or near the top of the heap well into the 20th Century.

AL SPALDING

etween 1871 and 1875, Al Spalding reeled off victory totals of 19, 38, 41, 52 and 55, totaling 205 while losing 53 for a .795 winning percentage. His Chicago mark was no less sensational, with a 47 and 12 in 1876. His next season was his last, a sort of half-a-loaf mixture of a little pitching here and a little infielding there as he began, more and more, to turn to executive responsibilities in the front office. By 1878 he had played his last professional baseball game.

Anson on Spalding, who with McVey, White and Barnes left Boston to play with the White Stockings. Concerning the first meeting between the two bitter rivals on Memorial Day, 1876, Anson had this to say about Spalding:

"The Big Four' were given a great ovation when they put in an appearance...The game that followed was, as might be expected, played under difficulties, but thanks to the excellent pitching of Spalding we won by the score of 5 to 1, and the Hubbites [Boston fans] were sorer than ever over the 'Big Four's' defection."

—Adrian Anson, *A Ball Player's Career*

FINAL STANGING FOR THE NL'S INAUGURAL YEAR

Team	W	L	Pct.	GB
Chicago	52	14	.788	
St. Louis	45	19	.703	6
Hartford	47	21	.691	6
Boston	39	31	.557	15
Louisville	30	36	.455	22
New York	21	35	.375	26
Philadelphia	14	45	.237	34.5
Cincinnati	9	56	.138	42.5

THE NATIONAL LEAGUE'S FIRST TOP SIX TWIRLERS

Name/Team	W-L-W%		ERA	SH	OBA	PR	DEF	TPI
Devlin, J; Louisville	30-35	.462	1.56	5	.224	51	1	7.3
Bradley, G; St. Louis	45-19	.703	1.23	16	.211	69	1	5.8
Spalding, A; Chiacgo	47-12	.797	1.75	8	.247	33	4	4.6
Bond, T; Hartford	31-13	.705	1.68	6	.220	29	5	3.2
Cummings, W; Hartford	16-8	.667	1.67	5	.239	15	-2	0.6
Manning, J; Boston	18-5	.783	2.14	0	.252	4	0	0.4

Other Baseball Highlights of 1876

- The National League of Professional Base Ball Clubs is formed, the first permanent major league, with eight teams.

- The player-run National Association folds.

- Chicago's Ross Barnes leads the NL in runs (126), hits (138), triples (14), total bases (190), batting average (.429), slugging average (.590) and on-base percentage (.462).

John Albert Schmitz—1948

Chicago Cubs Summit Season
Number 33

No. 33
JOHNNY SCHMITZ

BORN: November 27, 1920; Wausau, Wisconsin

Chicago Cubs: 1941-1942;1946-1951

SEASON AT THE SUMMIT: 1948

W-L-%	IP	CG	SH	SV	K/BB	PR	DEF	ERA
18-13 .581	242.0	18	2	1	100/97	35	5	2.64

An 18-13 record for a pitcher is commendable, though hardly spectacular.

An 18-13 record for a pitcher on the 1948 Cubs is spectacular. Really spectacular.

The '48 Cubs won only 64 games. They ranked at or near the bottom of the National League in home runs, stolen bases, errors, fielding percentage and runs allowed. How bad would it have been without **Johnny Schmitz**?

Schmitz, a 27-year-old left-hander, must have known early on what kind of season it would be. He made his 1948 debut on April 23 in the Cubs' home opener, throwing a two-hitter against St. Louis—and losing. The Cardinals got the only run of the game in the ninth when Erv Dusak walked and Ralph LaPointe, after fouling off two bunt attempts, swung away and doubled Dusak home. It ruined an eight-strikeout effort by Schmitz, and wouldn't be his first disappointment in the opening weeks of the season.

He lost on April 28, 8-1, to Cincinnati, and was beaten 3-1 by the Cardinals on May 3. So after three games, Schmitz was 0-3 and the Cubs had scored just one run for him while he was on the mound.

Schmitz took matters into his own hands in his next outing, May 8 against Brooklyn. He fired a five-hitter as the Cubs won 6-0, striking out nine Dodgers and getting into trouble only once, that in the ninth when Billy Cox singled and Duke Snider doubled. But Schmitz struck out Eddie Miksis to end the threat and wrap up his first victory of the season (and the first of six he would record against Brooklyn in 1948).

Getting the Breaks

Luck finally appeared to be on Schmitz's side in his next two starts. He outdueled Philadelphia's Curt Simmons on May 18—the Cubs won 3-2, with all of their runs the result of four Phillies errors—and evened his record at 3-3 on the 21st when he came on in relief of Hank Borowy, who left after 4⅔ innings with an 8-2 lead against New York. Had Borowy been able to stick around for one more out, he would have qualified for the win; as it was, Schmitz finished up, allowing just two hits the rest of the way.

A 4-1 six-hitter against Brooklyn on May 26—Gil Hodges' fifth-inning homer the only blemish—was Schmitz's fourth straight win, and he was on his way to No. 5 four days later against the Reds. He took a two-hit shutout into the eighth, but a single, fielder's choice and walk loaded the bases, and Grady Hatton unloaded them with a homer. Cincinnati added another single and homer and Schmitz was saddled with a 6-1 defeat to even his record to 4-4.

The Cubs fell out of the NL pennant race quickly, settling into last place from where they made only occasional forays into seventh (though they did, very briefly, reach sixth late in the season). Schmitz did what he could to further the cause through the remainder of the first half of the season—he stopped the Dodgers on a four-hitter on June 13 (again, Brooklyn's lone run came on a Hodges homer); he threw another four-hitter at the second-place Cardinals on June 29, beating Harry Brecheen, who entered the game with a 21-5 lifetime mark against the Cubs; and he closed out the first half of the season with a sparkling two-hit victory over the Pirates.

Going Strong
Despite being only 8-9, Schmitz was chosen for the All-Star Game, one of four Cubs on the NL team. But it was a less-than-stellar outing for Schmitz. Coming in in the fourth inning in relief of Ralph Branca with the score 2-2, he retired the first man he faced. But singles by Ken Keltner and George McQuinn and a walk to Birdie Tebbetts filled the bases. Then Vic Raschi drove home two runs with a single. That was it for Schmitz for the day as the American League went on to a 5-2 victory and he was tagged with the loss.

Schmitz won his first three decisions after the break. He four-hit the Phillies on July 18—three of the hits by Johnny Blatnik—winning when Robin Roberts hit two Cub batters with the bases loaded in the ninth. He stopped the Dodgers 6-3 on the 22nd, ending a five-game Cub los-

ing streak. And on August 2 he went 11 innings to beat Brooklyn 4-2, scoring the winning run himself after reaching on a fielder's choice, taking second on a single and scoring on Eddie Waitkus' double.

A 6-3 loss to the Braves' Johnny Sain—Schmitz hadn't won in Boston since June of 1942—was only a temporary setback, as he won his next four decisions to run his record to 15-10: a seven-hitter against the Reds on August 13, a five-hitter against the Cardinals four days later, and an eight-hitter versus the Reds on the 22nd. His finest effort came on the 27th when he not only stopped Sain and the first-place Braves 1-0 on six hits, but also scored the game's only run when he doubled in the ninth, took third on a single and came home on a fielder's choice.

He was knocked out early in his next outing, lasting only three innings against the Dodgers on September 1, but bounced back the following day, working four innings of relief in a 7-6 Cub victory over Brooklyn.

A Season Cut Short
Schmitz would suffer only two more losses the rest of the season—6-4 to Brooklyn on the 13th, when the Dodgers scored three runs in the seventh thanks to errors by Schmitz and Waitkus, and 8-1 to the Dodgers in a game in which he lasted just two-thirds of an inning, giving up two homers and three runs. He ran his record to 18-13 on September 21, beating the Giants 3-2 on Andy Pafko's three-run homer in the ninth, and appeared to have a good shot at 20 victories.

His season, though, was ended by a sore arm. Even without 20 wins, he had reason to be proud. His 18 victories accounted for 28 percent of the Cubs' total. Opponents batted just .215 against him, best in the National League. His 2.64 ERA was fourth best in the league. He was third in complete games with 18. And he allowed an average of just 6.92 hits per nine innings, another league-leading stat. It would be the best year of Schmitz's 13-year career. And had it been with a stronger team, it would have been spectacular. Really spectacular.

JOHNNY SCHMITZ'S

Two Other Great Cub Seasons

	Yr	W-L	IP	GS	GC	SH	SV	PD	K/BB	OBA	OB%	ERA	PR
1.	1946	11-11	224.1	31	14	2	2	2	135/94	.221	.302	2.61	20
2.	1947	13-18	207.0	28	10	3	4	2	97/80	.262	.330	3.22	19

From northern Wisconsin, they called Johnny Schmitz "Bear Tracks," and indeed, he left a few in the vicinity of the pitcher's mound at the Friendly Confines. After he traded uniforms with Uncle Sam for the colorful Cub flannels, he joined Charlie Grimm's third-placers in 1946, and went on to help out with a sixth-place 1947 finish and a tail-ender in 1948 as the Cubbies went into hibernation, progressing from worse to "worser" along the way. One wonders how deep they might have burrowed had it not been for one of the classier lefties in Cubs history! Schmitz's 1948, a career year, ranks a No. 33 spot on the summit list. All things considered, his '48 is a more singular achievement than the Cubs' greatest lefty, Hippo Vaughn, logged with his No. 37, 1918 season. That was accomplished with a far better ballclub.

Though his 1948 All-Star Game wasn't typical of his season, Johnny Schmitz's stint at Sportsman's Park in St. Louis summed up the futility of one of the Cub franchise's worst ballclubs—ever. Touched for three earned runs in only a third of an inning before being lifted, Schmitz, like the '48 Cubs' disastrous campaign, just didn't have it. Peter Golenbock commented in his *Wrigleyville* on what that can do to a ballplayer (Phil Cavarretta):
"Losing would bother me physically, because I wouldn't feel too good after losing game after game...I played a long time, but to me, another thing you do to be a success, it isn't whether you go 2 for 4. It's did we win or lose? A lot of guys will say, 'That's a pile of garbage what you say.' But that's the way I felt!'"

SCHMITZ: A NOTEWORTHY BOX SCORE

August 27, 1948

Schmitz beats first-place Boston and Johnny Sain on a six-hitter and scores the game's only run in the bottom of the ninth.

Boston	AB	R	H	RBI	PO	A	E	Chicago	AB	R	H	RBI	PO	A	E
Holmes, rf	4	0	0	0	3	1	0	Verban, 2b	3	0	0	0	6	1	0
Dark, ss	4	0	1	0	3	6	0	Jeffcoat, cf	4	0	1	0	3	0	0
M. McCormick, lf	4	0	1	0	3	6	0	Cavarretta, 1b	4	0	1	0	13	0	0
Elliott, 3b	2	0	1	0	0	2	1	Pafko, 3b	4	0	0	1	2	6	0
F. McCormick, 1b	4	0	0	0	9	0	0	Lowrey, lf	3	0	1	0	0	0	0
Conaster, cf	2	0	0	0	2	0	0	Nicholson, rf	3	0	0	0	1	0	0
Masi, c	3	0	2	0	4	0	0	Scheffing, c	3	0	1	0	0	0	0
Sisti, 2b	3	0	1	0	3	4	1	Smalley, ss	3	0	0	0	1	8	2
Sain, p	4	0	0	0	0	0	0	Schmitz, p	3	1	1	0	1	3	0
TOTALS	30	0	6	0	26	13	2	TOTALS	30	1	5	1	27	18	2

Boston	000	000	000	--	0
Chicago	000	000	001	--	1

Double--Schmitz. Triples--Dark, M. McCormick. Sacrifices--Sisti, Masi. Double plays--Boston 2, Chicago 2. Left on base--Boston 9, Chicago 4. Strikeouts--Sain, 4. Bases on balls--Schmitz, 4. Attendance--9,076. Umpires: Conlan, Stewart and Hamline.

Other Baseball Highlights of 1948

- Cleveland owner Bill Veeck signs 42-year-old Satchel Paige, and he goes 6-1 with a 2.48 ERA for the Indians.

- The Pirates make a record 19 outfield putouts on July 5.

- Frank Lane is hired as White Sox GM.

- The Negro National League disbands.

- Babe Ruth dies on August 18 at the age of 53.

Larry Corcoran—1884

Chicago Cubs Summit Season
Number 34

No. 34
LARRY CORCORAN

BORN: August 10, 1859; Brooklyn, New York
DIED: October 14, 1891; Newark, New Jersey

Chicago White Stockings: 1880-1885

SEASON AT THE SUMMIT: 1884

W-L-%	IP	CG	SH	SV	K/BB	PR	DEF	ERA
35-23 .603	516.2	57	7	0	272/116	33	7	2.40

The first no-hitter in the history of organized base-ball was thrown by Joe Borden of Philadelphia on July 28, 1875, against Chicago's Whites. **Larry Corcoran** pitched baseball's fifth, and the first of his three no-nos, against Boston in 1880, his freshman season. He followed that with another in 1882 and then on June 27, 1884, delivered his trump card against the Providence Grays to complete his no-hit hat trick. It was by far the most brilliant of his 35 conquests that summer. The *Chicago Tribune* summed up the masterpiece this way on June 28, 1884:

"The fact that Chicago has at least one pitcher was dem-onstrated very plainly in yesterday's game, in which the Providence team, composed of the heaviest batters in the league, failed to earn a single base in nine innings. This result was by no means due to extra-sharp fielding, but was in the main brought about by extraordinary pitch-ing."

Downs and Ups

Corcoran had opened with a pair of losses at New York, moved to a 2-5 record by mid-May and in general gave

little indication that 1884 was to be his finest major-league season. But on June 10 he closed out a Chicago homestand with a 2-0 win over Cleveland, and though there was a 20-9 lambasting at the hands of Buffalo's Bisons (Corcoran left that game in the fourth with a bruised hand), the team backed him with 13 runs on June 24 to beat Boston before the Whites returned home to the very friendly confines of West Side Park. Three days later Hoss Radbourn and his Grays came to town, and the tobacco chewing, hard-throwing right-hander (he was ambidextrous and batted left, incidentally) faced the Providence nine in the opener of a three-game se-ries.

He was ready. That day, the 27th, he entered the record books with baseball's 15th no-hitter. Though he didn't pitch against the Grays' Hall of Famer Radbourn in that one, the two hooked up in the second game of the se-ries, Corcoran again triumphant, 5-4.

Going Great Guns

The two Providence wins marked the beginning of a six-week run in which he unleashed a steady barrage of dominating hurling, adding up to a 14-3 mark between June 27 and August 6. While the rest of the pitching staff faltered until John Clarkson was added in mid-August, the only thing in Corcoran's way was sloppy fielding (uncharacteristic of an Anson ballclub) and mental lapses (more uncharacteristic still).

Going into the last weeks of the season, the small but stylish twirler, who signaled for his drop-curve by moving the wad of tobacco in his mouth, was about as arm-weary as Charlie Buffinton of Boston, Buffalo's Pud Galvin, and the Grays' ace Radbourn, the overworked workhorses of the league. But in the '80s and on into the '90s you simply picked up the ball and kept on throwing—as many as 400 to 600 innings a season. That took its toll. Corcoran tapered off to a 33-23 record going into the final series of the season with Philadelphia, but he pulled things together for two fine conquests in the City of Brotherly Love to close out his record at a glossy 35-23, featuring a 2.40 ERA, seven shutouts, a more than adequate .243 batting average, and his customary fielding brilliance. It had been *some* season!

Another First

Although Larry Corcoran didn't get to pitch in a World Series, he was responsible for a first, winning Chicago's first postseason game, and, consequently, the National League's first as well. After completing its inaugural American Association season in 1882, Cincinnati's championship team, ousted from the NL in 1880, agreed in October to a series that would pit the two major-league champs against each other. The games opened at the Reds' League Park on October 6, with Cincinnati's Will White, a 40-game winner that summer, whitewashing the Whites 4-0. Cincinnati was absolutely aglow.

That brought Chicago's ace, Corcoran, who had enjoyed an outstanding 27-12 season, to the mound for the second game. With 3,500 roaring Cincinnatians on hand, the little fellow proceeded to set down the AA champs with a calcimining of his own, shutting them down on three hits. The Whites came up with a pair of first-inning runs chiefly on the strength of another of those Anson innovations, the hit and run, with Ned Williamson punching the ball into the hole and setting up the runners in scoring position for the Captain. You could have bet the farm that Adrian would come through—and he did. The two-run opening salvo was all Anson's diminutive speedster needed. That cooled the Ohio atmosphere in a hurry and so incensed league president Dennis McKnight that he ordered the Reds not to play any more games in the series. And so it ended, 1-1, in favor of, at the very least, Larry Corcoran and the hit and run.

But the Finale Was A Sad One

One of the many early Chicago stars who died at a very young age, Larry Corcoran passed from the scene at 32. A combination of physical exhaustion, Bright's Disease, and the malady that plagued and cursed so many of the Whites, alcoholism, stilled his pitching artistry forever, seven short years after his career year in 1884.

LARRY CORCORAN'S

Three Other Great Cub Seasons

	Yr	W-L	IP	GS	GC	SH	SV	PD	K/BB	OBA	OB%	ERA	PR
1.	1880	43-14	536.1	60	57	4	2	6	269/99	.199	.236	1.95	25
2.	1882	27-12	355.2	39	38	3	0	1	170/63	.200	.234	1.95	38
3.	1883	34-20	473.2	53	51	3	0	1	216/82	.247	.277	2.49	34

Between 1880 and '84 Larry Corcoran fashioned 163 victories for A.G. Spalding's White Stockings, a 32.6 average per season. His TPI rating averaged 3.1 and his name appeared on just about every top-five listing for the various pitching categories. He burned up the league and no doubt his arm, and, sadly, himself during those meteoric years. And then it was over as suddenly as it all began. But while it lasted there were few better, and Cap Anson's boys were always at or near the top of the heap. His 1880, '82 and '83 seasons, gems in their own right, were nonetheless eclipsed by his career year, a season that propelled Anson's pint-sized ace into the No. 34 spot, just ahead of Cub favorite Stan Hack and Corcoran's teammate, Mike "King" Kelly.

In his book, *A Ball Player's Career*, Cap Anson had this to say about his bantam-sized pitcher, Larry Corcoran:

"He [Corcoran] was a very little fellow with an unusual amount of speed and the endurance of an Indian pony. As a batter he was only fair (i.e., by Anson's standards, Ed.), but as a fielder in his position he was remarkable, being as quick as a cat and as plucky as they made them."

CORCORAN: A NOTEWORTHY BOX SCORE

June 27, 1884

Corcoran no-hits Providence—the third such gem of his career.

Chicago	AB	R	H	PO	A
Dalrymple, lf	5	0	0	3	0
Gore, cf	5	0	0	0	0
Kelly, c	4	1	1	7	1
Anson, 1b	4	1	2	13	0
Pfeffer, 2b	4	2	1	3	5
Williamson, 3b	4	1	2	0	2
Burns, ss	4	1	2	0	3
Sunday, rf	4	0	0	1	0
Corcoran, p	4	0	0	0	6
TOTALS	38	6	8	27	17

Providence	AB	R	H	PO	A
Hines, cf	4	0	0	1	1
Radbourne, 2b	4	0	0	1	6
Start, 1b	3	0	0	16	0
Sweeny, p	3	0	0	0	5
Irwin, ss	3	0	0	1	4
Denny, 3b	3	0	0	3	2
Carroll, lf	3	0	0	2	0
Radford, rf	3	0	0	0	1
Gilligan, c	3	0	0	3	2
TOTALS	29	0	0	27	21

```
Providence    0 0 0   0 0 0   0 0 0  — 0
Chicago       0 0 0   0 0 0   0 3 3  — 6
```

Doubles: Burns; Home run: Pfeffer; Double plays: Corcoran-Kelly-Pfeffer, Pfeffer-Anson; Strikeouts: Corcoran, 6 and Sweeny, 4; Bases on balls: Corcoran, 6 and Sweeny, 4; Time: 1:45; Attendance: 2,000; Umpire: McLean.

Other Baseball Highlights of 1884

• Bud Hillerich introduces the Louisville Slugger bat to major league baseball.

• Freddie Dunlap (St. Louis of the Union Association) sets the record with 1.58 runs per game average.

• Charlie Sweeney of the Providence Grays strikes out 19. The record is not broken until 1986.

Stan Hack—1940

Chicago Cubs Summit Season
Number 35

No. 35
STAN HACK

BORN: December 6, 1909; Sacramento, California
DIED: December 15, 1979; Dixon, Illinois

Chicago Cubs: 1932-1947

SEASON AT THE SUMMIT: 1940

AB-R-H	BA	OB%	2B	3B	HR	RBI	BR	FR	SB
603-101-191	.317	.395	38	6	8	75	29	14	21

Of the many tributes written after **Stan Hack** died in 1979 was one that was especially touching. A Chicago columnist wrote not about Hack's 16-year Cub career, or about the two seasons he led the National League in hits, or about his four World Series appearances. Instead, the writer recalled the ever-present Stan Hack smile.

Hack was one of the best-liked Cubs, not only among fans but among other players as well. Or as one rival once put it: "That man has more friends than Leo Durocher has enemies."

Hack's career began in his hometown of Sacramento, California, where he worked as a bank clerk. The Pacific Coast League's Sacramento Solons lured him away from the banking business and signed him to a contract. After Hack hit .352 in his first season, he attracted the attention of the Cubs, who brought him to the majors in 1932.

It was the start of a career that would be marked by timely hitting, heads-up baserunning, good defense—

and that smile. "I enjoy playing baseball, and this grin is just my way of showing it," Hack once said.

If there was a season that would have tested that smile, it should have been 1940.

A Slow Start
Hack got off to a slow start—he didn't get his first hit until the third game of the season—and didn't reach the .200 level until the last week of April. Still, he was making contributions. On April 27, for example, his defense helped the Cubs beat St. Louis. He made a nice catch of a liner in the first inning, then in the third, with the game still scoreless and men on first and second, he smothered Joe Medwick's smash and turned it into a rally-killing double play.

Soon, though, his bat warmed up and days like his 3-for-6 effort against the Cardinals on the 29th helped him get his average to .236 by month's end.

The Cubs were plagued by bad weather and worse luck through the first month of the 1940 campaign. Two games in early May were snowed out, and there were several rainouts. Another problem was a lack of timely hitting—Claude Passeau lost one game 1-0 on a dropped third strike—and manager Gabby Hartnett began shuffling his lineup.

The bad fortune touched Hack on May 17 when he suffered a frightening injury. He had walked in the first inning of the Cubs' game against New York and had worked his way to third. Teammate Hank Leiber lined a foul that Hack couldn't duck, and he was struck in the head and knocked out. He was carried off the field on a stretcher and finally regained consciousness in the clubhouse, from where he was taken to a hospital. There was no fracture, but he did have a slight concussion and doctors decided to keep him overnight. The one-night stay, though, lasted until May 21 because of persistent dizziness.

Hack's first game back was the 25th when he pinch-hit for Billy Herman—himself nursing an ankle injury—and singled. Hack stayed in the game and added a second hit, raising his average to .271.

It would be a week before Hack got back in the swing, going 3 for 4 and 3 for 5 in a Memorial Day doubleheader against Philadelphia. But that type of day was relatively rare for Hack, who at one point was dropped from the leadoff spot by Hartnett in favor of Augie Galan. The experiment lasted one day, and Hack celebrated his return to the top of the order by opening the Cubs' June 4 game against the Phillies with a triple, sparking a three-run first, and later broke a 6-6 tie with a seventh-inning double.

One Good Swing

June ended with Hack at .295 and the Cubs in fourth place at 34-33, 9½ games back. He finally got his average to .300 on July 15 when he went 3 for 4 with two runs scored in a 5-3 victory over the Giants. A week-long slump—he went 4 for 26 over his next six games—dropped Hack to .288.

All four of Hack's hits during his slump came in the same game, July 19 against Brooklyn at Wrigley Field. That

game, though, was more memorable for its extracurricular activities. With the Cubs in the middle of a three-run rally in the eighth that would push their lead to 11-3, Brooklyn pitcher Hugh Casey hit Cub pitcher Passeau with a pitch. An infuriated Passeau retaliated by throwing his bat at Casey, and both benches emptied. The Dodgers' Joe Gallagher singled out Passeau and began pummeling him. Hartnett jumped into the pile and pulled Gallagher off his pitcher, at which time Hack—easy-going, always smiling Stan Hack—unloaded a haymaker that bloodied Gallagher's nose.

Hack got no hits the next day, on the field or in any fights, then embarked on a 16-game hitting streak during which he hit .424 to raise his average to .311. Among the highlights: three hits in five at-bats in a July 23 win over Boston; a 4-for-4 day August 2 in Brooklyn, when he doubled and scored the winning run on a Herman single in the seventh; and a 2-for-4 afternoon in a 5-3 win over the Reds on August 7.

A Batting Race

Once Hack's modest streak had ended, he still stayed hot, hitting .361 (39 for 108) for the month of August. He had slowly raised his average so that by the middle of September he was challenging for the league lead. On the 18th he hit two homers, part of a 4-for-5 day, to beat the Giants 6-4 and improve to .322, best in the league. A homer and single the next day brought him to .323, and it appeared he was on his way to a batting crown. But at that point league officials announced that Pittsburgh infielder Debs Garms, although he had played in only 93 games thus far (and hit .377), was eligible to be considered for the batting title.

Hack would finish at .317. Garms (.355), Cincinnati's Ernie Lombardi (.319) and Boston's Johnny Cooney (.318) all ended up with higher averages, but none had the requisite number of at-bats when the season ended to beat Hack out for the hitting crown. His 191 hits tied him for the league lead, he was second in stolen bases, fourth in doubles, and fifth in runs and on-base percentage. He also led NL third basemen in three defensive categories—putouts, assists and double plays.

All reasons to smile.

Four Other Great Cub Seasons

	Yr	GP	AB-R-H	BA	OB%	SA	K/BB	HR	RBI	SB	FR	BR
1.	1935	124	427-754-133	.311	.406	.436	17/65	4	64	14	11	18
2.	1938	152	609-109-195	.320	.411	.432	39/94	4	67	16	7	28
3.	1941	151	586-111-186	.317	.417	.427	40/99	7	45	10	-16	38
4.	1945	150	597-110-193	.323	.420	.405	30/99	2	43	12	18	32

Level-headed and even-tempered, Stan Hack was a Wrigley Field favorite through a fine, 16-year Bruin career. His 1940 season was a gem, netting him a ranking among Cub greats at the No. 35 summit spot. Signed personally by Bill Wrigley, he stayed on at the Cubs' North Side digs to manage the team from 1954-56. Stan Hack was a steady .300 hitter who rarely fanned and usually wound up the season having been aboard about two out of every five at-bats. An excellent baserunner, he was also a base-stealing threat with a high percentage of steals per attempt.

"Smiling Stan. Everybody loved Stan Hack. Stan was a very, very popular player. Stan was an outstanding stick. He hit from foul line to foul line, a line drive type of hitter. He was like Wade Boggs. He was a lifetime .301 hitter. He didn't have a great arm, but he had such a nice soft throw. It was never off the mark, and he'd always come up with the ball. He looked a little unorthodox, those knees would go together. Don Johnson and I would have a lot of fun imitating him."
—**Teammate Lenny Merullo, Cub shortstop, commenting on Cub hero Stan Hack**

HACK: A NOTEWORTHY BOX SCORE

August 17, 1940

Hack's fourth hit of the day, a two-out single in the 13th, beats the Pirates 6-5

Pittsburgh	AB	R	H	RBI	PO	A	E	Chicago	AB	R	H	RBI	PO	A	E
Gustine, 2b	4	1	0	0	6	7	0	Hack, 3b	5	0	4	2	3	5	0
Elliott, 2b	4	0	1	0	5	1	1	Herman, 2b	5	0	0	0	4	7	0
Garms, 3b	5	1	2	1	0	4	0	Bonura, 1b	5	1	1	0	20	3	0
Vaughan, ss	5	1	2	0	2	7	0	Leiber, cf	6	2	2	0	3	0	0
P. Waner, 1b	6	0	2	1	18	0	0	Gleeson, rf	5	1	2	0	1	1	0
Van Robays, lf	6	1	1	1	2	0	0	Dallessandro, lf	5	1	3	2	2	0	1
DiMaggio, cf	5	1	3	1	1	0	0	Todd, c	5	0	2	2	1	2	0
Davis, c	5	0	3	1	3	2	0	Warstler, ss	2	0	0	0	1	3	0
Fernandes, c	1	0	0	0	1	0	0	Nicholson, ph	1	0	0	0	0	0	0
Klinger, p	3	0	0	0	0	0	0	Mattick, ss	2	1	1	0	3	3	0
Brown, p	1	0	0	0	0	1	0	Mooty, p	1	0	0	0	0	1	0
L. Waner, pr	0	0	0	0	0	0	0	Root, p	1	0	0	0	0	1	0
MacFayden, p	1	0	0	0	0	1	0	Rogell, ph	1	0	0	0	0	0	0
								Page, p	0	0	0	0	0	2	0
TOTALS	46	5	14	6	36	20	1	Raffensberger, p	0	0	0	0	0	0	0
								Passeau, p	2	0	0	0	1	1	0
								Hartnett, ph	0	0	0	0	0	0	0
								TOTALS	46	6	15	6	39	29	1

Pittsburgh	0 1 0	2 2 0	0 0 0	0 0 0	0	--	5
Chicago	0 0 0	0 0 0	1 3 1	0 0 0	1	--	6

Doubles–DiMaggio, Leiber, Davis, Hack. Home run–DiMaggio. Sacrifices–Elliott, Vaughan, Hartnett, Todd, Mattick. Double plays–Pittsburgh 4, Chicago 3. Left on base–Pittsburgh 9, Chicago 11.

Other Baseball Highlights of 1940

- On September 4, the Red Sox become the first team to hit four home runs in an inning.

- Bob Feller no-hits the White Sox on April 16, 1940 to post baseball's only opening day no-hitter.

- Cincinnati's 40-year-old catcher, Jimmie Wilson, in a lineup shift to replace catcher Ernie Lombardi, winds up a hitting star at .353 in the World Series.

- Bobo Newson, the most traveled pitcher in baseball history, paces Detroit to the 1940 pennant with a 21-5 record.

Michael Joseph Kelly—1886

Chicago Cubs Summit Season
Number 36

No. 36
MIKE KELLY

BORN: December 31, 1857; Troy, New York
DIED: November 8, 1894; Boston, Massachusetts

Chicago White Stockings: 1880-1886
Hall of Fame: 1945

SEASON AT THE SUMMIT: 1886

AB-R-H	BA	OB%	2B	3B	HR	RBI	BR	FR	SB
451-155-175	.388	.483	32	11	4	63	44	3	53

"Mike Kelly was up to his old tricks again yesterday. He rolled around on the grass in seemingly great pain when McCormick rapped him on the knee with the ball in the third inning, but stole second in his old-time form ten minutes after."
—*Chicago Tribune*, May 19, 1886

There was no more exciting, colorful or popular player in the 19th Century than Mike "King" Kelly. Whether delivering a timely hit, sliding across the plate, making a terrific catch in the outfield or bamboozling an opponent, Kelly was always a crowd-pleaser.

He also exasperated management with his drinking, late hours and off-field escapades. One story that circulated at the time of his death in 1894 pretty much sums up his career. The White Stockings were in Cleveland for a series with the Spiders. Kelly and pitcher Larry Corcoran had spent a night on the town and returned to the team hotel extremely intoxicated as the sun came up. A group of Cleveland bettors, knowing that Corcoran was scheduled to pitch for Chicago that afternoon, bet heavily on the Spiders, figuring they had an advantage. But not only did Corcoran pitch, he threw a no-hitter, or so the story went. And the only run of the game was driven in by Kelly.

The tale isn't true, of course, but such was the Kelly legend. He broke into the National League in 1878 with Cincinnati, playing every position but pitcher and shortstop in his two years with the Reds. He came to Chicago in 1880 and helped Cap Anson's team to league championships in '80, '81 and '82. He followed that with a disappointing 1883—he hit .255, a dropoff of 50 points over the year before—as the White Stockings finished second to Boston. He rebounded in 1884, hitting .354, then slumped to .288 the following season, when the Whites regained the NL championship.

A Close Race From the Start
Big things were expected of the Whites and Kelly for the 1886 season from manager Anson and White Stockings president Al Spalding. And they didn't disappoint. Detroit and Chicago both jumped out of the starting gate

quickly, the Wolverines winning 16 straight in one stretch. On June 1, they led the league with a 20-4 record. But on their heels at 18-4 were the White Stockings.

Kelly, too, started fast. In typical fashion, he provided big hits when they were needed—two hits on May 6, when the Whites opened their home season with a victory over Detroit; a two-run single in the ninth to beat the Phillies on May 31; he drove in the tying run in the ninth then scored the winner minutes later in a win over New York on June 8. By the first week of June, he was well over .300 and Chicago was only a half-game behind Detroit.

Kelly was splitting his time between right field and the catcher's position. On July 3, he injured a finger while catching, an injury that had him in and out of the lineup over the next 10 days. He returned for good on the 12th, contributing a single and double in an 8-4 victory over St. Louis. The month ended with Detroit holding a 4½-game lead over Chicago, seemingly in command.

Taking Control
But the Whites kept chipping away at the Wolverines' lead, and on August 26 beat Boston 10-4—Kelly contributing a home run and a single—to move into first place. Two weeks later, Kelly led an impressive sweep of a double-header with New York—he had a double in Game 1 and a home run, single and three stolen bases in Game 2—that all but knocked the Giants out of contention.

Detroit came to town September 9, and again Kelly worked his magic, getting two doubles and two singles in one victory, and a double and two singles in another. Chicago won two of the three games to open a four-game lead with less than a month to go.

The Wolverines refused to surrender, though, and were within 3½ when they met the Whites in a four-game series starting September 20. Chicago won three of the four—Kelly sparked a victory in the opener with a single and double—to widen its lead to 5½ games. But then the Whites stumbled, losing six of seven in early October as Detroit moved back within striking distance. "Things are beginning to look rather shaky," Anson said after an October 6 loss to New York that, coupled with a Detroit sweep of Washington, cut Chicago's lead to 1½ games.

The race went down to the final days of the season, and Chicago didn't clinch until October 9 when it beat Boston 10-9—Kelly contributing three hits to the cause.

Postseason Disappointment
After the season, the White Stockings met the American Association's St. Louis Browns in what was billed as the World Series. Chicago won the opener behind John Clarkson's five-hitter, but St. Louis won Game 2 as Bob Caruthers held the Whites to two singles. Kelly's home run in Game 3 helped give Chicago a 2-1 series lead, but the Browns came back to win the next two games. Game 6 was tied at 3 in the 10th inning when the Browns got baserunner Curt Welch to third with one out. He then tried to steal home, but catcher Kelly saw it coming. He called for a pitchout, but Clarkson's toss was off the mark and Kelly bobbled the ball as Welch scored the series-winning run.

It was a disappointing ending for a magnificent season for Kelly. He batted .388 and scored 155 runs in 118 games—both league highs. He was third in doubles (32), fourth in slugging average (.534) and fifth in total bases (241). Kelly, though, wasn't able to enjoy his accomplishments. During the off-season he said he was through playing for Spalding and Anson, and within a week he was sold to Boston for the unheard-of sum of $10,000. It was a good deal for the King. His 1886 salary had been $2,250; Boston paid him $5,000.

Kelly's career was clearly on the decline. Only 30, he slipped to .322 in his first year in Boston. He fell to .318 the next year and .294 the next before joining with other unhappy players to form the Brotherhood League in 1890. Kelly split time in 1891 in the American Association and National League before closing out his career with New York in 1893.

The end came for King Kelly the next year. He was traveling from New York to Boston by boat to appear in a vaudeville show. The boat was caught in a snowstorm, and Kelly came down with a cold that quickly turned into pneumonia. Weakened by years of drinking, he succumbed on November 8, 1894, at the age of 36.

MIKE KELLY'S

Two Other Great Cub Seasons

	Yr	GP	AB-R-H	BA	OB%	SA	K/BB	HR	RBI	SB	FR	BR
1.	1881	82	353-84-114	.323	.352	.433	14/16	2	55	-	0	15
2.	1882	108	452-120-160	.354	.414	.524	24/46	13	95	-	-5	39

King Kelly had his own little fiefdom in Chicago, where he was a daring, colorful ballplayer for the better part of a decade. He was so good, in fact, that he brought White Stockings owner Al Spalding 10,000 big ones, an unheard of stack of baseball cash in the 1800s. But Kelly could play. Anywhere. It was inevitable that a chant like "Slide, Kelly, Slide!" would make the rounds of the ballparks, given his breakneck baserunning and head-first sliding. It would be hard to keep him off the franchise honor listings, and he appears on the summit list at No. 36 between Stan Hack and "Hippo" Vaughn. The two seasons cited above, and his 1886 season, which drove the White Stockings to their last pennant, are persuasive testimony to his athletic talents and productivity during the 1880s.

"Kelly was a general on the diamond, a born humorist, and an agreeable companion. As a batter and baserunner, Mike had few equals, and no man was ever of more value behind the bat. Contrary to the general opinion, he was not a hard man to get along with, and I would willingly have had him on the Chicago team at any time."

—Cap Anson

KELLY: A NOTEWORTHY BOX SCORE

October 20, 1886

Kelly's home run and two singles help Chicago beat St. Louis in Game 2 of their postseason series.

Chicago	R	H	PO	A	E	St. Louis	R	H	PO	A	E
Gore, cf	3	2	2	1	0	Latham, 3b, c	0	1	2	1	0
Kelly, c, 1b	2	3	5	3	1	Caruthers, p	0	1	2	2	4
Anson, 1b, c	0	0	11	0	1	O'Neill, lf	0	1	4	0	0
Pfeffer, 2b	1	1	3	2	0	Gleason, ss	0	0	6	3	0
Williamson, ss, p	1	0	1	3	0	Comiskey, 1b	0	0	6	2	0
Burns, 3b	2	2	1	0	1	Welch, cf	2	3	3	0	0
Ryan, rf, ss	1	2	1	1	0	Robinson, 2b	2	2	2	2	2
Dalrymple, lf	1	1	0	0	1	Hudson, rf	0	0	3	0	0
Clarkson, p, rf	0	0	0	5	3	Bushong, 3b	0	1	2	0	0
TOTALS	11	11	24	15	9	TOTALS	4	9	24	10	6

Chicago	2 0 0	1 1 2	3 2	-- 11	
St. Louis	0 1 0	0 0 2	0 1	-- 4	

Earned runs--Chicago 5, St. Louis 0. Home runs--Kelly, Gore. Triple--Burns. Doubles--Ryan, Welch. Total bases--Chicago 20, St. Louis 10. Stolen bases--Robinson (2), Clarkson. First base on errors--Chicago 1, St. Louis 3. Bases on balls--Gore, Kelly, Pfeffer, Williamson, Caruthers, O'Neil, Welch. Left on bases--Chicago 5, St. Louis 8. Passes balls--Kelly (3), Anson. Wild pitches --Clarkson (2); Williamson. Strikeouts--by Clarkson, 6; by Williamson, 2; by Caruthers, 1. Double plays--Chicago 1, St. Louis 1. Time--2:10. Umpire--John Kelly.

Other Baseball Highlights of 1886

▪Baltimore's Matt Kilroy no-hits Pittsburgh 6-0 on October 6.

▪Former NL player Frank "Terry" Larkin is arrested after pulling out two guns and challenging his former employers to a duel.

▪A new rule states that pitchers no longer have to keep both feet on the ground when delivering a pitch.

James "Hippo" L. Vaughn—1918

Chicago Cubs Summit Season
Number 37

No. 37
HIPPO VAUGHN

BORN: April 8, 1888; Weatherford, Texas
DIED: May 29, 1966; Chicago, Illinois

Chicago Cubs: 1913-1921

SEASON AT THE SUMMIT: 1918

W-L-%	IP	CG	SH	SV	K/BB	PR	DEF	ERA
22-10 .688	290.1	27	8	0	148/79	33	-1	1.74

I t was a game unlike anything anyone had seen.

On May 2, 1917, right-handers Fred Toney of Cincinnati and **Jim "Hippo" Vaughn** of Chicago locked up in a double no-hitter through nine innings. The Reds pushed a run across in the top of the 10th thanks to an error and a misplayed grounder, and Toney set the Cubs down in order in the home half to go into the record books with the no-hitter. Vaughn made it too, but with undeserved second billing. He clearly had outpitched Toney: He faced the minimum 27 batters through nine innings, having walked two men who were erased in double plays, and he struck out 10. Toney also walked two but fanned only three, two of them in the 10th.

It wouldn't be the first time Vaughn would be overshadowed by others or by events over which he had no control.

"Hippo" Vaughn—he ran with a peculiar side-to-side gait—began his major-league career with the American League's New York Highlanders in 1908. He was traded to Washington during the 1912 season and the next year came to the Cubs, going 5-1. His victory totals over the next seven years were 21, 20, 17, 23, 22, 21 and 19—team highs in six of those seven seasons. His finest year, the one that stands above the rest, was 1918.

Ace By Default

The big left-hander had had a mediocre spring but was still being counted on to carry the load, along with the newly acquired Grover Cleveland Alexander, who had been 33-12 and 30-13 the two previous seasons with Philadelphia. Before the season was two weeks old, however, Alexander would be out of the picture. With World War I raging in Europe, Alexander got the call from Uncle Sam. He pitched his last game of the season for the Cubs on April 26—beating St. Louis on a two-hitter—before going into the service.

That left the Cubs' pitching largely with Vaughn; veteran right-hander Claude Hendrix, coming off two sub-.500 seasons; and "Lefty" Tyler, who was 90-94 in nine years in the National League. Within a month, Vaughn had firmly established himself as the ace of the staff.

He picked up his first victory of the season on April 18, beating the Cardinals with a nine-hitter. He also helped himself with a pair of hits and two runs scored. He lost his next outing, but came back on April 24 to beat St. Louis in a masterful performance in the Cubs' home opener. He allowed only one hit, a second-inning single by Rogers Hornsby, struck out six and walked just two. It was an impressive performance according to the next day's newspapers, but one that was nearly lost amid the Opening Day hoopla.

"Vaughn was in tiptop form from start to finish," wrote James Crusinberry in the *Chicago Tribune.* "He had no trouble getting the ball over with all his best stuff on it, so it isn't remarkable that the Cardinals made only one hit in the game...

"[The Cardinals] didn't get a man to second base in the entire game, which would make quite a feature in itself if it hadn't been opening day, with the soldiers and sailors and bands and governors and flowers and everything to kill it. Not many who were present realized the feat turned out by the big southpaw."

No Stopping Him Or Cubs
Vaughn won three consecutive decisions, then lost two of his next three, setting the stage for a big series between the first-place New York Giants and second-place Cubs, opening May 25 at Weeghman Park.

The Cubs won the opener to pull within three games of the leaders. Vaughn won Game 2, 5-1 on a four-hitter, getting three hits and scoring two runs. Manager Fred Mitchell's team won the next day too, to cut the Giants' lead to one game. Chicago finally passed New York and moved into first on June 6, a position it would hold for the rest of the season.

Vaughn won four straight decisions between May 26 and June 10, then—weakened by the flu—got hammered by the Giants on June 14, dropping his record to 10-4. Over the next month, though, he was unbeatable. After stopping Brooklyn and Pittsburgh to run his record to 12-4, he handcuffed St. Louis 1-0 on a one-hitter on June 26, then blanked Cincinnati 2-0 three days later. Beating the Reds was Vaughn's second biggest thrill of

the day—that morning he became the father of an 8½-pound son.

Three more victories followed—one a 1-0 decision over the Giants in which Vaughn drove in the winning run with a 12th-inning single. By July 15, he was 17-4 and on his way to a most remarkable season. Then, however, real life intervened.

On July 19 the government announced that major-league players must "fight or work," in other words, enlist or obtain productive employment that would assist the war effort. Owners had tried to get an exemption for the players, but their request was turned down by the secretary of war, with the blessing of President Woodrow Wilson. After two weeks of meetings and haggling, the owners agreed to end the season a month early.

Second Banana to Babe Ruth
Vaughn, after back-to-back losses in mid-July, won three more games to run his record to 20-6, the third of the victories another one-hitter, against New York on August 1. He won just two of his last six decisions before the season ended, but the Cubs didn't need him—they ran away with the NL pennant, winning by 10½ games over the second-place Giants.

The World Series matched Vaughn and the Cubs against the Boston Red Sox and their 22-year-old phenom, Babe Ruth (13-7, 2.22 ERA, .300, 11 HRs). In the Series, Vaughn was tough, but as was the case in the double no-hitter 16 months earlier, he became a footnote. Ruth pitched 29⅔ shutout innings in the Series, which the Red Sox won in six games. Vaughn allowed a total of three runs in his three appearances—and lost two games. Ruth beat him 1-0 in the opener, Carl Mays bested him 2-1 in Game 3, and he finally beat Sam Jones 3-0 in Game 5. In 27 innings, Vaughn struck out 17, allowed 17 hits and walked five.

Vaughn had two more winning seasons for the Cubs, going 21-14 in 1919 and 19-16 in 1920. After a 3-11 mark in 1921 he retired from the majors and spent the next seven years playing semipro ball in Beloit, Wisconsin. He spent another nine years playing semipro ball around the Chicago area before finally hanging 'em up. Vaughn, who had a career 178-137 major-league record, died on May 29, 1966 in Chicago at the age of 78.

HIPPO VAUGHN'S

4 Four Other Great Cub Seasons

Yr	W-L	IP	GS	GC	SH	SV	PD	K/BB	OBA	OB%	ERA	PR
1. 1914	21-13	293.2	35	23	4	1	-1	165/109	.222	.299	2.05	24
2. 1916	17-15	294.0	35	21	4	1	1	144/67	.250	.298	2.20	14
3. 1917	23-13	295.2	38	27	5	0	3	195/91	.235	.300	2.01	23
4. 1919	21-14	306.2	37	25	4	1	-3	141/62	.234	.278	1.79	38

Leave it to the ballplayers. If there's something the least bit out of the ordinary, they'll notice it; then comes the "tag." In Jim Vaughn's case, it was his uncommon running stride that made him appear as though he rumbled along like a hippo. Voila: "Hippo." Don't make any mistakes about his pitching, however. He was simply the Cubs' greatest left-hander. Like Bill Lee a score of years later, he had a fantastic summit season, then pitched just as well in the 1918 World Series, only to lose 1-0 and 2-1 before winning Game 5 at Boston on a five-hit shutout. His 151 Cub career wins stand at No. 5 on the all-time list. And he ranks a proud No. 37 on the list of summit seasons.

"Hippo Vaughn was magnificent in the 1918 World Series. He threw three complete games, walked only five batters while striking out 17, and compiled a superb ERA of 1.00. Yet, he was only 1-2! In the opener the big left-hander threw a five-hitter but lost to Babe Ruth, 1-0...In Game 5 Hippo made sure, throwing a five-hit shutout to win, 3-0. In all three [WS] games, he gave up only one extra-base hit, a double."

—TSN Conlon Collection, card number 800.

VAUGHN: A NOTEWORTHY BOX SCORE

April 24, 1918

Vaughn allows just one hit—a Rogers Hornsby single—as the Cubs win their home opener.

St. Louis	AB	R	H	BB	PO	A	E	Chicago	AB	R	H	BB	PO	A	E
Betzel, rf	4	0	0	0	2	0	0	Hollecher, ss	3	0	0	0	3	3	1
Smith, cf	3	0	0	0	1	0	0	Barber, rf	3	0	0	0	1	0	0
Brock, ph	1	0	0	0	0	0	0	Mann, lf	4	0	1	0	1	0	0
Baird, 3b	3	0	0	1	1	2	0	Paskert, cf	3	1	2	1	1	0	0
Hornsby, ss	3	0	1	0	2	2	1	Merkle, 1b	2	0	0	0	8	0	0
Cruise, lf	3	0	0	0	1	0	0	Kilduff, 2b	2	0	1	1	4	1	0
Paulette, 1b	2	0	0	1	10	0	0	Deal, 3b	3	0	2	0	0	2	0
Niehoff, 2b	3	0	0	0	3	4	0	Killefer, c	3	0	0	0	8	2	0
Gonzalez, c	3	0	0	0	4	2	0	Vaughn, p	2	1	0	1	0	2	0
Meadows, p	3	0	0	0	0	3	0								
Snyder, ph	1	0	0	0	0	0	0	TOTALS	26	2	6	3	27	10	1
TOTALS	27	0	1	0	24	13	1								

```
St. Louis    0 0 0   0 0 0   0 0 0  --0
Chicago      0 1 1   0 0 0   0 0 x  --2
```

Struck out--by Vaughn, 6; by Meadows, 4. Double plays--St. Louis, 2; Chicago, 1. Wild pitch--Meadows, 2. Time--1:45. Attendance: 10,000 (est.). Umpires: Byron and O'Day.

Other Baseball Highlights of 1918

▪The season ends on September 2 because of World War 1.

▪While in the service, Christy Mathewson is accidentally gassed and subsequently contracts tuberculosis.

▪On August 30, the Giants beat the Dodgers 1-0 in a game that lasted only 57 minutes.

Billy Leo Williams—1972

Chicago Cubs Summit Season
Number 38

No. 38
BILLY WILLIAMS

BORN: June 15, 1938; Whistler, Alabama

Chicago Cubs: 1959-1974
Hall of Fame: 1987

SEASON AT THE SUMMIT: 1972

AB-R-H	BA	OB%	2B	3B	HR	RBI	BR	FR	SB
574-95-191	.333	.403	34	6	37	122	48	-3	3

It was the summer of 1956 when Cubs scout Ivy Griffin pulled off one of the greatest signing coups in baseball history. **Billy Williams**, an 18-year-old prospect from Whistler, Alabama, was being scouted by several teams. Griffin beat them all to the punch—and cut a pretty nifty deal in the process.

"I hate to say it, but the Cubs got me for a cigar and a bus ticket to Ponca City," Williams told *The Sporting News* in 1972. "At the time the highest bonuses were about $4,000 to $10,000. But I was so anxious to play baseball I just put my name on the dotted line. There was no money involved. My father got a cigar and I got a bus ticket to Ponca City."

Best Investment The Cubs Ever Made

Williams would go on to an 18-year Hall-of-Fame career that included a .290 lifetime average, a streak of 1,117 consecutive games played, more than 2,700 hits and nearly 1,500 RBIs. Still, Williams often played in the shadow of others. When he came up to stay in 1961—a year he would win NL Rookie of the Year honors—there was Ernie Banks. Later he played on teams featuring

such stars as Fergie Jenkins, Ron Santo and Randy Hundley. Williams—dependable, steady and productive— was often overlooked. Even in 1970, when he hit .322 with 42 homers and 129 RBIs and led the league in runs scored and hits, he didn't get the recognition he deserved, finishing a distant second to Cincinnati's Johnny Bench in the NL MVP voting.

But in 1972, there would be no overlooking Billy Leo Williams.

The 1972 campaign would be an abbreviated one—a 13-day players strike in the spring delayed the start of the season 10 days and wiped out 86 games. The Cub season opened April 15 at Wrigley Field, and the first of many heroic days for Williams came three days later when his three-run third-inning homer helped beat the Pirates 6-4. He also contributed a leaping, run-saving catch of a smash by Roberto Clemente.

The Cubs stumbled to a 2-4 start. Before a double-header against the New York Mets on April 23, manager Leo Durocher was forced to leave the team because of a fever and sore throat that had bothered him for two weeks. Coach Pete Reiser took over, and his first order of business was to juggle his lineup, moving Williams to first base for Game 1. He handled the shift flawlessly ("Did I look like a first baseman?" he asked reporters afterward), but went 0 for 4 and 1 for 6 at the plate as the Cubs were swept. They also dropped their next three games to run their losing streak to eight games and tumble into last place.

Durocher was back when the team opened a two-week homestand on April 28 against Cincinnati. Wrigley Field agreed with Williams and his teammates. The Cubs were 8-2 and Williams started getting into the groove with a nine-game hitting streak that included back-to-back 2-for-4 days against the Reds, and two singles and three RBIs against Atlanta.

May was a typical month for Williams, known as the classic streak hitter. He went 0 for 11 over one stretch, then followed the mini-slump with an 8-for-16 series against St. Louis and an 8-for-20 series against New York. The month ended with him at .287 and the Cubs in third at 20-18, eight games behind the first-place Mets.

Williams put together another impressive streak in mid-June to get his average near the .300 mark. On the 13th, he had a homer, double and three RBIs against San Diego; he homered and singled twice the next day; on the 15th—his 34th birthday—he hit his 10th and 11th homers of the season; he added a two-run homer the next day against the Dodgers. Four games, 9 hits in 18 at-bats, 10 RBIs.

A Remarkable Month

July, though, would be the month when Williams hit his stride. He finally went over the .300 mark with a 2-for-4 day against the Pirates on July 1. He was 7 for 14 in the series to raise his average to .319. The best was yet to come.

In a July 11 double-header against the Astros, Williams went 8 for 8: a homer and two singles in Game 1, and a double, homer and three singles in the nightcap. He raised his average 18 points to .328 and his four RBIs gave him 50 for the year. But Williams wasn't done. He was 3 for 5 with three RBIs the next day. He went 4 for 5 with three more RBIs two days later against Atlanta. Two hits the next day; two more on the 17th; three more on the 18th. When Williams' eight-day tear—22 for 38 (.579)—ended, he was at .338 and the talk of baseball.

Williams was added to the NL All-Star team by manager Danny Murtaugh and went 1 for 2 in the game, scoring the tying run in the ninth in a 4-3, 10-inning NL victory. But the big news out of Atlanta during the break was the firing of Cubs manager Durocher. The Cubs were 46-44, 10 games back and going nowhere when owner Philip K. Wrigley ended Durocher's seven-year reign on the eve of the All-Star Game. Whitey Lockman took over and would go 39-26 as the Cubs finished a distant second to Pittsburgh.

Williams wound up July with a 4-for-4 day against the Cardinals on the 31st. He batted .438 for the month with nine homers and 29 RBIs, numbers that earned him NL Player of the Month honors.

He cooled off during the first week of August—a 1-for-17 slump dropped his average to .336—but then got hot again when the Cubs returned to Wrigley Field on the 8th. He went 2 for 2, including a two-run homer in the seventh, as the Cubs beat Montreal 6-5. The two hits gave him a .403 (75 for 186) average at Wrigley Field. August would also include a 10-game hitting streak that helped Williams get in the thick of the NL batting race.

A First Batting Crown

September started with Billy at .340, two percentage points behind Houston's Cesar Cedeno. The two of them, and later Atlanta's Dusty Baker, spent the first two-thirds of the month neck and neck. By September 20, Williams was at .335, Baker at .328 and Cedeno at .326. A week later, Williams had a 10-point lead over his nearest challenger and had virtually wrapped up the batting title. At that point, though, people were talking Triple Crown. After the games of September 26, he led the league in hitting (.333) and was within striking distance of league leader Bench in homers (40-36) and RBIs (122-121).

After picking up just one homer and RBI in the next two games, though, Williams conceded the race to Bench. He took the next two days off to protect his average—"I just didn't want to gamble after getting this close to winning my first batting title"—before going 1 for 3 in the Cubs' October 4 finale.

He finished at .333 with a .606 slugging average, both tops in the NL—and figures that made it impossible for him to be ignored. After the season The Sporting News named him its Player of the Year.

Give that man a cigar.

BILLY WILLIAMS'

Three Other Great Cub Seasons

	Yr	GP	AB-R-H	BA	OB%	SA	K/BB	HR	RBI	SB	FR	BR
1.	1965	164	645-115-203	.315	.380	.552	76/65	34	108	10	0	46
2.	1970	161	636-137-205	.322	.393	.586	65/72	42	129	7	8	35
3.	1971	157	594-86-179	.301	.384	.505	44/77	28	93	7	7	24

The press forgot about Billy Williams a good deal more than pitchers around the league did. But not even the scribes could pass him by during a summit season that found him atop the league with a spiffy .333 batting average and a .606 slugging average to go with it in 1972. He was the Player of the Month in July that year, and finished second to Johnny Bench in the MVP voting. His '72 vaulted him into the summit listing at No. 38, just ahead of a couple of other great Cub outfielders, Andy Pafko and Hank Sauer. They got around to a day for Billy at Wrigleyville in 1969, and well they should have. He had quietly led the Cub uprising, putting them on the pennant-bound express. Even though derailed, the consensus was that without their main man the train never would have left the station.

"I don't really feel I'm quiet. I get excited, but I hear people say I'm not an exciting ballplayer. I go out there and catch the ball and hit the ball and play the game like it should be played and try to do my best, try to give 100 percent."

—Billy Williams after his big 1972 season

Other Baseball Highlights of 1972

• White Sox slugger Dick Allen (37 homers, 113 RBIs) is the AL MVP.

• Roberto Clemente dies in an airplane crash on New Year's Eve. Other obituaries: Jackie Robinson, Pie Traynor, Zach Wheat, Gabby Hartnett and Gil Hodges.

• San Francisco's Jim Barr retires a major-league record 41 consecutive batters over two games.

WILLIAMS: A NOTEWORTHY BOX SCORE

July 21, 1972

Williams homers and doubles and drives in six runs in a victory over the Astros.

Chicago	AB	R	H	RBI		Houston	AB	R	H	RBI
Monday, cf	5	1	0	0		Metzger, ss	4	0	1	0
Kessinger, ss	4	2	1	1		Cedeno, cf	3	1	2	1
Williams, lf	6	1	4	6		Wynn, rf	4	1	2	1
Cardenal, rf	5	1	1	0		L. May, 1b	4	0	0	0
Pepitone, 1b	4	2	2	1		Watson, lf	4	0	1	0
Beckert, 2b	5	1	2	0		Edwards, c	4	0	0	0
Santo, 3b	3	1	1	0		Rader, 3b	3	1	1	1
Hundley, c	5	1	1	0		Helms, 2b	3	0	1	0
Bonham, p	2	0	1	0		Forsch, 2b	2	0	0	0
Martin, ph	1	1	1	1		Culver, p	0	0	0	0
Aker, p	0	0	0	0		Griffin, p	0	0	0	0
						Gladding, p	0	0	0	0
TOTALS	40	11	14	9		Miller, ph	1	0	0	0
						York, p	0	0	0	0
						TOTALS	32	3	8	3

Chicago	002	101	061	— 11	
Houston	010	101	000	— 3	

Errors--Helms, Rader. Double play--Houston 1. Left on base--Chicago 11, Houston 3. Double--Williams. Home runs--Rader, Williams, Wynn, Pepitone, Cedeno.

Chicago	IP	H	R	ER	BB	SO		Houston	IP	H	R	ER	BB	SO
Bonham(W, 1-0)	7	7	3	3	0	4		Forsch (L, 5-5)	7⅓	10	6	6	2	2
Aker	2	1	0	0	0	3		Culver	⅓	1	3	3	2	1
								Griffin	0	1	1	1	2	0
								Gladding	⅓	0	0	0	1	0
								York	1	2	1	1	2	0

Save--Aker. Hit by pitch--by Bonham (Cedeno). Wild pitch--Griffin. Time--3:00. Attendance--23,415.

PAFKO
48

Andrew Pafko—1948

Chicago Cubs Summit Season
Number 39

No. 39
ANDY PAFKO

BORN: February 25, 1921; Boyceville, Wisconsin

Chicago Cubs: 1943-1951

SEASON AT THE SUMMIT: 1948

AB-R-H	BA	OB%	2B	3B	HR	RBI	BR	FR	SB
548-82-171	.312	.375	30	2	26	101	32	13	3

Andy Pafko had it figured out.

"Cub fans seem to kind of pick out one guy they like and stick with him," he once said. "You go to other parks and maybe they make every guy on the club a hero. It's a pattern you don't see in other ballparks. Cub fans always seem to have a soft spot for certain players, I guess. I was lucky enough to be one of them."

Pafko was always a hero to Cub fans. But never more so than in 1948.

The Cubs had discovered Pafko, a native of Boyceville, Wisconsin, playing in the Wisconsin State League. After a couple of seasons in the minors, he was brought up late in the 1943 season and was soon their regular center-fielder, a position where he earned All-Star honors in 1947.

Now Playing Third Base...

For 1948, though, changes were in order for Pafko and the Cubs. Manager Charlie Grimm wanted to use rookie Hal Jeffcoat in center, so he offered Pafko the vacant third base job—Stan Hack had retired after 16 seasons—in spring training. Handy Andy began working out there and was soon playing third in spring exhibitions. And he was the starting third baseman on Opening Day, part of a revamped infield that included rookie Roy Smalley at short and former part-time third baseman Hank Schenz at second.

Only two games into the season, Pafko began his 1948 heroics. On April 21, he had a home run, single and stolen base in a 6-3 victory over Pittsburgh. An injury—he split his right index finger in pregame practice—relegated him to pinch-hitting duties over a two-week period in late April and early May, but he returned to the lineup in a big way.

On May 14 his eighth-inning homer beat Cincinnati. Two days later in a losing cause against the Reds, he had two homers, a double and two singles. On the 28th and 29th he went 3 for 4 and 3 for 5 in a pair of games against Cincinnati. And in a Memorial Day double-header against the Pirates, he had two homers, his sixth and seventh of the year, and three singles. The month ended with Pafko at .295 with seven homers and 22 RBIs.

The Cubs, though, after showing some early foot, had tumbled to eighth place at 14-22, seven games out of first. They still demonstrated enough occasional spunk to make life difficult for others. The first-place New York Giants came to town in early June and left town as the second-place New York Giants after losing three straight at Wrigley.

National Recognition

Pafko, too, was having a good month—his home run, part of a 3-for-4 day, helped beat Brooklyn on the 13th; he added a three-run homer and single in an 8-5 win over first-place Boston three days later; and an 11-for-18 stretch June 19-24 raised his average to .342.

By now not only Cub fans were cheering him. On June 28 he moved into the lead in nationwide fan voting to pick the starting lineups for the All-Star Game. He would briefly lose his lead to the Pirates' Frank Gustine, but a big late push put him over the top, 1,047,886 votes to Gustine's 984,624 out of more than 4 million ballots cast in the voting, conducted by the *Chicago Tribune* through 452 newspapers, radio stations and magazines in 47 states.

Pafko closed out the first half with a rush, going 10 for 19—in the last game before the break his seventh-inning home run off Ernie Bonham beat the Pirates 1-0—to raise his average to .342. He went hitless in two at-bats in the All-Star Game, a 5-2 American League victory, but then picked up where he left off, going 15 for 30 with three doubles and three homers in his next seven games.

Even so, Pafko's hitting wasn't enough to get the Cubs out of last place. By mid-August they had lost 18 of their last 23 games and were a distant 32½ games back. They had to content themselves with trying to catch seventh-place Cincinnati—they actually climbed to sixth, briefly, in the last month of the season—and being spoilers.

On August 26, Pafko went 3 for 6 as the Cubs swept two from the first-place Braves; five days later the new league leaders, Brooklyn, came to Wrigley Field, and in front of 45,531 fans the Cubs swept another double-header—Pafko contributing three hits to the offense.

Dramatic Homers

Over the closing two months of the season, Pafko solidified his spot in the hearts of Cub fans. There was a homer through a window of a house on Waveland Avenue on August 20 that helped beat the Reds. And a 4-for-5 day, which included his 21st home run, that helped beat the Pirates on September 3 and moved the Cubs into seventh place for a day. Two more homers two days later in a double-header in Pittsburgh. A ninth-inning three-run homer—his 25th—on September 21 to beat the Giants 3-2 and end a 10-game Cub losing streak. And three RBIs the following day to beat the Giants again.

His average, though, slid slowly over the last weeks of the season. Once as high as .353 in July, he ended that month at .328. He was back at .333 in early September, but hit just .182 over his last 11 games to finish at .312. His 26 homers, 171 hits and 101 RBIs were all team highs. His move to third was less successful—although he led the league in assists with 314, he also made 29 errors, most among regular NL third basemen and second on the team to Smalley's 34—and the experiment ended the next season when he was moved back to the outfield.

But no matter where Grimm played him, the fans loved Andy Pafko. To a point.

He once recalled the day in 1951 when the Cubs traded him to Brooklyn. "We were playing a three-game set with the Dodgers in Wrigley," he said. "I came home to have dinner after the first game and the Cubs called me to tell me I'd be playing for Brooklyn the next day. I was, and hit a home run, in fact.

"They booed me in Wrigley. First time that ever happened."

ANDY PAFKO'S

Two Other Great Cub Seasons

	Yr	GP	AB-R-H	BA	OB%	SA	K/BB	HR	RBI	SB	FR	BR
1.	1947	129	513-68-155	.302	.346	.454	39/31	13	66	4	7	9
2.	1950	146	514-95-156	.304	.397	.591	32/69	36	92	4	-1	43

Andy "Pruschka" Pafko, a hardy Pole from northern Wisconsin, was a strong-armed outfielder-third baseman who hit in the clutch, helped the Cubs to their last pennant in 1945, and put together a super season in 1948 that landed him in 39th place on the all-time Cub summit list. He was involved in one of the Cubs' most unpopular trades, moving along to Brooklyn and finally along to his native Wisconsin with the Braves. Wherever he went he gave it the full blast, piling up 17 seasons under the Big Tent—and with distinction. Three successive bleacher shots in 1950 was a career highlight, as was his selection to four All-Star teams as a Cub.

Dewey Williams, reserve catcher for the Cub pennant winners in 1945, recalled the fun those Cubs had that summer. Here's a cameo involving Andy Pafko:

"We had so much fun. I can remember after a Sunday game against St. Louis, we were on our way home. Andy Pafko was sitting next to me and Don Johnson was sitting across the aisle. I began talking to Johnson, but I was just moving my lips, and he was doing the same thing. Pafko was going, 'Huh? Huh?' Andy thought he was going deaf!"

PAFKO: A NOTEWORTHY BOX SCORE

September 21, 1948

Pafko's three-run homer in the ninth beats the Giants 3-2 and ends a 10-game Cub losing streak.

Chicago	AB	R	H	RBI	PO	A	E	New York	AB	R	H	RBI	PO	A	E
Mauch, 2b	3	0	1	0	3	2	0	Lohrke, 3b	4	0	0	0	2	0	0
Waitkus, lf	5	0	0	0	4	0	0	Lockman, cf	4	1	1	1	1	0	0
Cavarretta, 1b	4	1	1	0	10	0	0	Gordan, lf	3	0	0	0	2	0	0
Pafko, 3b	3	1	2	3	1	3	0	Frey, pr	0	0	0	0	0	0	0
Nicholson, rf	4	0	0	0	2	0	0	Mize, 1b	4	0	0	0	7	2	0
Scheffing, c	3	0	2	0	2	0	0	Thomson, rf	3	1	0	0	3	0	0
Jeffcoat, cf	3	0	0	0	3	0	0	Rigney, 2b	1	0	0	0	8	3	1
Walker, ph	1	0	0	0	0	0	0	Yvars, c	2	0	0	0	4	0	0
Lowrey, cf	0	0	0	0	0	0	0	Rhawn, ss	1	0	0	0	0	0	0
Smalley, ss	4	0	1	0	2	2	0	Kerr, ss	2	0	0	0	0	5	1
Schmitz, p	2	0	0	0	2	0	0	Cooper, ph	1	0	0	1	0	0	0
Lynch, ph	1	1	1	0	0	0	0	Milne, pr	0	0	0	0	0	0	0
Dobernic, p	0	0	0	0	0	0	0	Westrum, c	0	0	0	0	0	0	0
Chipman, p	0	0	0	0	0	0	0	Webb, p	3	0	1	0	0	3	0
TOTALS	33	3	8	3	27	9	0	TOTALS	28	0	2	0	27	13	2

Chicago	000	000	003	–	3
New York	000	000	011	–	2

Home runs--Pafko, Lockman. Sacrifices--Schmitz, Pafko, Mauch. Double plays--Chicago 1, New York 1. Left on bases--Chicago 11, New York 3. Bases on balls--Webb 5, Schmitz 3, Dobernic 1. Strikeouts--Schmitz 2, Webb 4. Hits--Schmitz, 1 in 8 innings; Dobernic, 1 in 0 (faced two batsmen); Chipman, 0 in 1. Winning pitcher--Schmitz. Losing pitcher--Webb. Attendance--7,177. Umpires--Barlick, Barr, Driscoll and Ballanfant.

Other Baseball Highlights of 1948

• Joe Gordon of the Cleveland Indians hits a record-setting 32 HRs (for a second baseman).

• Ted Williams has .497 on-base percentage to lead the major leagues.

• Stan Musial loses a Triple Crown by one homer.

• The Indians beat the Red Sox in the American League's first playoff for pennant. They go on to win the World Series over the Boston Braves.

Henry "Hank" John Sauer—1952

Chicago Cubs Summit Season
Number 40

No. 40
HANK SAUER

BORN: March 17, 1917; Pittsburgh, Pennsylvania

Chicago Cubs: 1949-1955

	SEASON AT THE SUMMIT: 1952								
AB-R-H	BA	OB%	2B	3B	HR	RBI	BR	FR	SB
567-89-153	.270	.361	31	3	37	121	32	17	1

When the Cubs left their new spring training home in Mesa, Ariziona, in April 1952, there were no great expectations. They had finished last in the National League standings in three of the four previous seasons. And the one year they weren't eighth they had climbed only to seventh. So when the Cubs charged out of the gate in 1952 and positioned themselves near the top of the standings for the first month of the season, they attracted some attention. And when they stayed in the race for another month, they became the talk of baseball.

Leading manager Phil Cavarretta's ballclub was **Hank Sauer**, a 35-year-old slugging left-fielder known for his home runs—he hit 19, 32, 23 and 22 the previous four seasons—and an ever-present chew of tobacco.

Before the season had started, New York Giants manager Leo Durocher was asked by *The Sporting News* to assess the Cubs. "In the outfield, there's Hank Sauer," Durocher said. "Well, Sauer is Sauer. Certainly he isn't going to get any better."

A New Sauer

Sauer did his best to prove Leo wrong, starting with the Cubs' season-opener April 15 in Cincinnati, when his grand slam helped beat the Reds 6-5. A week later, he went 3 for 4 in a victory over St. Louis, and on April 28 he homered and singled and had four runs batted in in a 4-3 win against the Cardinals.

In some ways, Sauer was still being Sauer, the longball hitter with four home runs in the first two weeks of the season. But there was a new aspect to his game, something he had not done in his seven previous seasons: He was starting to hit to the opposite field.

Teams had learned to defense the right-handed-hitting Sauer by deploying three infielders between second and third, and swinging the outfield to the left so that the right-fielder was positioned in right-center. The strategy worked. Sauer had never hit above .275 since becoming a regular during the 1949 season. But in 1952, Sauer started to go the other way, at Cavarretta's suggestion, with great success.

"It forces you to keep your eye on the ball more," Sauer explained. "You follow it better because you swing late hitting to right field."

Of Sauer's first 25 hits, six were to right field. He was no longer just a longball threat; he was just as apt to punch the ball through the right side for a single or double. And it showed in his average. Two weeks into the season he was hitting .304. By the end of May he was around .320 and climbing. On June 4 he was second in the NL—first among regulars—at .349 ... and still climbing.

By the first week in June, the Cubs were on the verge of becoming a phenomenon. Pitcher Bob Rush was a surprising 8-2, including a stretch of 32 consecutive shutout innings; the Cub outfield of Frank Baumholtz, Gene Hermanski and Sauer was hitting a Murderer's Row-like .321, .354 and .347, respectively; the team won 10 of 13 at one point, and on June 13 was in third place at 32-19, only four games behind the league-leading Dodgers and 1½ games behind Durocher's second-place Giants.

But almost as quickly as the Cubs had taken the league by surprise, the bubble burst. And no one was brought back to earth as suddenly—or harder—than Hank Sauer.

The Bottom Drops Out
He was terrorizing opponents' pitching—on June 4 he had a homer and single in a 6-2 victory over the Giants; two days later he went 3 for 4, driving in his league-leading 49th and 50th runs of the season in a 3-2 win over Philadelphia; his average was up to .350. Then came his biggest game yet.

On June 11, he hit three home runs—all to left field, interestingly—to give the Cubs a 3-2 victory over the Phillies at Wrigley Field. His big day gave him the league lead in home runs (18), runs batted in (58) and average (.352) and set off a frenzy in Chicago.

The newspapers the next morning pointed out that Sauer's 18 homers in 51 games matched Babe Ruth's pace from 1927, when he hit 60. And hours after his big day at Wrigley, Sauer was mobbed by fans and reporters

during a personal appearance at umpire Jocko Conlan's new batting range at River Road and North Avenue.

It seemed as though it couldn't get any better for Sauer and the Cubs. And it didn't.

In his next six games, Sauer went hitless in 24 at-bats. Ten of the 24 trips ended in strikeouts. He hit the ball solidly only twice—both easy fly balls to center field. He ended the skid, briefly, on the 18th with a single, double and homer in a loss to Brooklyn, but by the 19th had fallen from the league batting lead to fourth at .320, a drop of 32 points in a week.

Looking For Reasons
What happened? The papers pointed out that Sauer had taken 10 minutes of batting practice at Conlan's facility. Did that throw off his batting eye? Did the fact that opposing teams started playing him straight-away, so he no longer had the right side to punch the ball through, cut into his effectiveness? Or was it just a case of the averages catching up with Sauer? It may have been a combination of all three.

Whatever the reason, Sauer cooled off considerably. Between June 12 and August 1, he hit just .197 with seven homers and 25 RBIs, dropping his average to .279. He had nine homers and 31 RBIs in August, hitting .276, and finished the season at .270. He hit just three homers in the final month of the season—the last on September 11—and finished with 37, sharing the league lead with the Pirates' Ralph Kiner. The Cubs likewise tailed off, going just 45-58 after Sauer's three-homer afternoon, and finished fifth at 77-77, 19½ games behind the pennant-winning Dodgers.

Despite his disappointing finish, Sauer still put up quite impressive stats. In addition to sharing the home run title, he led the league in RBIs (121) and was second in slugging average (.531) and total bases (301). The numbers added up to a year good enough to earn Sauer the NL Most Valuable Player Award, the first time a player from a fifth-place club was so honored—as well as a spot among the 50 greatest Cub seasons.

HANK SAUER'S

Two Other Great Cub Seasons

	Yr	GP	AB-R-H	BA	OB%	SA	K/BB	HR	RBI	SB	FR	BR
1.	1951	141	525-77-138	.263	.325	.486	77/45	30	89	2	0	7
2.	1954	142	520-98-150	.288	.379	.563	69/70	41	103	2	-2	30

The NL's 1952 MVP, big Hank Sauer, enjoyed a season of stature with top-of-the heap totals in homers (37) and RBIs (121). Another of those genial giants, he really had Curt Simmons' number, twice blasting three of his pitches over the Wrigley vines, once in 1950, and again in '52. As a Cub All-Star, he crushed one of Bob Lemon's better offerings in the 1952 contest to win the game for both the NL and teammate Bob Rush, 3-2 in a rain-shortened game at Philadelphia. One hundred and ninety-eight of his 288 career homers were hit in a Cub uniform, good for seventh on the all-time franchise list. And his 1952 summit season ranks No. 40. That's because his timely hitting and his unheralded but effective defensive work combined to make up the best season he had in his 15-year career.

A story Phil Cavarretta tells about Frankie Baumholtz, 1950's Cub outfielder, involves Hank Sauer:

"On his [Baumholtz's] left was Hank Sauer, the right fielder. They were roomates, two great people. On his right was Ralph Kiner (1953 season). Sauer and Kiner were two guys who couldn't run as fast as an elephant could. And just about everyday Frankie was playing out in center field. The ball would be hit out to right center. All you heard from Sauer was, 'Come on, Frankie. Go catch that ball.' Even if Hank was closer than poor Frankie Baumholtz."

—**From Peter Golenbock's *Wrigleyville***

SAUER: A NOTEWORTHY BOX SCORE

June 11, 1952

Sauer hits three home runs in a 3-1 victory over Philadelphia, giving him 18 homers and 58 RBIs in 51 games.

Philadelphia	AB	R	H	RBI	PO	A	E		Chicago	AB	R	H	RBI	PO	A	E
Ashburn, cf	5	0	0	0	2	0	0		Miksis, 2b	4	0	1	0	3	4	1
Hamner, ss	5	0	2	0	0	2	0		Fondy, 1b	4	0	0	0	6	0	1
Wyrostek, rf	5	0	1	0	2	0	0		Serena, 3b	4	0	1	0	0	3	0
Burgess, c	5	0	2	0	7	0	0		Sauer, lf	4	3	3	3	5	1	0
Mayo, lf	4	0	2	0	2	0	0		Pramesa, c	3	0	0	0	9	1	0
Lohrke, 3b	4	1	0	0	0	1	0		Hermanski, rf	4	0	2	0	1	0	0
Ryan, 2b	1	0	1	0	3	3	0		Jeffcoat, cf	4	0	0	0	2	1	0
Brown, 1b	2	0	1	1	8	1	0		Smalley, ss	2	0	1	0	1	2	0
Simmons, p	3	0	0	0	0	1	0		Lown, p	2	0	0	0	0	0	0
Nicholson, ph	0	0	0	0	0	0	0		Leonard, p	0	0	0	0	0	0	0
Caballero, pr	0	1	0	0	0	0	0									
									TOTALS	31	3	8	3	27	12	2
TOTALS	34	2	9	1	24	8	0									

Philadelphia	000	100	001	-- 2		
Chicago	010	001	01 *	-- 3		

Doubles–Burgess, Hamner. Home runs–Sauer (3). Stolen base–Hamner. Sacrifice--Lown. Double plays–Chicago, 2. Left on base–Philadelphia 11, Chicago 7. Struck out–Lown, 6; Leonard, 1; Simmons, 7. Hits–Lown, 9 in 8⅓ innings; Leonard, none in ⅔; Simons, 8 in 8. Runs earned–Lown, 2-1; Leonard, 0-0; Simmons 3-3. Winning pitcher–Lown (3-2). Losing pitcher–Simmons (4-2). Attendance--10,765. Umpires–Donatelli, Ballanfant, Barlick and Gorman.

Other Baseball Highlights of 1952

- Billy Goodman, Red Sox utility player, becomes the only player in major-league history to win a batting crown without having a regular position.

- The Phils clinch the pennant on the season's last day in the 10th inning with Dick Sisler's home run against the Dodgers.

- Early Wynn wins the AL ERA crown with a 3.20, the highest ERA in major-league history by a league leader.

NOT THE LEAST OF THESE...

41) Bill Lee, 1938, P
42) Larry Jackson, 1963, P
43) Phil Cavarretta, 1945, 1B
44) Jimmy Ryan, 1888, CF
45) Bob O'Farrell, 1922, C

46) Frank Chance, 1904, 1B
47) Cap Anson, 1888, 1B
48) Johnny Evers, 1912, 2B
49) Ken Holtzman, 1970, P
50) Mark Grace, 1989, 1B

Heavy hitters, pitchers who could bring it, and slick-fielding, brainy ballplayers are jammed tightly into our final grouping of Cubbies who distinguished themselves with a season worthy of summit honors. Though their 41-50 rankings might at first glance imply "bottom of the barrel" status, remember, if you will, that these players still wind up near the top of the more than 7,500 individual seasons contributed by some 1,750 players who have worn Cub uniforms.

Frank Chance, Cap Anson and Johnny "the Crab" Evers, three hallowed Hall of Fame names, cluster together at Nos. 46-48, lending a distinctive touch to the final 10. Big Bill Lee, with his pace-setting 22-9 for the 1938 pennant winners, leads off this 41-50 segment. Two other pitchers, Larry Jackson and southpaw Kenny Holtzman, add a dimension of grit and outstanding craftsmanship that made for exceptional years in 1963 and 1970. Holtzman, with his crackling heater and biting curveball, will be remembered as the author of two no-hitters in 1969 and 1971. Jackson is in the No. 42 spot. The husky Idahoan enjoyed outstanding seasons in both 1963 and 1964 for middle-of-the-road Wrigleyville teams.

Two first basemen, each from different eras and each as different as the next, are positioned at No. 43 (Phil Cavarretta), and at the very end of the summit line (Mark Grace). Cavarretta's 1945 career year fueled the Cubs' last pennant winner. Grace, perhaps the finest fielding first baseman in Cub history, adds a classy No. 50 to the franchise honors list.

Jimmy Ryan, the outspoken pepperpot and bon vivant of Anson's 1880s and '90s ballclubs, and Bob O'Farrell, whose exceptional 1922 season rates as one of the greatest any Cub catcher ever had, are often overlooked by those who make lists of "greatest this and thats." They're not forgotten here—and deservedly so.

Our concluding 10 carry a TPR average rating of 3.63. That's still a very fine season, make no mistake about it. But it does put the herculean efforts of those in the top 10, who managed a 6.89 aggregate rating, in sharp relief of the other lesser but still great seasons. From Johnny Clarkson, with his stratospheric 8.9, on through to No. 50, Grace—there you have it, the Chicago Cubs' 50 greatest individual seasons.

William C. Lee—1938

Chicago Cubs Summit Season
Number 41

No. 41
BILL LEE

BORN: October 21, 1909; Plaquemine, Louisiana
DIED: June 15, 1977; Plaquemine, Louisiana

Chicago Cubs: 1934-1943; 1947

SEASON AT THE SUMMIT: 1938

W-L-%		IP	CG	SH	SV	K/BB	PR	DEF	ERA
22-9	.710	291.0	19	9	2	121/74	37	1	2.66

Much of what occurred during the Cubs' pennant-winning season of 1938 is often forgotten. An entire season—89 victories, two managers, a 20-3 run down the stretch to the pennant—is obliterated by one image: Gabby Hartnett being mobbed by fans after his "homer in the gloamin'," arguably the most memorable moment in team history.

But Hartnett's home run wouldn't have meant anything— he might not have even had a chance to bat against Pittsburgh's Mace Brown that September afternoon—if not for **Bill Lee**.

Lee was the dominating pitcher not just in the National League, but in all of baseball in 1938. There wouldn't have been a pennant race for the Cubs without him.

Lee came to Chicago for the 1934 season, a strapping 24-year-old right-hander who had won 21 games for Columbus of the American Association the year before. He went 13-14 his rookie season, then blossomed during the pennant-winning campaign of 1935, going 20-6 (best winning percentage in the majors) with a 2.96 earned-run average. A good 1936 (18-11) was followed

by a disappointing 1937 (14-15). The question for 1938 was, were Bill Lee's best years behind him?

Early in the season, he continued his form of 1937. He wasn't the pitcher of record in his first outing, April 22, against St. Louis. After surrendering two runs in the first inning, he cruised through the Cardinals' lineup. But an error, single and walk in the ninth knocked him out and let St. Louis tie the game, which the Cardinals went on to win.

Lee had an effective relief appearance three days later, working two-thirds of an inning against Pittsburgh. But on the 28th he again ran out of steam, this time against Cincinnati. He had a 12-0 lead going into the ninth, but the Reds strung together seven hits for five runs, and Clay Bryant had to come in and put out the fire.

Unfinished Business
Lee's workdays got shorter and shorter as he tried to find a groove during the first month of the season. On May 2, he was in control against St. Louis through six innings then got KO'd in the eighth for his first loss of the season. His next time out, on the 6th, he lasted only four-

plus innings against Boston. Then on May 10, he was knocked out in the first inning of a 5-1 loss to New York, facing only eight men.

Manager Charlie Grimm considered taking Lee out of the rotation for a week or 10 days so he could work on his mechanics. Lee got one more chance, May 15 against Pittsburgh, and made the most of it. He scattered five hits over seven innings and left with the score tied 3-3. Grimm saw enough to convince him that Lee should stay in the rotation. And Lee didn't disappoint.

On May 19, he allowed New York just five singles as the Cubs won 1-0 on Billy Herman's RBI single in the 10th. Only two Giants reached second—one on a steal, the other on an error—as Lee evened his record at 2-2. He beat Boston, which had won seven straight, 4-1 on May 23, then followed that with consecutive shutouts of Pittsburgh, Cincinnati and Boston. His scoreless inning streak reached 35 before the Giants' Mel Ott homered off Lee on June 7. He went on to beat New York 4-2, making him 7-2 and giving the Cubs a 1½-game lead in the NL pennant race.

Lee ran into more problems over the next month—there was a 1-0 loss to Boston, he was knocked out of games in the third and fourth innings, he surrendered three runs in an inning of relief—but reached the All-Star break at 9-4. (In the summer classic, Lee pitched one-hit ball over three innings as the Nationals posted a 4-1 victory.)

He also lost his next decision, beaten by Johnny Vander Meer and Cincinnati on July 10, but then won his next two, five-hitters against Philadelphia and Boston, to go 11-5.

A Busy Guy
The Cubs, though, had slipped in the standings and were treading water in third place. With his team not going anywhere, Grimm decided to step down, and Hartnett became player-manager. Hartnett soon decided Lee was his iron man and increased his workload. On July 23, for example, he beat New York 7-4, going all the way. The next afternoon Hartnett brought Lee on in relief against the Giants in the ninth and left him in for seven innings (Lee got the win on Stan Hack's homer off Carl Hubbell in the 15th). A week later it was the same story—8⅓ innings one day, then back in relief the next. A weary Lee lost three straight decisions, falling to 13-8 by early August. But he righted himself and won three of his next four, standing at 16-9 as September arrived.

The month started with the Cubs in fourth place, seven games behind the leading Pirates. They went on a tear that would see them win 20 of 23 games and a relentless Lee win his last six decisions.

He beat Pittsburgh 3-0 on September 5, contributed 1⅓ innings of scoreless relief in a win over St. Louis two days later, shut out the Cardinals on four hits on the 11th, blanked New York on the 17th, then won his 20th on September 22, again by shutout, beating Philadelphia 4-0. His scoreless streak ended at 39 innings on September 26 in a 6-3 victory over St. Louis. It was the Cubs' seventh win in a row and 17th in their last 20 games. More importantly, it set the stage for a three-game showdown with first-place Pittsburgh.

A Crucial Showdown
The Pirates came to town on September 27 with a 1½-game lead. The series turned out to be a Cub sweep engineered by Lee and Hartnett. In the opener, he relieved Dizzy Dean in the ninth and struck out Al Todd to preserve a 2-1 victory that moved the Cubs within a half-game of first. The next day he worked a scoreless inning of relief to set the stage for Hartnett. With dusk closing in—had the game not been so important the umpires likely would have stopped play—two out and two strikes against him, Hartnett launched a Brown fastball over the left-field wall in the ninth for a 6-5 victory that moved the Cubs into first. Then Lee—making his fourth appearance in as many days—drove a nail in the Pirate coffin, beating them 10-1 the next afternoon.

The Cubs went on to win the pennant by two games. Their prize? A date with the Yankees in the World Series. But this was a tired Cub team—and these were the Yankees. New York swept the Cubs in four games, with Lee the principal victim. His teammates scored just one run in his 12 innings on the mound and committed two crucial errors behind him.

A disappointing Series, to be sure. But the Cubs wouldn't have even been there without Lee. He finished 22-9—the most victories and highest winning percentage (.710) in either league. His nine shutouts and 2.66 ERA were also the best in baseball.

Hartnett may have earned a spot in every Cub fan's heart and in the history books with his home run—but without Bill Lee, it would have been just another late September ballgame.

BILL LEE'S

Three Other Great Cub Seasons

	Yr	W-L	IP	GS	GC	SH	SV	PD	K/BB	OBA	OB%	ERA	PR
1.	1935	20-6	252.0	32	18	3	1	0	100/84	.251	.314	2.96	30
2.	1936	18-11	258.2	33	20	4	1	1	102/93	.246	.314	3.31	21
3.	1939	19-15	282.1	36	20	1	0	1	105/85	.272	.325	3.44	15

Bill Lee, the big-framed bayou beauty, was an imposing sight on the mound. And his high-kick delivery added more than an ounce or two of intimidation. His 1938 effort was the cornerstone of the pitching staff's contribution to the pennant that year and his World Series hurling was nothing to be ashamed of, even though he was tagged for two losses. It all added up to a superb season with league leadership in shutouts, ERA and pitching runs, good for a No. 41 ranking at the head of the list of the final 10 summiteers. The General, whose career was ultimately hampered by eyesight problems, and finally declared legally blind, battled on much like Ed Reulbach did years before him. Two fine professionals—two fine gentlemen.

"There are still a few iron men left in baseball. One of them is William Crutcher Lee Jr., the statuesque Louisiana gentleman who yesterday pitched himself and Cub mates to the victory that probably decided the eventual destination of the National League flag...The all-important victory that just about put to rest the flag hopes the Pirates had been nourishing since last July, really was a triumph of Lee's courage and stamina. It was a fitting climax for a fellow who throughout the year has been the mainspring of an otherwise shaky pitching corps..."

—Irving Vaughan in the *Chicago Tribune* on September 30, 1938, after Lee made four appearances in four days—all Cub victories—that all but locked up the pennant.

LEE: A NOTEWORTHY BOX SCORE

May 19, 1938

Lee holds the first-place Giants to five hits, all singles, and scores the game's only run himself in the 10th inning.

Chicago	AB	R	H	RBI	PO	A	E	New York	AB	R	H	RBI	PO	A	E
Hack, 3b	4	0	0	0	0	2	0	Moore, lf	4	0	1	0	4	0	0
Herman, 2b	5	0	1	1	0	4	0	Bartell, ss	4	0	1	0	3	7	0
Galan, lf	4	0	0	0	3	0	0	Ripple, rf	4	0	0	0	1	0	0
Demaree, rf	4	0	1	0	4	0	0	Ott, 3b	4	0	0	0	1	3	0
Cavarretta, rf	1	0	0	0	0	0	0	Berger, cf	4	0	0	0	5	0	0
Hartnett, c	4	0	1	0	3	0	0	McCarthy, 1b	4	0	2	0	12	0	0
Reynolds, cf	4	0	2	0	5	0	0	Chiozza, 2b	3	0	1	0	1	3	1
Collins, 1b	3	0	0	0	14	0	0	Danning, c	4	0	0	0	3	1	1
Jurges, ss	4	0	0	0	1	6	1	Gumbert, p	3	0	0	0	0	1	0
Lee, p	3	1	1	0	0	1	0								
TOTALS	36	1	6	1	30	13	1	TOTALS	35	0	5	0	30	15	2

```
Chicago      000   000 000   1 -- 1
New York     000   000 000   0 -- 0
```

Stolen bases--Reynolds, Bartell. Double play--New York. Left on base--New York 5, Chicago 9. Bases on balls--by Gumbert, 4. Strikeouts--by Lee, 3; by Gumbert, 2. Umpires--Parker, Moran and Magerhurth. Time--2:04. Attendance--7,339.

Other Baseball Highlights of 1938

- Detroit's Hank Greenburg hits 58 homers to lead the AL.

- The Reds' Johnny Vander Meer throws back-to-back no-hitters vs. Boston on June 11 and Brooklyn on June 15.

- Pittsburgh's Mace Brown wins 15 games in relief.

- Lou Gehrig hits the last of his career 23 grand slams.

JACKSON
46

Lawrence Curtis Jackson—1963

Chicago Cubs Summit Season
Number 42

No. 42
LARRY JACKSON

BORN: June 2, 1931; Nampa, Idaho
DIED: August 29, 1990; Boise, Idaho

Chicago Cubs: 1963-1966

SEASON AT THE SUMMIT: 1963

W-L-%		IP	CG	SH	SV	K/BB	PR	DEF	ERA
14-18	.438	275.0	13	4	0	153/54	22	2	2.55

Larry Jackson had the distinction of being part of two of the biggest Cub trades of the 1960s: He came to Chicago from St. Louis along with Lindy McDaniel and Jimmie Schaffer in exchange for George Altman, Don Cardwell and Moe Thacker in October 1962, and was sent to Philadelphia in April 1966 in a deal that brought Ferguson Jenkins and Adolfo Phillips to Chicago.

A native of Idaho, Jackson started his professional career with Pocatello of the Pioneer League, going 3-11 in 1951. The next year with Fresno of the California League he was 28-4 with a 2.85 earned-run average, striking out 351 hitters in 300 innings. Jackson broke into the majors with the St. Louis Cardinals in 1955, going 9-14. He didn't have another losing season until his first year with the Cubs, when he went 14-18 on a mediocre seventh-place ballclub. Despite that record, Jackson's 1963 campaign is worthy of recognition as one of the Cubs' 50 top seasons.

Jackson picked up his first victory as a Cub—he lost his debut—on April 14 when he outdueled San Francisco ace Juan Marichal, allowing only three hits in 8⅔ innings

as he beat the Giants 3-1. He would have had a shutout had not Lou Brock dropped a fly ball in the ninth.

He lost his next start, to the Giants and Marichal, then closed out April with two impressive performances, beating Pittsburgh and Philadelphia to run his record to 4-2 with a 1.98 ERA.

Happy May Days

As May wore on, Jackson, relying on a good but not great fastball, sometimes-wicked slider and considerable baseball savvy, established himself as a key member of the Cubs' rotation. There was a 5-4 victory on May 7 that knocked the league-leading Pirates into second place (and left the Cubs three games over .500, the first time they'd been in that heady territory since 1958); on May 25 he scattered five singles in beating Houston 4-1; five days later, buoyed by a 10-run fourth inning, he blanked New York 12-0.

But if any game that month demonstrated what kind of pitcher Jackson was, it was on May 16 against Cincinnati. The Reds sent Chicago Back of the Yards product

Jim O'Toole, who was off to a good start and was 10-4 lifetime against the Cubs, to the mound against Jackson. The Cubs led 2-0 when the Reds mounted a serious threat in the seventh. Cincinnati had men on second and third with none out, and Jackson bore down. Marty Keough—the third of six consecutive left-handed hitters Reds manager Fred Hutchinson would send to the plate—lined to Ernie Banks at first. Rookie Pete Rose popped to short for the second out. Vada Pinson walked, loading the bases. Jackson got Jerry Lynch on a popup to end the threat. He held on for the 2-0 victory, his first shutout as a Cub and 16th of his career, and lowered his ERA to 2.25.

No Pushovers

The Cubs surprised a lot of people in 1963. Behind the pitching of Jackson and Dick Ellsworth—having a career year—and the relief work of McDaniel, they challenged for first place for more than a third of the season. Winning 11 of 13 in late May and early June, they grabbed a share of first by beating the Giants on June 6. They were swept by the Dodgers in a three-game series June 7-9, however, and tumbled to third. And although they played respectably the rest of the season, they were unable to do any better than seventh, at 82-80.

Jackson was only 7-9 at the end of June. In July, though, he would have his best month. He failed to get a decision in his first start, a 3-2, 11-inning Cub victory over the Phils on the 5th (he allowed one earned run through seven innings before leaving for a pinch-hitter). Four days later he got the win in the National League's 5-3 All-Star victory, despite allowing two runs and four hits in two innings of work.

On July 14 he finally beat his old St. Louis teammates, winning 7-3 thanks to homers by Banks, Brock and Ron Santo; and four days later he ran his record to 11-7 with a 3-2 win over Milwaukee. Jackson should have also won his next outing on the 23rd when he allowed just one run in nine innings against the Reds, but the Cubs were handcuffed by Jim Maloney's one-hitter, and Jackson was a 1-0 loser.

Jackson won three of his first five starts in August—the best of the lot a 4-0 complete-game seven-hitter against

the Mets on the 10th—and was 14-11 after beating the Reds on the 18th.

That would prove to be Jackson's last victory of the season. He lost his next seven decisions although he certainly deserved better. There was a four-hitter against Houston on September 8 that he lost 2-1 when he balked in the second Colt run, an 8-3 defeat on September 12 to the streaking Cardinals, who had won 15 of 16, and a 1-0 loss at the hands of Pittsburgh—the run was unearned—on the 16th. He finished 14-18 but with a 2.55 ERA.

A New Attitude

Despite the losing record, some good came out of Jackson's season. After it ended, he returned to his home in Boise, "and I started telling myself I was a 20-game winner," he would later recall. "I continued selling myself on the 20-victory theme in [1964] spring training. It was foremost in my thoughts."

Jackson's positive mental approach paid off—he led the majors in 1964 in victories (he went 24-11), was second in the NL in innings pitched, third in complete games and fourth in opponents' on-base percentage. His Total Pitcher's Index was an impressive 3.0 and his ERA 3.14—very good numbers, but still inferior to the 4.1 and 2.55 of his 1963 season.

Jackson slipped to 14-21 the next season, and when the Cubs got off to a bad start in 1966 manager Leo Durocher shipped him to Philadelphia, where he went 15-13, 13-15 and 13-17 in three seasons with the Phillies. He was chosen by Montreal in the expansion draft, but chose instead to end his major-league career after 14 years and 194 victories.

He returned to his lifelong home in Boise and went into politics, serving four terms in the Idaho legislature. He even ran for governor, losing in the Republican primary in 1978. He also worked as a lobbyist and started his own insurance business. Early in 1990, Jackson was diagnosed with cancer, and seven months later, on August 29, died. He was 59.

LARRY JACKSON'S

*O*ne Other Great Cub Season

Yr	W-L	IP	GS	GC	SH	SV	PD	K/BB	OBA	OB%	ERA	PR
1. 1964	24-11	297.2	38	19	3	0	7	148/58	.235	.273	3.14	13

Lawrence Curtis Jackson fashioned a 4.1 Total Pitcher's Index in 1963. Though it looks completely out of whack, that 14-18 season was a greater achievement than his 1964 season (above), rated at a 3.0 TPI. Why? Here are a couple of telling comparisons: 1963 PRs: 22; '64: 13; '63 ERA: 2.55; '64: 3.14; '63 DEF: 2; '64: 7. In '63 his team hit a paltry .238 behind him, scoring just under two runs per game. In '64, when he won 24, they scored at a four per game average, while hitting at a .251 pace. Like Dick Ellsworth, whom he followed in 1964 as the team's staff ace, he had only one big winning year with the Cubs. But at least he had that! With any respectable help at all in 1963, he would easily have won 22-25 games.

"For a dozen years in a row Jackson won 13 or more games . . . A fine fielding pitcher, he led all hurlers in chances and fielding average several times. Rather than report to the expansion Expos in 1969, Jackson returned to Idaho, becoming a sportswriter, and later, a state legislator."

—From *Who's Who in Baseball* by Lloyd Johnson and Brenda Ward

JACKSON: A NOTEWORTHY BOX SCORE

June 20, 1963

Jackson, with help from Billy Williams' two home runs, beats Houston 5-0 on a four-hitter.

Houston	AB	R	H	RBI	E	Chicago	AB	R	H	RBI	E
Spangler, lf	4	0	1	0	0	Landrum, cf	4	1	1	0	0
Temple, 2b	3	0	0	0	0	Rodgers, ss	4	0	0	0	0
Davis, rf	4	0	1	0	0	Williams, lf	3	3	3	3	0
Warwick, cf	4	0	1	0	0	Santo, 3b	3	1	3	1	0
Runnels, 1b	3	0	0	0	0	Banks, 1b	4	0	1	1	0
B. Aspromonte, 3b	3	0	0	0	0	Hubbs, 2b	4	0	0	0	0
Lillis, ss	3	0	0	0	0	Burton, rf	4	0	0	0	0
Campbell, c	2	0	0	0	0	Bertell, c	4	0	3	0	0
Drott, p	1	0	1	0	0	Jackson, p	4	0	0	0	0
McMahon, p	0	0	0	0	0						
Hartman, ph	1	0	0	0	0	TOTALS	34	5	11	5	0
Kemmerer, p	0	0	0	0	0						
Staub, ph	1	0	0	0	0						
Woodeshick, p	0	0	0	0	0						
TOTALS	29	0	4	0	0						

```
Houston     0 0 0   0 0 0   0 0 0  -- 0
Chicago     1 0 0   0 3 0   0 0 *  -- 4
```

Doubles--Bertell, Santo, Banks, Williams. Home runs--Williams (2). Double plays--Cubs, 1. Left on base--Houston 4, Chicago 7.

	IP	H	R	ER	BB	SO
Drott (L, 2-5)	4⅓	8	4	4	2	2
McMahon	⅔	0	0	0	0	0
Kemmerer	2	3	1	1	0	0
Woodeshick	1	0	0	0	0	1
Jackson (W, 8-6)	9	4	0	0	2	3

Attendance--7,442. Umpires--Donatelli, Crawford, Venson, and Steiner

Other Baseball Highlights of 1963

• On March 30, Pete Rose, a nonroster player for the Reds, goes 2-for-2 in his first major-league exhibition game. He goes on to become NL Rookie of the Year.

• Rogers Hornsby and Home Run Baker die.

• On September 13, the three Alou brothers—Felipe, Matty and Jesus—briefly play together in the outfield in the same game.

Phil Cavarretta—1945

Chicago Cubs Summit Season
Number 43

No. 43
PHIL CAVARRETTA

BORN: July 19, 1916; Chicago, Illinois

Chicago Cubs: 1934-1953

SEASON AT THE SUMMIT: 1945

AB-R-H	BA	OB%	2B	3B	HR	RBI	BR	FR	SB
498-94-177	.355	.449	34	10	6	97	49	-1	5

He was the local kid who made good. Very good.

In September of 1934, three months out of Lane Tech High School, only two months past his 18th birthday, **Phil Cavarretta** made his debut in a Chicago Cubs uniform. It would be the start of a 20-year Cub career that included three pennant winners—1935, '38 and, perhaps most memorably, 1945.

There wasn't a lot for Cub fans to cheer in the first weeks of the '45 season as their team hovered around the .500 mark. More attention was on the White Sox, who jumped into first place in the American League; the lousy spring weather that saw 28 of baseball's first 103 scheduled games postponed because of rain, snow or cold; and the defeat of Germany and Italy.

Cavarretta also started his season slowly, a hit here, a couple of hits there, only occasionally breaking out—a 3-for-3 day with two walks in a victory over Pittsburgh on April 28, for example, or a 2-for-4 effort May 5 in a win over St. Louis that raised his average to .302. Soon,

though, he was regularly playing the role of hero: Moved to the cleanup spot in the batting order, supplanting a slumping Bill Nicholson, he had four hits and a walk May 11 to help beat Philadelphia 7-1 (and raise his average to .365); a three-run homer in the seventh the next day helped spark a 13-12 win over the Phils; he had a 3-for-11 series as the Cubs took two of three from second-place Brooklyn. He also was playing flawless defense at first base; he didn't commit his first error until May 26 when he let third baseman Stan Hack's throw get by, his first error in 298 chances.

By the end of the month Cavarretta was seventh in the National League in hitting with a .346 average. The Cubs were less successful, sitting in fifth, 6½ games behind the first-place New York Giants.

To The Outfield And Back
In an effort to get more punch in his lineup, manager Charlie Grimm decided to put Heinz Becker at first and move Cavarretta to the outfield. The experiment, which started on June 3, was only four days old when Becker got a notice from the draft board in his hometown of

Dallas to report for a physical on the 18th. He left the team after the game of the 14th and Cavarretta moved back to first.

He celebrated his return to his natural position the next day in a double-header sweep of Cincinnati. In Game 1, his first-inning single drove in two runs and his second homer of the season brought in another. In the second game, he tripled home a run in the first and later singled and walked. For the day he reached base in eight of nine trips to the plate, raising his average to .341 as the Cubs improved to 25-22.

Becker was rejected by his draft board, but Grimm was reluctant to dislodge the red-hot Cavarretta from first base. After his big double-header against the Reds, he went 7 for 10 in his next three games, all Cub victories. By the end of June, the Cubs were third, five games back, poised to make their move. And Cavarretta was the man who led the way.

The Cubs and Boston Braves opened a four-game set on July 3, a series made all the more interesting by the head-to-head duel between Cavarretta and the Braves' Tommy Holmes, who came in having hit safely in 29 straight games. The Cubs won the opener 24-2, with Cavarretta going 5 for 7 to boost his average to .363 while Holmes went 3 for 4 to climb to .402. Cavarretta went 5 for 11 and Holmes 5 for 14 through the rest of the series, which the Cubs swept.

Chicago followed that four-game sweep with another, this one against the Phillies. Cavarretta had four hits and four RBIs in a 12-6 victory on July 8, the Cubs' ninth win in a row, which moved them into first place. That's where they would remain, though tenuously at times, for the rest of the season.

A Slump And An Injury

Cavarretta suffered a mild slump through the middle of the month, going 0 for 19 at one point. But the Cubs were winning without him, going 12-3 in the last two weeks of July and winning 31 of 37 over one stretch. He was at .350 on August 1, 20 points behind Holmes, who had had his hitting streak snapped at 37 by the Cubs' Hank Wyse on July 12.

Holmes began tailing off and Cavarretta got hot in the first week of August, closing the gap to four percentage points (.368 to .364). But Cavarretta suddenly saw his bid for a batting title, and the Cubs' chances, threatened by injury.

On August 12 in Philadelphia, he collided with Phils baserunner Fred Daniels and suffered a badly bruised shoulder. He would miss 12 games, during which time the Cubs' lead shrank to 3½ games. He returned to the lineup for two games late in the month, but the shoulder again sidelined him for 13 more games.

When he returned September 9, Cavarretta found himself leading the league at .361, thanks to a 3-for-24 slump by Holmes (.357). The two would take their race down to the wire, with the Cub captain ekeing out the batting title .355 to .352.

The pennant race came down to the Cubs and defending champion Cardinals. St. Louis was just 1½ games back after beating the Cubs 11-6 on September 26, but the Cubs swept the Reds the next afternoon to clinch at least a tie, then swept the Pirates on the 29th to wrap it up and earn a World Series date against the Detroit Tigers.

Can't Hold Those Tigers

Cavarretta and the Cubs looked unbeatable in Game 1 as they shelled Hal Newhouser and throttled the Tigers 9-0. He had a single in a four-run first and a two-run homer in the seventh to lead the way. Detroit won Game 2, but Claude Passeau's one-hitter in Game 3 put Chicago back ahead. The Tigers won Games 4 and 5—Cavarretta getting just one hit in seven trips—and went for the clincher on October 8. The Cubs, though, refused to die, winning 8-7 in the 12th on Hack's double and sending the Series to a deciding Game 7.

Hank Borowy, who was 11-2 with a 2.13 ERA for the Cubs after coming over from the Yankees in July, was shelled in the first inning, and Detroit went on to a 9-3 romp and world championship.

There was some consolation for Cavarretta. He was the Cubs' leading hitter in the Series at .423. And his regular-season stats—the .355 batting average and .449 on-base percentage, 177 hits, 34 doubles and 97 RBIs—earned him NL MVP honors. He would spend 10 more years in Chicago, eight with the Cubs, two with the Sox, concluding his 22-year career in 1955.

PHIL CAVARRETTA'S

Four Other Great Cub Seasons

	Yr	GP	AB-R-H	BA	OB%	SA	K/BB	HR	RBI	SB	FR	BR
1.	1942	136	482-59-130	.270	.365	.363	42/71	3	54	7	6	13
2.	1944	152	614-106-197	.321	.390	.451	42/67	5	82	4	-7	31
3.	1946	139	510-89-150	.294	.401	.435	54/88	8	78	2	1	30
4.	1949	105	360-46-106	.294	.374	.444	31/45	8	49	2	9	12

P hil "Philibuck" Cavarretta was a Chicago boy who spent 22 years in Chicago uniforms as a Cub, and in 1954-55, as a White Sox handyman. His Bruin longevity mark will probably stand for a good long while. So will his summit effort in 1945, arguably one of the very best of the wartime years by a position player. Without hesitation, it was ranked as an honors list entry alongside the Larry Jackson and Jimmy Ryan seasons. He was a team leader almost from his youthful starting days, playing first and the outfield, and doing what was required to win. At 18, he was the Cubs' first baseman and at 35 he was still on the scene, manager, first baseman and ace pinch-hitter with 12 pinch hits in 1951. In 1941, he joined with Stan Hack and Bill Nicholson to hit three consecutive home runs, a franchise record, and he stands fifth in Cubs games played and triples.

"I've thought of it. Then I get upset, and I stop thinking about it."
—Phil Cavarretta, asked whether he ever thinks about how much money he'd be paid today.

CAVARRETTA: A NOTEWORTHY BOX SCORE

July 8, 1945

Cavarretta's four hits and four RBIs help beat the Phillies
and move the Cubs into first place.

Chicago	AB	R	H	RBI	PO	A		Philadelphia	AB	R	H	RBI	PO	A
Hack, 3b	6	2	2	1	1	0		Mott, ss, 2b	5	1	3	3	1	3
Johnson, 2b	4	2	1	0	3	2		Antonelli, 3b	5	1	3	0	2	0
Nicholson, rf	4	2	1	0	5	0		Wasdell, cf, lf	5	0	2	1	3	0
Cavarretta, 1b	5	2	4	4	6	0		Crawford, rf	5	0	1	0	5	1
Pafko, cf	4	1	1	2	2	1		DiMaggio, cf	2	1	1	0	3	1
Lowrey, lf	5	1	2	3	2	0		Monteagudo, lf	2	0	0	0	0	0
Williams, c	5	0	1	0	3	0		Dinges, 1b	5	1	4	0	7	0
Merullo, ss	3	1	1	0	5	4		Daniels, 2b	1	0	0	0	0	1
Erickson, p	3	1	1	0	0	1		Flager, ss	3	0	0	0	1	0
Vandenburg, p	1	0	0	0	0	1		Spindel, c	4	1	1	0	5	0
Prim, p	1	0	0	0	0	0		Wyatt, p	1	0	0	0	0	0
								Grate, p	0	0	0	0	0	0
								Scott, p	0	0	0	0	0	0
TOTALS	41	12	12	10	27	9		Foxx, ph	1	0	1	1	0	0
								Chapman, p	2	1	1	0	0	1
								TOTALS	41	6	17	5	27	7

```
            Chicago         0 0 3    5 0 0    0 0 4   – 12
            Philadelphia    1 0 0    2 0 0    0 3 0   –  6
```

Errors--Mott, Wasdell, Flager. Doubles--Antonelli, Johnson, Merullo, Chapman, Cavarretta. Triple--Cavarretta. Stolen bases--Nicholson, Crawford, Merullo. Sacrifice--Daniels. Double plays--Chicago 1, Philadelphia 1. Left on base--Chicago 7, Philadelphia 10. Bases on balls--by Wyatt, 1; by Grate, 1; by Chapman, 3; by Erickson, 1. Strikeouts--by Erickson, 2; by Chapman, 1; by Prim, 1. Hits--Erickson, 11 in 4 1/3; Vandenberg, 6 in 6 2/3; Prim, 0 in 2, Wyatt, 4 in 2 1/3; Grate, 5 in 1 1/3; Scott, 1 in 1/3. Chapman, 4 in 5. Winning pitcher--Prim. Losing pitcher--Wyatt. Umpires--Reardon, Goetz and Jorda. Time--2:36.

Other Baseball Highlights of 1945

- Hank Greenberg's grand slam on the last day clinches the AL pennant for Detroit.

- Brooklyn signs Jackie Robinson.

- The All-Star Game is canceled because of the war—the only cancellation in history.

- The Cubs sweep 20 double-headers.

Jimmy Ryan—1888

Chicago Cubs Summit Season
Number 44

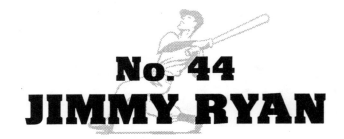

No. 44
JIMMY RYAN

BORN: February 11, 1863; Clinton, Massachusetts
DIED: October 26, 1923; Chicago, Illinois

Chicago White Stockings: 1885-89; 1891-1900

SEASON AT THE SUMMIT: 1888

AB-R-H	BA	OB%	2B	3B	HR	RBI	BR	FR	SB
549-115-182	.332	.337	33	10	16	64	34	4	60

Baseball came of age in the 1880s, replete with the introduction of what we would today call marketing and the commercialization of the game and its players, national coverage in newspapers and magazines, and the celebration of its first idols. The ascendancy and ultimate domination of the Windy City's White Stockings over their National League rivals coincided with baseball's first golden era. America, it seemed, was simply taken by what was soon to be dubbed the National Pastime.

And Chicago? The prospering, tempestuous, barely-under-control metropolis and its wildly supportive fans, much like those in the other of the big-time baseball capitals, couldn't get enough of their ballplaying heroes.

The White Stockings franchise was led by A. G. Spalding, by this time well into the ownership and general manager phase of his brilliant baseball and merchandising career. The ballclub itself was in the hands of one of the all-time greats, the Captain Extraordinaire, Adrian Anson. Featuring a cast of earthy characters, rich in talent and

derring-do, they taunted, brawled, outplayed and outlasted the best in the league season after season. And it often seemed that the old ballgame was only a prelude to the really big event of the day: more brawling, carousing and riotous bar-hopping well into the wee hours of those sticky Chicago summer nights.

One of the more beguiling of the Whites' swashbuckling crew was **Jimmy Ryan**, a stocky, powerful young Irishman they called "Pony," who hit and guzzled with the very best of the team's Kellys, Williamsons and Dalys. Afternoons, Ryan roamed Chicago's outfield, an Anson reliable, who usually hit around .320, helped out the pitching staff here and there, stole 25-30 bases a season, and otherwise found endless ways and means to irritate opposing teams to distraction. Pony was one of those baseball rarities who, like Pete Reiser, Rickey Henderson, or Oscar Gamble, threw from the portside and hit from the starboard side.

By 1888 the Whites were a tad beyond their glory days. Ryan's first full season came with the 1886 champs, but that was to be Chicago's last pennant winner for a while. One of the reasons the ballclub continued to demand respect around the league even though stars like Kelly and John Clarkson had been peddled elsewhere, was Jimmy Ryan. His career best 1888 season was one of the stronger factors in the club's second-place finish. He was the catalyst of the attack from his leadoff spot, pushing his boss (he led the batting championship race as late as the first week in September), Cap Anson, who led the league with a .344 mark.

A Wild One

For Ryan, one of the summer high spots came at Detroit's Recreation Park on July 28 against the league's defending champion Wolverines. The box score that day looked like a Phillies-Cubs tilt played in 1930.

That neither Chicago's "Lady" Baldwin nor Mark Baldwin of Detroit had it that day would be the understatement of 1888. Of the 39 hits ricochetting around Recreation Park, five belonged to Pony Ryan, who authored a "cycle," the first of his club record two (a second came during the 1891 season). He also found time to relieve Mark Baldwin, who took a severe enough pounding in Detroit's five-run second for Anson to bring on Ryan. Some day, right? Rest assured, the evening hours, awash in the bubbly, were even better!

But as far as playing the game is concerned, some of the more knowledgeable baseball researchers, Saberites Brenda Ward and Lloyd Johnson among them, suggest that Jimmy Ryan was one of the best 19th Century ballplayers not elected to the Hall of Fame. While similar cases might be made for Ned Williamson and Freddie Pfeffer, teammates of Ryan, and still others, the premier Chicago center-fielder of his day has much to offer to substantiate the claim.

During his summit season Ryan had league-leading numbers in base hits, doubles, homers and outfield assists, running up 34 of them in a day and age when center-fielders often became the sixth infielder. A league-leading .515 slugging average was a rarity for a leadoff-type hitter in those days, but the power and pop in his stick was more than a sometime thing—a bonus of the first order included in the Ryan package. Beyond all that, he swiped bases at a career-high clip, adding 60 to his total of 418 during his 15-season White Stocking tenure. More? How about a 4-0, 3.05 ERA pitching effort.

Solid Hitting

Although the White Stockings finished a distant second to a strong Giants team loaded with future Hall of Famers like Mickey Welch, Buck Ewing and "Orator Jim" O'Rourke, they battled down to the very end in the only way an Anson-led team could: all-out every inning, never quite believing they had lost a game. Pony Ryan fit the mold to a T.

In 1888 the National League averaged a rather anemic .239 while the pitchers posted a collective 2.83 ERA, New York leading the way with a snappy staff ERA of 1.96. In that pitching-rich environment Ryan staked his claim to a super season with a substantial .332 average, including 34 batting runs, which ranked him directly behind the season's top sluggers, Hall of Famer Dan Brouthers (47), Roger Connor (45), and Anson (41).

Ryan's 1888 is just too good to leave off the franchise's top-50 list. While it's not a middle-range season the likes of Lee Smith's 1983 or Bob Rush's 1952, it's still right near the top of the "Bottom 10." That's near the bottom of the list's very best, but infinitely better than winding up the best of the "also-rans."

JIMMY RYAN'S

Three Other Great Cub Seasons

	Yr	GP	AB-R-H	BA	OB%	SA	K/BB	HR	RBI	SB	FR	BR
1.	1889	135	576-140-177	.307	.388	.498	62/70	17	72	45	6	29
2.	1894	108	474-132-171	.361	.425	.487	23/50	3	62	11	9	10
3.	1898	144	572-122–185	.323	.405	.446	—/73	4	79	29	-7	34

The three seasons listed are Pony's best after his big 1888 season; 1889 is the best of these due to its steady, balanced hitting, including his career-high 17 homers. His 45 stolen bases put him in scoring position often, and note his 140 runs scored, another career high. Even though he hit .361 in 1894, his other numbers and overall contribution to the team were not up to the other two listed. During his 15 seasons in a White Stockings uniform, he played many positions, as in 1892 and 1889, adding versatility to the lineup. By the 1894 and 1898 seasons he had been restricted to outfield duty only. With the release of the great Captain Anson in 1897, the days of the White Stockings came to an end, and though Ryan's last great season was in 1898, already into the "Orphans Era," it should be remembered that Jimmy Ryan's career was one of the great White Stocking chapters written during those glorious days of Chicago supremacy.

Some years after Ryan's hell-raising baseball days were over, Johnny Evers recalled one of the better antics in which Pony and his pals were involved. Tom Daly, Elmer Foster, Fritz Pfeffer and, of course, the fun-loving Ryan, "came close to dropping a half-empty keg of beer four stories onto (manager) Anson's head." So much for peace and quiet after hours!

RYAN: A NOTEWORTHY BOX SCORE

July 28, 1888

The Whites, with Ryan's help at the plate
and on the mound, outlast Detroit.

Chicago	AB	R	H	P	A		Detroit	AB	R	H	P	A
Ryan, cf-p	6	3	5	1	5		Hanlon, cf	6	3	3	1	1
Sullivan, lf	5	0	1	1	1		Brouthers, 1b	5	2	3	10	1
Duffy, rf	6	3	3	2	0		Lowe, ss	6	3	2	1	5
Anson, 1b	6	3	2	10	1		White, 3b	6	2	3	1	4
Pfeffer, 2b	6	0	0	1	5		Ganzel, 2b	6	1	1	8	5
Williamson, ss	4	3	3	2	5		Sutcliffe, c	6	1	1	5	5
Burns, 3b	5	3	2	0	2		Twitchell, lf-p	6	1	0	0	2
Baldwin, M, p-cf	4	2	1	1	0		Baldwin, C, p-lf	6	2	1	0	2
Daly, c	5	4	3	9	0		Campau, rf	5	2	1	1	0
TOTALS	47	21	20	27	19		TOTALS	52	17	15	27	25

Chicago	2 2 0	4 3 3	2 2 3	— 21
Detroit	1 5 1	0 4 0	0 6 0	— 17

Doubles: Ryan, Williamson, Brouthers, Rowe, White, Sutcliffe; Triples: Daly, Ryan (2); Home runs: Ryan, Anson (2), Duffy. Strikeouts: M. Baldwin, 3; C. Baldwin, 4; Ryan and Twitchell, 0; Bases on balls: M. Baldwin, 4; C. Baldwin, 6; Ryan and Twitchell, 0; Wild pitches: C. Baldwin, 1; Ryan, 2; Twitchell and M. Baldwin, 0. Winning pitcher: Ryan; Losing pitcher: C. Baldwin.

Other Baseball Highlights of 1888

- *Casey at the Bat* is published.

- New York wins the NL pennant and beats St. Louis of the American Association in the World Series, six games to four.

- Chicago's Jimmy Ryan leads the NL in hits (182), doubles (33), homers (16), total bases (283) and slugging percentage (.515).

- NL pitcher Tim Keefe wins 19 straight games.

- The National League adopts a three-strikes-and-you're-out rule. (Previously, batters were allowed four strikes.)

Robert Arthur O'Farrell—1922

**Chicago Cubs Summit Season
Number 45**

No. 45
BOB O'FARRELL

BORN: October 19, 1896; Waukegan, Illinois
DIED: February 20, 1988; Waukegan, Illinois

Chicago Cubs: 1915-1925; 1934

SEASON AT THE SUMMIT: 1922

AB-R-H	BA	OB%	2B	3B	HR	RBI	BR	FR	SB
392-68-127	.324	.439	18	8	4	60	19	16	5

Mr. William K. Wrigley took complete control of the Cubs franchise, bought the Los Angeles Angels of the Pacific Coast League, sent his ballclub to his private island off the coast of California, Catalina by name, and installed a new manager—all in 1921. That year he was also investing heavily ($7.8 million) in his and Chicago's unique, white terra cotta showpiece, the Wrigley Building. And the Wrigley purse strings were just starting to loosen in earnest.

His first love, above all, was that North Side ballclub, and it needed help. Plenty of it. That meant top-notch players and, if possible, big-name attractions. Grover Cleveland Alexander had already checked in, and they kept on checking in until Marse Joe McCarthy and his late '20s fence-bashers finally put his Cubs in the winner's circle.

Nice Guys - No Cigars

Between the 1918 and 1929 pennants, there were a number of fine ballplayers on the Cub roster, but never in sufficient number to bring home the bunting. Names like Charlie Hollocher, Ray Grimes, Hack Miller, Bernie Friberg, Vic Aldridge, George Grantham, John "Sheriff" Blake and Tony Kaufman drifted into and out of Cub lineups. All had their moments and some put together a strong season or two, but, of course, it took the Hartnetts, Wilsons, Malones, Hornsbys, et al., to put the Cubs on top. Much as he liked them all, Wrigley insisted on a pennant. He kept at it doggedly, methodically.

The 1922 season was one of those years that the Bruins inched closer to the pot at the end of the rainbow. Gabby Hartnett debuted that year. He was with the ballclub the entire season, but his was a minor, weak-hitting role. The reason he wasn't in the lineup to stay was spelled O'-F-a-r-r-e-l-l.

He Hailed from Jack Benny's Town

Bob O'Farrell, a sturdy young lad from Waukegan, just north of Chicago, got in his first big-league licks at 18 and had been around the Cubs' clubhouse since 1915. It took some time, but when manager Bill Killifer put his catching gear aside to lead the '22 ballclub,

O'Farrell got his chance. Before the year was out the 25-year-old catcher had authored a summit season, No. 45 on the Cubs' top 50 listing. He was one of the prime movers in the Cubs' jump from their seventh-place 1921 finish to the top of the second division, at fifth. Another fine O'Farrell season in 1923 helped move the club into the first division, and Wrigley was beginning to feel as though the organization was finally headed in the right direction.

A Summit Season In the Making

Grimes, Hollocher, utility player Friberg, "Jigger" Statz, Alexander and Aldrige were all vital cogs in the 1922 Cub lineup. But it was O'Farrell who fashioned the team's top all-around performance that year. As early as May he was recognized as one who was headed for one headliner of a season. Chicago's correspondent to *The Sporting News*, Oscar Reichow, filed this report in the May 25 issue: "...he (manager Bill Killifer) now has one of the greatest catchers in baseball in Bob O'Farrell who has finally come to life and is playing as few catchers are playing today. Not only is he throwing out runners by feet to spare, but...he is handling the pitchers with as clever judgement at they were ever handled before."

O'Farrell's 1922 Season At A Glance

Here are some of the strong-armed catcher's 1922 numbers of note:

1) As the best catcher in the National League he was its leader in putouts, assists, double plays and fielding runs.
2) He had a second-place NL tie in walks (79) and a third-place ranking behind teammate Grimes with an on base average of .439.
3) He hit a career-high .324 and garnered 19 batting runs.
4) He led all major-league catchers with a 3.8 TPR. Only the White Sox's Hall of Famer, Ray Schalk, pressed him (2.8) for honors.
5) As an added fillip, he recorded the final out of the season with Alexander as the Cubs won the City Series, four games to three, breaking a string of seven consecutive White Sox series wins dating back to 1911.

Surging

After Alexander had staked the North Siders to opening game victories both at home and on the road, the Cubs soon found themselves nose-diving into the league's nether regions, and though O'Farrell hit at a steady .300 tempo, it seemed that neither he nor Grimes, the Cubs' hard-hitting first baseman, could dislodge the team from its second-division moorings. It often took "overtime" to win games that had already been won, then lost or tied. Extra innings were the order of the day. An example was the game played at Boston on June 16, when O'Farrell contributed four singles to a 7-6 win in the 12th.

But there was a surge—both for the contact-hitting O'Farrell and for the Wrigleymen. He put together a 10-for-15 spurt the end of June that raised his average to .309 as the club moved all the way to the third spot, when finally it began to look as though the pitching would come around. On July 4 a double-header sweep of Pittsburgh marked the start of the Cubs' strongest showing of the year. They were still third. But then troubles bedeviled them in the form of injury, some tough luck and a plain everyday relapse into their former shortcomings.

Oh, Those August Dog Days

On the strength of a pair of O'Farrell two-baggers, the Cubs won at Boston behind Kaufman, 5-0. Then came one of those Alexander classics at New York before a full house, a 2-1, 11-inning squeaker (O'Farrell added another double in a 2-for-4 day). St. Louis then edged them into fourth and from there on it was only a matter of time before they finished the season in first place—of the second division, that is. There was one August record-setter: on the 25th they were involved in *the* slugfest of 1922, a 26-23 encounter with the Phillies. O'Farrell, Grimes, Miller and Co., with the help of the Phils, rifled some 51 hits around the ballpark that day!

By September 13, O'Farrell had been involved in 110 of his team's 133 games, was hitting .319 and directed the Cub defense superbly. He was on his way to a 3.8 TPR year, the best Cub rating in a hit-happy, New York kind of season. At season's end he stood at a perky .324, his career high—in his career year!

While the New Yorkers were into their subway World Series, Chicagoans were into their crosstown City Series. Though he didn't hit as well in the series as he had during the regular season, it didn't matter. For once they had whipped the Sox. In Chicago, who could ask for anything more?

BOB O'FARRELL'S

One Other Great Cub Season

Yr	GP	AB-R-H	BA	OB%	SA	K/BB	HR	RBI	SB	FR	BR
1. 1923	131	452-73-144	.319	.408	.471	36/67	12	84	10	1	22

Bob O'Farrell logged 21 major-league seasons, including an MVP year in 1926 with the Cardinals. That was the season Alexander and Hornsby & Co. dominated the headlines, while O'Farrell was quietly going about his business and, as usual, turning in his top-rate year. In 1927 he managed the Cards, leading them to within a game and a half of the pennant, only to be relegated to second-string catching duties the following year. Figure that one out! His 1923 season with the Cubs featured his highest major-league total for batting runs in a single season (22) and was a year almost on a par with 1922. From 1918 to 1940, O'Farrell and Gabby Hartnett kept the Cubs in A-1 No. 1 in catching. That's a remarkable span of years matched by very few franchises.

THE MAJOR LEAGUES' 1922 TOP 10 RECEIVERS:
A comparative rundown

	GP	BA	OBA	BR	PO	A	DP	FR	TPR
1) O'Farrell, (CHI, NL)	128	.324	.439	16	446	143	22	16	3.8
2) Schalk, (CHI, AL)	142	.281	.379	0	591	150	16	20	2.8
3) Schang, (NY, AL)	124	.319	.405	9	456	102	12	0	1.5
4) Severeid, (STL, AL)	137	.321	.356	-2	481	117	11	9	1.3
5) Bassler, (DET, AL)	121	.323	.422	9	421	113	12	-3	1.2
5) Henline (PHL, NL)	111	.324	.407	7	400	113	13	2	1.2
6) Snyder, (NY, NL)	104	.343	.387	11	272	74	10	-3	0.9
7) Gooch, (PIT, NL)	105	.329	.403	5	382	102	10	0	0.8
8) Gharrity, (WAS, AL)	96	.256	.351	-1	285	86	9	3	0.7
8) Gowdy, (BOS, NL)	92	.317	.391	3	204	63	8	1	0.7
8) Hargrave, (CIN, NL)	98	.316	.371	12	261	60	5	-9	0.6
9) Ainsmith, (STL, NL)	119	.293	.343	4	428	99	14	-2	0.6
9) O'Neill, (CLV, AL)	133	.311	.423	15	450	116	9	-14	0.6
10) Wingo, (CIN, NL)	80	.285	.343	-4	211	81	6	4	0.2

Discussion: Note how the players listed above cluster in the .310 to .330 batting average range. In the 1922 season, there was no lack of .300 hitters. Among players who played in 100 or more games in the NL that year, 30 hit .300 or better. There were, further, 1,055 homers in the bigs. By 1922 the dead ball era had been asnooze a couple of seasons and the *really* big fireworks were yet to come!

By the way—Bob O'Farrell came off pretty well in that list, didn't he? Good reason for his No. 45 summit rating.

How many of those catchers' names do you recognize? Would a similar listing from, say, 1965 to 1985 raise the recognition level any? There's at least one message here: Those fellows who put the pads on are among baseball's most unsung and unknown. For all the battering they take, one simply has to wonder.

Other Baseball Highlights of 1922

- St. Louis' Rogers Hornsby sets NL records with 42 homers, 152 RBIs and a .722 slugging average. He also hits .401.

- Ray Grimes of the Cubs drives in at least one run in 17 straight games.

- The Supreme Court rules that baseball is a sport, not a business, and therefore isn't subject to anti-trust laws.

- Sudden deaths: Cardinals catcher Pickles Dillhoefer of typhoid fever, and Cardinals outfielder Austin McHenry of a brain tumor.

Frank Leroy Chance—1904

Chicago Cubs Summit Season
Number 46

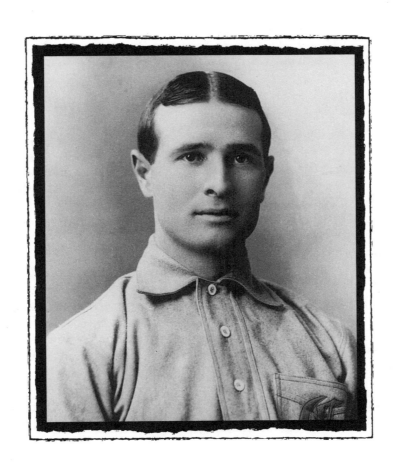

No. 46
FRANK CHANCE

BORN: September 9, 1877; Fresno, California
DIED: September 15, 1924; Los Angeles, California

Chicago Colts/Cubs: 1898-1912
Hall of Fame: 1946

SEASON AT THE SUMMIT: 1904

AB-R-H	BA	OB%	2B	3B	HR	RBI	BR	FR	SB
451-89-140	.310	.382	16	10	6	49	27	1	42

There was absolutely nothing in the world of base-ball to compare with the heated, bitter rivalry between the New Yorks and Chicagos of the early 1900s. Each inning of every game was played as though the fate of the franchise hung in the balance, to say nothing of the pennant. And more often than not, it did!

Made To Order for Frank Chance

Into that cauldron of white-hot contention strode **Frank Chance**, the California collegian. Ox strong, a wondrously endowed athlete, he played ball as well as the game of life on his own terms, and he was ready, literally, to fight to make his point or win the day. In the clubhouse, on the diamond, in the boardroom, or at the corner tavern—it made no difference to "Husk." He was the Chicago counterpart of New York's Muggsy McGraw and used anything, any tactic, anyone, any way or means—whatever it took—to succeed.

1904

By 1904 the converted catcher had become a line-drive-hitting first baseman, the anchor of the legendary Colt and later Cub infield that featured the keystone combi-nation of Joe Tinker and Johnny Evers. Under manager Frank Selee he had already become the team leader and before another season or two would become known not only as Chicago's, but indeed, baseball's Peerless Leader.

With a .327 season in 1903 behind him, Chance was ready to continue a five-year run that turned out to be the highlight years of his playing career. Among them, 1904 was his finest. It was the final full season he was able to devote to playing day by day without the added burdens of managing the ballclub. He made the most of it.

Watch Out, Pittsburgh!

It was clearly evident that the ballclubs in the nation's Nos. 1 and 2 cities were primed and ready to give Pittsburgh's NL champs all they could handle in the 1904 pennant chase. That's exactly what happened as the race, at least in its earlier stages, involved all three. But 1904 was the year of the Giant. Though manager Selee's Colts forged into an early season lead on the strength of the greatest May record in franchise history (they won

19 of 25 that month), there was just too much to contend with in New York's earlier day M and M boys, immortals Mathewson and McGinnity.

Confrontation at West Side Grounds

The July 21 game with archrival New York was typical of the razor-sharp competition between the Giants and the Colts that summer. The Giants started with Joe McGinnity, who was to win 35 that season, and wound up using Christy Mathewson in a two-inning relief stint to subdue Selee's charges 4-3 with a ninth-inning inside-the-park home run by *outfielder* Roger Bresnahan. Chance that day had an inside-parker of his own to knot the score at 3 in the seventh. It was one of his best games of the summer with timely hitting and flawless defensive work.

The next day the two went at it again in a Sunday feature that drew what the *Chicago Tribune* called a "monster crowd." (Estimates placed attendance at near 25,000 for the biggest number of fans ever jammed into the tiny West Side Grounds facility.) They saw Matty beat "Miner" Brown 5-1 in a game that just about sealed the fate of the Chicagoans, who finally finished 13 games off the winning pace of the hated Giants.

Goose Eggs At the Polo Grounds

In an early season series at the Polo Grounds, Bob Wicker, who won 17 and lost 8 in 1904, shut down the New Yorkers without so much as a hit through nine innings, finally giving up a single in the 10th. But the Colts pushed across the winning tally in the 12th, giving the big left-hander a 1-0 one-hitter. Two days later, in the final game of the series on June 13, Chance hit for the cycle, the third franchise player to accomplish that rare feat. Indeed, the Colts beat the McGrawmen that day, too.

The 1904 Numbers

By the end of May, Chance had pushed his batting average beyond the .300 mark after a dismal, frustrating start. At season's end he settled for a .310 average, one of the top 10 hitters in the league. More important than his .300 average, however, was his team-leading on-base percentage and the timeliness of his hitting, underscoring his reputation as one of the more dangerous clutch hitters of his day. His 1904 numbers included team leadership in stolen bases (his 67 thefts in '03 set the still-standing club record), slugging average, runs, home runs (6), and defensively, a league-leading 12 fielding runs. That reminds us that his classy play at first base was on a par with the deft defensive wizardry of his accomplished teammates Tinker and Evers. Small wonder the poets got busy trying to capture the threesome's artistry in verse!

No, Frank Chance and his Chicago entourage didn't win the 1904 pennant despite his season of Colt summitry. But the boys from Carl Sandburg's city with broad shoulders were on their way. Halcyon days were around the corner. The Peerless Leader would see to that!

FRANK CHANCE'S

Three Other Great Cub Seasons

	Yr	GP	AB-R-H	BA	OB%	SA	K/BB	HR	RBI	SB	FR	BR
1.	1903	125	441-83-144	.327	.439	.440	-/78	2	81	67	-3	37
2.	1905	118	392-92-124	.316	.450	.434	-/78	2	70	38	2	34
3.	1906	136	474-103-151	.319	.419	.430	-/70	3	71	57	-1	34

The Colt/Cubs captain was at his best from from 1903 to 1906, and though his 1904 season was his finest, the other three pressed hard for summit honors. Each of the three above is in the range of 3-4 wins attributable (again, above the league-average player) to Chance's play. All things considered, Husk belongs in the top 50 on playing ability alone, but his most valuable contribution to the Cubs' franchise history is as a gifted leader who brought all the intangibles necessary for winning. Though some are dubious about his Hall of Fame credentials, there is sufficient evidence to make a convincing case for the Peerless Leader.

As far as doing the "little things" that make for the *Compleat Baseball Man*, Cub catcher Jimmy Archer (1909-17) had this to say:

"Chance was great on balls in the dirt. He'd step back to take them waist high or step into them. I never saw a better first baseman on the play. He wasn't fast, but he stole plenty of bases. He knew how to get the jump on the pitcher."

—**Charles B. Cleveland,** *The Great Baseball Managers*

CHANCE: A NOTEWORTHY BOX SCORE

July 21, 1904

It takes McGinnity and Mathewson to subdue Chicago, which got an inside-the-park homer from Chance.

New York	AB	R	H	P	A		Chicago	AB	R	H	P	A
Bresnahan, cf	4	1	1	1	0		Slagle, lf	5	0	1	3	0
Browne, rf	5	0	0	0	1		Casey, 3b	4	0	2	1	2
Devlin, 3b	2	1	0	2	4		Chance, 1b	4	2	3	11	0
McGann, 1b	3	1	1	14	2		McCartney, cf	4	1	1	1	0
Mertes, lf	4	1	2	1	1		Kling, c	4	0	1	3	0
Dahlen, ss	4	0	1	2	5		Evers, 2b	3	0	0	4	4
Gilbert, 2b	4	0	0	2	3		Tinker, ss	4	0	2	2	2
Bowerman, c	3	0	0	3	0		Williams, rf	4	0	2	2	0
McGinnity, p	2	0	0	0	2		Weimer, p	4	0	0	0	3
Mathewson, p	2	0	0	2	1							
TOTALS	33	4	5	27	19		TOTALS	36	3	12	27	11

New York	003	000	001	- - 4
Chicago	000	002	000	- - 3

Doubles: McGann, Dahlen; Home runs: Bresnahan, Chance; Strikeouts: by Weimer, 2; by Mathewson, 1; by McGinnity, 0; Bases on balls: Weimer, 4; Mathewson, 0; McGinnity, 1; Double plays: New York, 2; Chicago, 0; Time: 1:40. Attendance: 11,000. Umpires: O'Day and Emslie.

Other Baseball Highlights of 1904

- New York's Jack Chesbro wins 41 games, but his wild pitch on the last day of the season gives Boston the AL pennant.

- New York Giants manager John McGraw wins his first pennant, then refuses to play the AL champion in the World Series.

- Jim O'Rourke, 54, a former NL catcher from 1872-93, is brought back by the New York Giants to catch one game, their pennant clincher, on September 22. He goes 1 for 4.

Cap Anson—1888

Chicago Cubs Summit Season
Number 47

No. 47
CAP ANSON

BORN: April 11, 1852; Marshalltown, Iowa
DIED: April 14, 1922; Chicago, Illinois

Chicago White Stockings: 1876-1897
Hall of Fame: 1939

SEASON AT THE SUMMIT: 1888

AB-R-H	BA	OB%	EXBH	HR	RBI	BR	FR	SB
515-101-177	.344	.400	44	12	84	41	9	28

Those extraordinary talents who could so significantly affect not only the outcome of a game but *how* the game itself is played have been a part of the lure and lore of professional baseball since its infancy. Known today as impact players, their talent, flair and innovative genius are still capable of commanding respect and admiration, bringing the game to new heights of artistry.

During their glory years, the White Stockings had the good fortune—and distinction—of having had several of these gifted, intrepid ballplayers in their clubhouse. It began right off the bat with Al Spalding in 1876 and continued through the long and distinguished career of **Adrian Constantine "Cap" Anson**, the highly respected captain of the team. There were other Chicagoans: batterymates Michael J. "King" Kelly and John G. Clarkson during the 1880s; Fritz Pfeffer and Jimmy Ryan; and finally Clark Griffith and on to Frank Chance, who would bridge the 19th and 20th Centuries. These players, and others throughout the National League, moved the game along, sometimes in quantum leaps forward, to make it an attraction that captured the imagination and following of a national audience.

Batting Title at Age 36

Most movements have their shakers and movers. Among ballplayers and front office people during baseball's hectic and formative years, Spalding and Anson were in the first rank of that vanguard. In the case of Anson, there's plenty to consider beyond his outstanding 1888 season. But his 1888 was, at the venerable baseball age of 36, his 18th season of professional baseball, one that turned out to be something special. In a year when he claimed the batting championship once again, he was in the midst of a highly productive stretch (1886-1890), during which he played the best ball of his career, and at a time when the Whites needed his very best not only as a player, but as their manager and team leader.

These were years of Chicago descendency. Not rapid or precipitous, but just enough to frustrate the players and their fans; it was a time of change and testing. Into those somewhat shaky and uncertain times, the big fellow brought his best—especially in 1888.

During his lengthy, 27-year Hall-of-Fame career, the Whites' line-drive hitting first sacker hit for a higher average than his league-leading .344 in 1888 on no less than seven occasions, topping out with a .399 in 1881, another batting crown season that was almost as good as his summit season. He's the career franchise leader in hits, doubles, RBIs, and runs, and second in games played, runs and triples.

Aside from the leadership and managerial skills he brought to the team, Anson's contribution in 1888 was surpassed only by Ryan's top-notch effort. Ryan gets the edge over Anson at the No. 42 spot —but not by much. Second baseman Pfeffer also played extremely well, but the threesome needed far more help to pull off another championship than the spotty hitting, sub-par pitching and often shoddy fielding (this, from the stone wall of infield brilliance) provided. There were still other causes for alarm during that troubled season: the growing and virulent threat of a players' revolt; increasing hostility from fans who were fast getting fed up with the tantrums, fights and beer hall indiscretions of professional ballplayers; and, for Windy City fans, the sinking fortunes of their still proud but stumbling heroes.

Managerial Duties Came First

Anson spent most of the first half of the 1888 season preoccupied with getting his pitching staff on target and otherwise trying to get an increasingly errant infield to settle down. And to some extent it worked even though the Giants gave early notice that the race would come down to a Chicago-New York affair, with defending champ Detroit offering troublesome but unconvincing credentials for the top spot. The Whites held on atop the league into July, about the time Anson's bat warmed to the task, enabling him to shake his earlier hitting miseries and surge to within sight of the .300 mark.

Then came a crucial three-game set at Detroit's Recreation Park marred by errors, defensive lapses and lackluster pitching, and with it, three straight embarrassments. The Ansonmen tumbled out of first place and into Pittsburgh for more humiliation, never to regain the lead. Though the Anson bat began booming, and he began throwing serious leather, as we are inclined to describe it these days, the pennant train had been derailed and the New York Express rolled on toward its first National League pennant. It was fueled by the best pitching in the league: right-handers Tim Keefe and Mickey Welch (both HOF'ers), and a lefty, Cannonball Titcomb. You can just imagine what Titcomb's strikeout pitch was.

Anson Begins His Barrage

It was during the late July-through-September span of the season that three-, four- and five-hit games began to boom off the Anson bat, narrowing the race to the batting crown.

In a season dominated by outstanding pitching, the two Chicago stars, Anson and Ryan, were the class of the league, Anson finally winning the crown, .344 to .332. Mike Kelly, now with Boston, was third at .318, followed by Dan Brouthers (.307) and Buck Ewing, the Giants' top hitter (.306), in a league that averaged but .239. In what was clearly a pitcher's year, the feisty old Captain had won it all. Handsomely.

A Showdown at the Polo Grounds

One of 1888's better games was played at the first Polo Grounds field near Coogan's Bluff on August 13 with nearly 10,000 enthusiasts crammed into and around the park. Mark Baldwin handcuffed the first-place New Yorkers through eight innings, giving up but a single hit going into the ninth, outdueling the Giants' Welch. In their last at-bat the Giants rocked Baldwin with a four spot, tying the game at 5-5 and sending it into extra innings. The pitchers dueled through another four frames before darkness called a halt to the tie. The star hitter of the day was Anson, with four sizzling line drives to go with three gems afield, one of which was a catch over his shoulder as he ran into the fans who had spilled onto the field of play.

Two-for-three games and a 5-for-5 day spiced the late-season stretch run when the Chicagoans trounced Detroit's Wolverines, 14-4. In a September Boston series, he led a sweep over Kelly and his Boston teammates (that pleased him) with an eight-hit spree. On September 13, he logged a perfect three-hit day to help his team beat the Giants, once again in New York, by a 5-3 count.

The Captain was a big, sturdy, broad-shouldered 220-pounder who asked no quarter and surely gave none. Straight-arrowed and straightforward, one of baseball's early impact players par excellence, he was the first player ever to reach 3,000 hits and ranked first in the hearts of Chicagoans. The fans raised more than $50,000 for him when he was released, but he turned it down, explaining that the fans and baseball didn't owe him a thing, while he, in turn, was indebted to baseball. Even if he hadn't really merited it, we would have found a way, somehow, to get Cap into the summit 50!

CAP ANSON'S

4 Four Other Great Cub Seasons

	Yr	GP	AB-R-H	BA	OB%	SA	K/BB	HR	RBI	SB	FR	BR
1.	1881	66	309-61-110	.356	.380	.450	8/12	2	59	-	13	16
2.	1890	84	343-67-137	.399	.442	.510	4/26	1	82	-	7	35
3.	1889	125	504-117-187	.371	.433	.544	19/59	10	147	29	8	39
4.	1884	139	504-95-157	.312	.443	.401	23/113	7	107	29	1	33

While shouldering the manager's responsibilities, keeping track of his fun-loving and too-often celebrating charges, and working on the many strategic innovations he brought to the game, Cap Anson still found time to whale the tar out of big-league pitching. Around the house, in the clubhouse, and in secret hiding places the legendary Chicagoan stashed enough lumber to build a home or two, forever picking up boards, unmilled chunks and odd pieces that simply looked to him like potential war clubs. This one was the complete package!

On the subject of putting a winner together, Anson said:
"Round up the strongest men who can knock a baseball the farthest the most often, put yourself at first base—and win!"

—Harvey Frommer, in *Primitive Baseball*

ANSON: A NOTEWORTHY BOX SCORE

August 13, 1888

Anson's 4-for-6 performance at the plate and some sterling plays in the field help Chicago salvage a 5-5 tie against the powerful New York Giants

Chicago	AB	R	H	PO	A		New York	AB	R	H	PO	A
Ryan, cf	5	1	1	2	0		Ward, ss	6	1	0	2	9
Van Haltren, 1f	5	1	3	3	0		Richardson, 2b	5	1	1	5	3
Duffy, rf	6	0	0	5	0		Tiernan, rf	5	1	0	1	0
Anson, 1b	6	1	4	17	0		Connor, 1b	4	0	1	17	0
Pfeffer, 2b	6	1	2	4	3		O'Rourke, 1f	4	1	0	2	1
Williamson, ss	5	0	2	0	4		Ewing, c	4	0	1	7	2
Burns, 3b	6	1	1	0	2		Whitney, 3b	5	0	0	1	8
Daly, c	6	0	0	8	5		Slattery, cf	4	1	1	3	1
Baldwin, p	5	0	1	0	14		Welch, p	4	0	0	1	10
TOTALS	50	5	14	38	28		TOTALS	41	5	4	39	34

Chicago	2 0 0	3 0 0	0 0 0	0 0 0	0	--5
New York	0 0 0	1 0 0	0 0 4	0 0 0	0	--5

Attendance: 9,000   Umpire: Lynch

Game called, darkness

Other Baseball Highlights of 1888

• Tim Keefe wins four World Series games as the Giants win over the St. Louis' Browns.

• Silver King wins 45 games for St. Louis of the American Association.

• The American Association votes to grant gate percentage to visiting teams.

• The Colts set a double-play record with 112 twin-killings.

John Joseph Evers—1912

Chicago Cubs Summit Season
Number 48

No. 48
JOHN EVERS

BORN: July 21, 1881; Troy, New York
DIED: March 26, 1947; Albany, New York

Chicago Colts/Cubs: 1902-1913
Hall of Fame: 1946

SEASON AT THE SUMMIT: 1912

AB-R-H	BA	OB%	2B	3B	HR	RBI	BR	FR	SB
478-73-163	.341	.431	23	11	1	63	29	6	16

There always seems to have been some of those pugnacious little fellows around, usually short-stops or second basemen who were short on power and brute strength and long on guts and brains. **Johnny Evers**, labeled "the Crab," because of the way he sidled up to grounders (it was more than coincidental that the sobriquet suited his persona, as many have re-marked), was one of them. Weighing in at 140 pounds dripping wet, the Troy, New York native, who labored in a collar factory before baseball found him, drove himself and those around him to that next level beyond "merely very good." He wound up, inexorably, in the Hall of Fame, one of its most combative and cantankerous hon-orees. The story of this tortured, oft-injured, much-hated and yet widely respected Cub hero who more than once tottered at the raw edges of a nervous breakdown has been rehearsed again and again, usually emphasizing his brainy, inside-baseball exploits. And, of course, they're as fascinating as they are a treasured and true part of both Cub and baseball lore.

1912

But there is also 1912, the most uncharacteristic season of Evers' odyssey through the ballparks of the National League. It happens to be summit season No. 48 on the Cubs' honors list of single seasons.

For one thing, he hit a boisterous .341, some 60 points above his lifetime seasonal average. For another, he was less a storm center than a unifying and steadying influ-ence on a Chicago franchise that was broiling in conten-tion and inner turmoil. Then too, it would be the last time the frail-looking second sacker would appear in the same lineup with his famed partners, Frank Chance and Joe Tinker—and that but once. Beyond all that, 1912 was another championship year for New York's John McGraw and his brawling minions, always a source of irritation for Evers. And, of course, not winning the pen-nant meant another of those City Series fracases with the hated South Siders at Comiskey Park. More often than not, that meant the loser's share—which he also despised.

Off and Feuding

Chance, still not through feuding with Cub owner Charlie Murphy over almost everything from contracts to signing ballplayers to managing, somehow got his charges down to New Orleans for spring training. Between spring and the year's windup, he would take on the season grind, wind up in the hospital undergoing a blood clot operation, be released as the team's manager and conclude his storied stay with the team he loved. In between he relied more and more on his trusted players, and it was here that John Joseph Evers helped immeasurably in keeping the team on an even keel.

For Openers

The 1912 season opened in Cincinnati where "they'd gone about as fer as they could go," with a new stadium ready for dedication, complete with a sunken garage outside the main entrance for the "gas wagons" of the day, as they were quaintly dubbed by *Tribune* sportswriter I. E. Sanborn. At the same time Fenway Park, which was to be the site of the World Series in its very first year, opened and, on a more foreboding note, the newspapers were covering the progress of the Titanic as she made her way to New York.

By April 13 the Bruins had absorbed a pair of losses to the Reds to open at 0-2. They next headed for St. Louis to meet manager Roger Bresnahan's Cardinals. Another 25,000 Opening Day crowd turned out to see the Cubs go down in 12 innings, and even as reports began to filter in that evening and the next day, April 15, about the sinking of the huge ocean liner that couldn't possibly sink, St. Louisans gathered for the second game of the series. This time, behind Larry Cheney, the Cubs' ace who that season recorded a league-leading 26 wins, the Chicagoans won their first 1912 ballgame 9-2, to bring their record to 1-3. The Crab had a 2 for 4 afternoon and keystone partner Joe Tinker 2 for 3.

A First-Division Season

As the months wore on, spring into summer, it became evident that the club just didn't have enough horsepower offensively, defensively or on the mound to match the Giants and Fred Clarke's Pirates. New York and Pittsburgh

pitching throttled the Cubs, especially Rube Marquard, the 22-year-old sensation who was after his 20th straight victory in a 26-11 season on July 8.

And so the handsome young southpaw tangled with Jimmy Lavender (16-13 that year) at West Side Park with a roped-off, SRO crowd on hand. You could just see the wheels turning under that Evers cap. It was a day meant for "the Trojan." Before it was over he had turned in a perfect 2-for-2 day, including a triple, two sacrifices that put runners in scoring position, and one sweetheart of a play on a line smash. Down went the Giants 7-2 and down went Marquard's winning streak.

It was vintage Cubs—with a seasoned, if not vintage lineup. And it was a vintage Evers day.

Toward the end of August the North Siders moved to within 5½ of the front-running Giants, and into second place with a 6-0 win at Brooklyn behind Cheney, but by season's end the log read 91-59, simply not good enough to get past the World Series-bound Giants. In the 6-0 Brooklyn win Evers had another three hits, including a two-bagger, keeping his batting average up around the .345 mark. Banging the ball hard all summer long, he rang down the curtain with a .341 average, fourth in the league to teammate Heine Zimmerman's league-leading .372. He paced the National League in on base average with a career-high .431. His 11 triples were also a career high.

Salute

For all Evers' troubles, injuries and demons, real or imagined, that bedeviled this proud, overachieving baseball warrior, there is still much more to be said for a truly remarkable career. The Hall of Fame stamp was on it as early as the 1906-10 championship era he helped fashion.

Before another season opened, Chance was gone and the little battler was installed in his place. Now he was the field general in *every* respect. That, too, was predictable.

JOHNNY EVERS'

Three Other Great Cub Seasons

	Yr	GP	AB-R-H	BA	OB%	SA	K/BB	HR	RBI	SB	FR	BR
1.	1904	152	532-49-141	.265	.307	.318	—/28	0	47	26	31	-5
2.	1908	126	416-83-125	.300	.402	.375	—/66	0	66	36	0	23
3.	1913	136	446-81-127	.285	.361	.372	14/50	3	49	11	30	6

In 1904, Johnny Evers led the league in putouts, assists and fielding runs. Note those 31 fielding runs, a telltale sign of superior defensive performance. Thirteen years later he came back with another 30 fielding runs. Swift afoot and sure of hand, he was the ideal pivotman to team with Tinker and Chance. Evers' No. 48 ranking, anchoring the bottom end of the summit season performers with Hall of Fame class, is due largely, of course, to his cerebral play, most consistently evident on defense. Though he couldn't change the course of a game with one swat, he could and did affect its outcome with all those celebrated "little things" that so often mark the difference between victory and defeat. That was his gift, his special forte.

EVERS: A NOTEWORTHY BOX SCORE

September 22, 1908

The "Evers game" was played at the Polo Grounds in New York City.

Among the Top 10 games played in major league history, this clash between the Giants and the Cubs, was a contest of supreme skills, wills, and the ceaseless vigilance of one John Evers. The usual boxscore of a pivotal or special game during an honoree's summit season is waived in order to be able to include this spine-tingler (and its consequences which unfolded in the next weeks). Often and rather insensitively referred to as "the Merkle Boner Game," it necessitated a playoff that matched the great Mathewson with the Cubs' winner, Miner Brown. Here is the box score of the game that reverted to a 1-1 tie, rather than ending in a 2-1 New York victory.

Chicago	R	H	P	A	E		New York	R	H	P	A	E
Hayden, rf	0	0	1	0	0		Herzog, 2b	1	1	1	1	0
Evers, 2b	0	1	4	7	0		Bresnahan, c	0	0	10	0	0
Schulte, lf	0	1	0	0	0		Donlin, rf	0	1	2	0	0
Chance, 1b	0	1	11	1	0		Seymour, cf	0	1	1	0	0
Steinfeldt, 3b	0	0	1	0	1		Devlin, 3b	0	2	0	2	0
Hofman, cf	0	1	0	0	0		McCormick, lf	0	0	1	0	0
Tinker, ss	1	1	8	6	2		Merkle, 1b	0	1	10	1	0
Kling, c	0	1	0	1	0		Bridwell, ss	0	0	2	8	0
Pfiester, p	0	0	1	0	0		Mathewson, p	0	0	0	2	0
TOTALS	1	5	27	15	3		TOTALS	1	6	27	14	0

```
         Chicago     000   100   000  —  1
         New York    000   010   000  —  1
```

Home run: Tinker; Double play: Tinker-Chance (2); Evers-Chance; Mathewson-Bridwell-Merkle; Bases on balls: Pfiester, 2; Hit by pitch: by Pfiester, 1; Strikeouts: Mathewson, 9; Pfiester, 0; Time: 1:30. Umpires: O'Day and Emslie.

Other Baseball Highlights of 1912

• Tris Speaker sets AL record for doubles with 53.

• Red Sox open Fenway Park with an AL championship and a World Series victory: Smoky Joe Wood wins 34, 16 in a row.

• Ty Cobb is suspended for attacking a heckler in the stands on May 15 in New York.

Kenneth Dale Holtzman—1970

Chicago Cubs Summit Season
Number 49

No. 49
KEN HOLTZMAN

BORN: November 3, 1945

Chicago Cubs: 1965-1971; 1978-1979

SEASON AT THE SUMMIT: 1970

W-L-%	IP	CG	SH	SV	K/BB	PR	DEF	ERA
17-11 .607	287.2	15	1	0	202/94	21	0	3.38

Time for a trivia question.

Ken Holtzman wore two uniforms in 1970, the year he won 17 games. One was of the Chicago Cubs. What was the other?

OK, it was a trick question. Holtzman's other uniform in 1970 was that of a member of the Illinois National Guard. The 24-year-old left-hander had his season interrupted several times as he had to report for weekend national guard duty. Still, he turned in what would be his best Cub season ever, particularly over the second half, when he was among the toughest pitchers in the National League.

In the first month of the season, the Cubs were the hottest club in the league. They moved into the NL East lead by beating St. Louis on April 22—it was their seventh victory in a row—and eventually extended their streak to 11 games. The string ended on the 28th when second-

place Pittsburgh—behind two long home runs by Manny Sanguillen—beat Holtzman and the Cubs.

It was Holtzman's second loss in five decisions and snapped a personal three-game winning streak that included an 8-1 four-hit victory over Montreal and a 6-3 five-hitter over the Houston Astros, whom he had held hitless through the first five innings.

He would lose his next start as well—he had surrendered four runs through 5⅔ innings against Atlanta when he was ejected for arguing a ball-and-strike call—but then won his next five decisions.

His victory over Cincinnati on May 8 ended a six-game Cub losing streak and eight-game Reds' winning streak. After a no-decision on May 12—it followed a weekend national guard stint—he didn't allow an earned run in a 3-2 win over St. Louis on the 16th.

Holtzman's next outing was something of a curiosity. The Cubs built a 4-0 lead against New York on May 22, but let the Mets come back to tie. Holtzman was ahead 6-4 with two out in the fifth—one out from qualifying for the win—when manager Leo Durocher replaced him. The Cubs went on to win, and afterward Durocher said that "Unless some things change in the near future, there may be some new guys in the regular pitching rotation."

Six Weeks Without A Loss

Holtzman may have calmed his manager with his next start—a complete-game seven-hitter against the Pirates on the 26th—but returned to shaky ground with three consecutive no-decisions. He righted himself with back-to-back victories over Los Angeles and San Francisco—he had gone six weeks without a loss—but then lost four of his five next starts (the other was a no-decision) to fall to 8-7 with a 4.09 ERA. He ended the slump on July 12 with a complete-game 10-2 victory over Philadelphia, leaving him 9-7 and the Cubs third at 43-42 at the All-Star break.

The second half started with two more Holtzman losses, neither of which he deserved. On July 16, he went seven innings, allowing just two hits, but lost to Houston 2-1. Both Astros runs were unearned and came in a second inning that featured a rare Glenn Beckert error and an Astro-Turf single that scooted past the reliable Don Kessinger at short. As a further Astrodome insult, Billy Williams hit a towering fly down the right-field line in the ninth that hit one of the Dome's speakers and fell in foul territory. A home run in almost any other ballpark, it became just another foul ball. "I'm beginning to think I'm snakebit," Holtzman said.

More Frustration

His next start was even more frustrating. On July 20 in Atlanta, Holtzman went into the bottom of the ninth having retired 10 Braves in a row and with the score tied at 1. Up stepped Hank Aaron, who had been scheduled to have the night off to rest an injured knee but who was pressed into service because regular first baseman Orlando Cepeda had developed a severe headache before the game. Being cautious, Holtzman walked him on four pitches. The next batter was Tommie Aaron, who had replaced Rico Carty earlier after Carty pulled a muscle. Tommie Aaron then homered to give the Braves a 3-1 victory.

But the bad breaks were out of Holtzman's system.

Helped by a 16-hit attack, he beat the Braves 11-1 with a

six-hitter on July 24. Five days later the Cubs spotted him a 6-0 first-inning lead—he needed all the help he could get on a day when he didn't have his best stuff—and he coasted to a 9-2 win over the Astros. He left his next outing in the ninth with the Cubs ahead, but the bullpen let the Reds tie the score and he wasn't the pitcher of record. No matter. Holtzman, with the best curveball of his career and a renewed confidence in his changeup, was just getting cranked up.

On A Roll

On August 6—his last scheduled start before two weeks of national guard duty in Camp McCoy, Wisconsin—he entered the eighth inning against Montreal without having allowed a hit. Holtzman, who had thrown a no-hitter on August 19, 1969, lost this one when John Boccabella singled leading off the eighth. He settled for a three-hit, 4-2 victory.

On August 15, having rejoined the Cubs on a weekend pass, he beat Los Angeles 13-2 to run his record to 13-9.

Then on August 22 came another near-gem. Holtzman allowed only one hit—Hal Lanier's line single to center with one out in the eighth—to beat the Giants 15-0.

His five-game winning streak ended on August 26 against the Dodgers, his first bad outing in more than two months, and he had two losses and a no-decision in his next three starts (in the latter, he allowed just two runs in 8⅔ innings; in one of the losses he fanned the first five Mets only to lose the game on two cheap hits).

The race came down to the last two weeks of the season. On September 15, Holtzman improved to 15-12 with a 5-3 win over the Cardinals that left the Cubs in third place, one game behind the first-place Mets and Pirates. They were a game and a half back after Holtzman, their ace, their stopper, beat Montreal 8-4 on the 19th.

The Cubs were fading, though, despite Holtzman's efforts. He beat the Cardinals 7-1 on a seven-hitter on the 24th—it would be his last win of the season—to keep them within 2½ games of first. But losses the next two days coupled with a Pittsburgh victory on the 27th gave the Pirates the division title.

Holtzman finished 17-12 with a 3.38 ERA. Good, but not mind-bending stats. For the second half of the season, though, he was 8-2 with a 2.72 ERA, as good as any pitcher in either league.

KEN HOLTZMAN'S

Two Other Great Cub Seasons

	Yr	W-L	IP	GS	GC	SH	SV	PD	K/BB	OBA	OB%	ERA	PR
1.	1967	9-0	92.2	12	3	3	0	0	62/44	.222	.314	2.53	9
2.	1969	17-13	261.1	39	12	6	0	-1	176/93	.247	.314	3.58	0

Master of the strike zone, Kenny Holtzman finessed his way through a very respectable major-league career that started and ended with the Cubs, though there were a few stops here and there along the way. His summit season is surrounded by years in which he tossed no-hitters against the Braves (1969) and Reds (1971). His '67 season, interrupted by service time, was a spotless effort, promising more than could rightfully be expected. Holtzman's 1970 season for the second-place Cubs (Eastern Division), with a 3.4 TPI, is a strong enough rating in the mix of "summit credentials" to earn a spot on our honors list just ahead of Mark Grace at No. 50. Many a fine pitching career was crafted on concentration and know-how. Kenny's was, to be sure.

"Ken doesn't get enough credit for being a competitor. When he gets the ball and goes to the mound, he goes to beat you. You are going to get 100 percent from him every time."

—Cub catcher Randy Hundley in 1970

Other Baseball Highlights of 1970

- On April 22, Tom Seaver sets a major-league record by fanning 10 Padres in a row.

- The Seattle Pilots move to Milwaukee, where they become the Brewers.

- Hank Aaron gets his 3,000th hit.

- The Angels' Tom Egan sets a modern major-league record by being hit by pitches 50 times.

HOLTZMAN: A NOTEWORTHY BOX SCORE

August 22, 1970 at Cincinnati

The only thing between Holtzman and his second career no-hitter is Hal Lanier's eighth-inning single.

Chicago	AB	R	H	RBI	E	Cincinnati	AB	R	H	RBI	E
Kessinger, ss	4	2	2	0	0	Bonds, cf	4	0	0	0	0
Popovich, ss	0	1	0	0	0	Fuentes, 2b	4	0	0	0	0
Beckert, 2b	5	3	2	1	0	Henderson, rf	4	0	0	0	0
Williams, lf	3	3	2	2	0	McCovey, 1b	2	0	0	0	1
James, lf	1	0	0	0	0	Hart, lf	1	0	0	0	0
Hickman, 1b	4	1	2	3	0	Dietz, c	1	0	0	0	0
Banks, 1b	1	0	1	1	0	Gibson, c	1	0	0	0	0
Pepitone, cf	5	3	2	2	0	F. Johnson, lf-1b	3	0	0	0	0
Santo, 3b	3	0	2	2	0	Gallagher, 3b	2	0	0	0	0
Gagliano, 3b	2	1	1	0	1	Lanier, ss	3	0	1	0	0
Callison, rf	4	0	1	2	0	Perry, p	0	0	0	0	0
Spangler, rf	0	0	0	0	0	Carrithers, p	1	0	0	0	0
Hundley, c	5	0	2	1	0	Bryant, p	1	0	0	0	0
Holtzman, p	5	1	1	0	0	Robertson, p	0	0	0	0	0
						Hunt, ph	1	0	0	0	0
TOTALS	42	15	18	14	1	Davison, p	0	0	0	0	0
						TOTALS	28	0	1	0	1

```
Chicago          3 6 0   2 2 0   1 1 0  — 15
San Francisco    0 0 0   0 0 0   0 0 0  — 0
```

Doubles—Pepitone, Santo, Williams, Hickman. Triples—Kessinger, Santo. Home runs—Pepitone, Williams. Sacrifice fly—Banks. Double plays—Chicago 1, San Francisco 1. Left on base—Chicago 9, San Francisco 4.

	IP	H	R	ER	BB	SO
Holtzman (W, 14-9)	9	1	0	0	3	7
Perry (L, 17-12)	1 1/3	7	8	7	1	1
Carrrithers	2	4	3	3	2	1
Bryant	3	4	3	3	3	2
Robertson	1 2/3	2	1	1	2	0
Davison	1	1	0	0	0	0

Wild pitch—Perry. Attendance—11,046. Umpires—Weyer, Olsen, Burkhardt, and Pryor. Time—2:50.

GRACE
17

Mark Eugene Grace—1989

Chicago Cubs Summit Season
Number 50

No. 50
MARK GRACE

BORN: June 28, 1964; Winston-Salem, North Carolina

Chicago Cubs: 1988-

SEASON AT THE SUMMIT: 1989

AB-R-H	BA	OB%	2B	3B	HR	RBI	BR	FR	SB
510-74-160	.314	.407	28	3	13	79	27	13	14

Mark Grace stood in the Cubs dressing room, surrounded, as usual, by an army of reporters, minicams and microphones. It was July 30, 1989, and the Cubs had just staged another of their patented late rallies to beat New York 6-4. This day, Grace was the hero, hitting a two-out homer in the bottom of the ninth off Mets relief ace Randy Myers.

"There's nothing tricky to it," Grace told the media's inquiring minds. "This team just believes in itself. This team will never quit."

The 1989 Cubs were heart-stoppers. Ultimately, they were heartbreakers. But the trip to the NL East title and the League Championship Series was a roller-coaster ride of twists, turns and thrills that no one who witnessed it would soon forget.

The Cubs came out of spring training with a 9-23 record and no shortage of optimism. A better pitching staff was one reason. Rookie prospect Jerome Walton was another. There was a core of proven veterans—Andre Dawson,

Ryne Sandberg, Rick Sutcliffe, Greg Maddux, Vance Law, Shawon Dunston. And then there was Mark Grace.

Grace had debuted with the Cubs the previous May, getting two hits in his first game, and going on to hit .296 with seven homers and 57 RBIs for the fourth-place, 77-85 Cubs. He finished second to Cincinnati's Chris Sabo in the NL Rookie of the Year voting, and was selected the top rookie by *The Sporting News*.

A Hero A Day
Cub fans got a taste of what they were in for within the first week of the season. In the April 4 opener, the Cubs beat Philadelphia 5-4. The highlight: Sutcliffe's steal of home. The Oh-My-God thrill: reliever Mitch ("I'm pitching like my hair's on fire") Williams loading the bases in the ninth on three singles then striking out the side.

Two days later against Pittsburgh it was Grace's turn to be a hero. With the score tied at 5 and Dawson on second in the bottom of the sixth, Grace lined a double to the wall in left-center to send home what proved to be the winning run. It was Grace's second hit—he started a four-run second with a single—to go with two walks.

The Cubs spent much of April in first place and were in third at 8-4 when it ended. By the end of May they were in first.

Grace started the month on the right foot, driving in three runs in a 4-3 victory May 1 in San Francisco. Injuries and a five-game losing streak during which they hit a paltry .161 dumped the Cubs into fourth place midway through May. But manager Don Zimmer's ballclub snapped out of its lethargy behind various guest heroes like Jeff Pico, who stopped Atlanta on four hits through seven innings on May 15; Lloyd McClendon, who was called up because of injuries and who hit a three-run homer in his first at-bat to beat the Braves; and Calvin Schiraldi, who got consecutive saves on the 22nd and 23rd as the Cubs moved back into first.

One constant was Grace, whose consistency is evident in his month-by-month averages. At the end of April he was hitting .321. At the end of May he was at .318. On July 1 he was at .316. A good July lifted him to .326, and he finished September at .315 and the season at .314.

His Old Pal, Frank DiPino

Grace spent much of June nursing a sore shoulder, an injury he suffered in a June 4 brawl with St. Louis. The Cubs had hit three homers in the fifth inning to take a 6-3 lead. The Cardinals brought in reliever Frank DiPino. The first batter he faced was Grace, who wasn't exactly DiPino's pal when they were Cub teammates the year before. After DiPino's first pitch was waist-high and tight, Grace tossed his bat aside and charged the mound. In the ensuing roughhousing, Grace suffered a shoulder separation that kept him sidelined for 18 days.

July began with the Cubs third, 2½ games behind first-place Montreal. It would be the month that would define this team, and Grace's biggest month as well.

On the 5th, he went 4 for 4—a three-run homer, three doubles and three RBIs—as the Cubs rallied to beat San Diego. The big night at Wrigley Field gave him a .405 average (15 for 37) over his last 11 games. He would have other big days—a couple of hits against Los Angeles on the 8th, a three-run homer to spark a 6-3 victory over the Dodgers on the 17th, a 7-for-16 series against the Giants to raise his average to .341, and, saving the best for last, that two-run homer on July 30 that beat New York 6-4, completing a three-game sweep of the Mets.

Late-inning heroics became a staple of this team. On July 20 the Cubs trailed the Giants 3-0 with two out in the ninth and rallied to win in the 11th; on the 28th they were behind 5-2 to the Mets in the seventh before winning; on August 5 in Pittsburgh, they trailed 2-1 in the ninth and came back to win; on the 17th in Cincinnati they trailed 2-1 with two out in the ninth before rallying to win; on August 25 they were down 3-2 with two out in the eighth but came back to beat Atlanta; two days later they rallied from a 2-1 deficit with two out in the ninth to beat the Braves.

A Fun-Filled August, September

The Cubs began August two games behind the first-place Expos. They moved within a game on August 4 by beating Pittsburgh 3-2—Grace contributing his eighth homer of the year and third in the last seven games. A victory the next day gave them a short-lived share of first, but they were in second when Montreal came to Chicago for a three-game series starting August 7. The Cubs wound up sweeping the series, capped by Grace's game-winning homer in the seventh inning of the third contest, to take over first for good. Their lead would shrink to as little as a half-game in early September, but they were able to hold on, finally clinching the NL East title on September 26 with a 3-2 victory in Montreal.

The Cubs' wild ride came to a sudden halt in the NLCS, thanks to the Giants and Will Clark. He had six runs batted in in the opener, an 11-3 San Francisco romp. The Cubs came back to win Game 2, 9-5 (Grace going 3 for 4 with four runs batted in). But the Giants swept the next three games, taking the best-of-seven series in five games. Clark was the hitting hero for San Francisco, batting .650 (13 for 20) with two homers and eight RBIs. Grace nearly matched him, batting .647 (11 for 17, eight RBIs), but it wasn't enough.

For the regular season, Grace's .314 batting average was fourth in the league, as was his .407 on-base percentage. He had a .996 fielding percentage, and a TPR of 3.3, slightly better than his 1996 mark.

"It was a crummy ending to a wonderful season," Grace said the day of the playoff elimination. "I had a blast. This is the most fun I've ever had. I'm going to cherish this."

MARK GRACE'S

Three Other Great Cub Seasons

	Yr	GP	AB-R-H	BA	OB%	SA	K/BB	HR	RBI	SB	FR	BR
1.	1990	157	589-72-182	.309	.377	.413	54/59	9	82	15	1	9
2.	1992	158	603-72-185	.307	.384	.430	36/72	9	79	6	9	23
3.	1996	142	547-88-181	.331	.396	.455	41/62	9	75	2	7	31

Frank Thomas, the other first baseman in town, could have been getting all the publicity. But there is another hard-hitting first sacker in the Windy City named Mark Grace—no dunce when it comes to playing the game. *The Sporting News'* choice for the Rookie of the Year in 1989, he worked hard to improve his game and gradually snuck up on the league to assume defensive leadership and a line-drive, timely hitting role in the Cub scheme—and a 3.0 TPR, the best hitting and fielding combination the Cubs have had at first since the days of Bill Buckner.

"Nobody believed in us. We're making believers of them."
—Mark Grace after another come-from-behind victory for the Cubs.

GRACE: A NOTEWORTHY BOX SCORE

July 30, 1989

Grace's two-out, two-run homer in the ninth completes a three-game sweep of the Mets.

New York	AB	R	H	RBI	Chicago	AB	R	H	RBI
Samuel, cf	4	0	1	0	Walton, cf	5	2	3	0
Magadan, lb	4	0	0	0	Sanberg, 2b	5	1	1	0
H. Johnson, 3b	3	0	0	0	Grace, 1b	3	1	2	2
Strawberry, rf	3	1	0	0	Dawson, rf	2	0	0	1
McReynolds, lf	4	1	1	0	McClendon, lf	2	0	0	1
Jefferies, 2b	4	0	0	1	Smith, lf	1	0	0	0
Myers, p	0	0	0	0	Berryhill, c	4	0	1	0
Carter, c	3	1	1	0	Law, 3b	4	0	0	0
Elster, ss	2	1	1	1	Dunston, ss	3	2	1	1
Ojeda, p	2	0	0	0	Bielecki, p	2	0	0	0
Hernandez, ph	1	0	1	2	Williams, p	0	0	0	0
Darling, pr	0	0	0	0	Lancaster, p	1	0	0	0
Aguilera, p	0	0	0	0					
Teufel, 2c	0	0	0	0	TOTALS	32	6	8	5
TOTALS	30	4	5	4					

Chicago	0 0 0	0 2 0	2 0 0	— 4				
Cincinnati	1 0 1	1 0 1	0 0 2	— 6				

Two outs when winning run scored.

Errors--Carter, Elster, McReynolds. Left on base--New York 3, Chicago 7. Doubles--McReynolds, Elster. Home runs--Dunston, Grace. Stolen base--Walton. Sacrifices--Grace, Bielecki. Sacrifice fly--Dunston, Elster.

New York	IP	H	R	ER	BB	SO	Chicago	IP	H	R	ER	BB	SO
Ojeda	6	6	4	2	4	2	Bielecki	6²/₃	4	4	4	3	2
Aguilera (L, 6-6)	2²/₃	1	1	1	0	4	Williams	0	1	0	0	0	0
Meyers	0	1	1	1	0	0	Lancaster (W, 3-0)	2¹/₃	0	0	0	0	1

Williams faced one batter in the seventh; Myers faced one batter in the ninth.
Wild pitches--Wiliams, Augilera. Attendance--36,837. Umpires--West, Crawford, Williams, McSherry. Time--2:34.

Other Baseball Highlights of 1989

•The completion of the A's-Giants World Series is delayed 10 days by a Bay Area earthquake.

•Pete Rose is banned from baseball for his gambling activities.

•Commissioner Bart Giamatti dies of a heart attack.

•Wade Boggs has his seventh consecutive 200-hit season.

10 NOTEWORTHY SEASONS

Extraordinary individual seasons such as those cited in our Cubs Top 50 are rare exceptions, especially when the year-after-year grind of so many seasons by so many players is taken into consideration. That's bound to make for serious contention among the Top 50, as we have seen. Further, there are a number of noteworthy seasons that pressed hard for inclusion on the honors list. From among these "also-but-not-quite contenders" we've chosen 10. These players are presented in chronological order with a statistic line and a thumbnail sketch to help identify their best Cub years. The likes of "Kiki" Cuyler, Riggs Stephenson and Augie Galan will be found among these noteworthies, and the great seasons they fashioned challenged seriously for summit 50 honors. Here's our "Top 10:"

John "Jocko" Flynn (RHP)

Born: 6/30/1864 - Died: 12/3/1907; White Stockings: 1886-1887

1886: 23-6, .793; 29 GS; 28 GC; 146/63 K/BB; 31 PR; 2 DEF; 2.24 ERA

"Jocko" Flynn was one of the reasons the White Stockings won their fifth pennant in seven years during the '80s. Cap Anson didn't use him during the World Series with Charlie Comiskey's St. Louis Browns because, as usual, he was several sheets to the wind the night before he was supposed to take his turn. In fact, this meteor, who shot through Chicago skies with one burst of glory, was never heard from again after 1886, a victim of disillusion and excessive drinking.

Carl Leonard Lundgren (RHP)

Born: 2/16/1880 - Died: 8/21/1934; Colts/Cubs: 1902-1909

1907: 18-7, .720; 21 GC; 7 SH; 84/92 K/BB; 30 PR; 0 DEF; 1.17 ERA

Another in the peerless Cub pitching stable of the early 1900s, Carl Lundgren enjoyed the best season of his career in 1907, logging the ninth lowest ERA in the game's history. Like "Jocko" Flynn, he didn't get to appear in a World Series. Unlike Flynn, it wasn't because he was sloshed. There were simply too many other frontliners to go around in a 4-zip thrashing of the Tigers in 1907. That season he also recorded the lowest opponents' batting average (.185) in the bigs. In his later years he coached the University of Michigan baseball team.

Arthur "Circus Solly" Hofman (OF)

Born: 10/29/1882 - Died: 3/10/1956; Colts/Cubs: 1905-1912; 1916

1910: 477-83-155, .325 BA; .406 OB%; 43 EXBH; 86 RBI; 29 SB; 33 BR; 5 FR

Circus catches in the outfield by the Cubs' slick center-fielder earned him the nickname "Circus Solly." Hofman put it all together in the Cubs' last pennant-winning season (1910) of the 20th Century's first decade. He hit at a .325 clip in 1910 and was right around the .300 mark in three World Series. Invaluable as a handyman, he played where he was needed and was capable of a key hit or a stolen base to keep things moving. Under iron-fisted Frank Chance, he once waited until the season was over before getting married when his mid-September request was turned down.

Samuel James "Jimmy" Sheckard (OF)

Born: 11/23/1878 - Died: 1/15/1947; Cubs: 1906-1912

1911: 539-121-149, .276 BA; .434 OB%; 41 EXBH; 147/58 BB/K; 32 SB; 15 FR

Jimmy Sheckard set a National League record for walks with 147 in 1911 and racked up a league-high on-base percentage with .434 in what turned out to be his last great season. That season he stole 32 bases (his career total was 465), leading the league with 121 runs scored. Swift and sure-handed, he was one of Chicago's better acquisitions, brought from Brooklyn, where he was a fan favorite. He was born, raised and died in Pennsylvania Dutch country.

Oscar Ray Grimes Sr. (1B)

Born: 9/11/1893 - Died: 5/25/1953; Cubs: 1921-1924

1922: 509-99-180, .354; .572 SA; 81 EXBH; 99 RBI; 75/33 BB/K; 45 BR

In an injury-shortened career, Ray Grimes proved one thing: He could hit. Socking the ball at a .354 clip in 1922, the compact first sacker also led his teammates in runs and RBIs. During his best season he drove in at least one run in 17 straight games, a still-standing major-league record. With an on-base percentage of .422 and his career-best slugging average of .572, Grimes was one of the reasons the Cubs finished as high as they did (fifth) in an otherwise lackluster season.

Jackson Riggs "Old Hoss" Stephenson (OF)

Born: 1/5/1898 - Died: 11/15/1985; Cubs: 1926-1934

1927: 579-101-199, .344; .415 OB%; 46 2B; 65/28 BB/K; 8 SB; 36 BR

Old Hoss would have cracked the Top 50 list of single-season honorees had he been a better glove man with a stronger arm. His contact hitting, and plenty of it, kept him in the outfield, piling up enough hits to rank as the Cubs' all-time career leader with a snappy .337 average. In 1927 he cracked a league-leading 46 doubles and missed the 200-hit level by a single bingle. He's probably best remembered as a part of the only outfield in major-league history in which all three outfielders (Hack Wilson and Kiki Cuyler were the other two) drove in more than 100 runs each in one season.

Hazen Shirley "Kiki" Cuyler (OF)

Born: 8/30/1899 - Died: 2/11/1950; Cubs: 1928-1935

1930: 642-155-228, .355; .428 OB%; .547 SA; 80 EXBH; 37 SB; 36 BR; 12 FR

Michigan-born Kiki Cuyler had himself quite a 1930, leading the NL in stolen bases (37) for a fourth time in five seasons, and helping the Wrigleyville cause along considerably with a boisterous .355 batting average, fashioned on the strength of a career-high 228 base hits, one fewer than the Cub standard set by Rogers Hornsby in 1929. With 50 doubles and 134 RBIs it took Hack Wilson's orbital 1930 season to outdo him. He's the only Hall of Famer on our "Noteworthy" list, elected by the Veterans Committee in 1968.

August John "Augie" Galan (OF)

Born: 5-25-1912 - Died: 12-28-1993; Cubs: 1934-1941

1935: 646-133-203, .314; .399 OB%; 22 SB; 53/87 K/BB; 31 BR; 7 FR

Leading the NL in stolen bases and runs scored in his sophomore season, Augie Galan set a record by *not* hitting into a double play in 646 at-bats. Ironically, he *did* hit into a triple play that same season! No matter. The speedster, always a hustling, popular favorite at the Friendly Confines, was a switch hitter who became the major leagues' first player to hit one out from both sides of the plate (1937). Often injured because of his all-out style, Galan was a prime figure in the Cubs' 1935 NL pennant year.

Henry Washington "Hooks" Wyse (RHP)

Born: 3-1-1918;   Cubs: 1942-1947

1945: 22-10, .688; 34 GS; 23 GC; 2 SH; 55/77 BB/K; 35 PR; 2 DEF; 2.68 ERA

Tough-minded, stocky Hank Wyse never had a better year than the one he put together for the Cubs' last pennant winner. A 4-F'er during World War II, he often wore a special supportive corset to stabilize his spinal column. It must have helped a great deal in '45 when he zapped 22 foes and lost but 10 times. That year he completed 23 games and rang up a super 2.68 ERA. The sinker-balling power pitcher, who enhanced his 1945 masterpiece with a near-no-hitter against the Pirates, was the go-to pitcher on Charlie Grimm's pitching staff.

Milton Stephen "Gimpy" Pappas (RHP)

Born: 5-11-1939; Cubs: 1970-1973

1972: 17-7, .708; 28 GS; 10 GC; 3 SH; 80/29 K/BB; 15 PR; -2 DEF; 2.77 ERA

They called him "Gimpy" and he checked into Wrigleyville the early part of 1970 after barnstorming around both leagues the better part of 15 years. And then, after all that time, came his career topper, a 1972 beauty that featured 17 W's and a fine 2.77 ERA for the NL Eastern Division's second-place Cubbies. That season Pappas and his hard slider led the league with only 1.34 walks per game. During his short, four-year Chicago career, after which he retired, Pappas found time to add a pair of no-hitters to his career win total of 209—and, oh yes, that super 1972 season.

During the past quarter-century, the Cubs have kept in dogged pursuit of the National League's pennant laurels, alas, unsuccessfully. Not since 1946, in commemoration of the 1945 pennant year, has the No. 1 banner rippled in the Wrigleyville breeze. Nonetheless, there have been a number of fine seasons turned in by more recent Cub players whose names have not appeared on our list of summit seasons.

You may have wondered about that, taking issue here or there with the honorees selected, while puzzling over the omission of an Andre Dawson or a Dave Kingman. Those were tough calls to make, as were the placements of Augie Galan and Kiki Cuyler. These players all contributed seasons that were just a cut below those listed in the "Not the Least of These," final 10 players.

For those of you who've been looking for Hawk or Big Dave, here is our Modern Era Cubs List, once again arranged chronologically.

Bill Madlock (3B)

Born: 1-2-1951; Cubs: 1974-1976

1975: 514-77-182, .354 BA; .406 OB%; 64 RBI; 34/42 K/BB; 27 BR; -11 FR

Bill Madlock made contact during his Cub years, winning two batting crowns by spraying line drives around the outfields of the National League. After his Chicago stint he repeated in Pittsburgh with another pair of batting championships, the only player in major-league history to accomplish such a feat. His 1975 season would have been a summit season qualifier had his defensive work, always a bit of a liability, been up to or above par.

Ivan DeJesus (SS)

Born: 1-9-1953; Cubs: 1977-1981

1977: 624-91-166, .266 BA; .330 OB%; 31 2BH; 90/56 K/BB; 24 SB; 36 FR

Ivan DeJesus' Chicago career was marked by two outstanding seasons, his first, in 1977, and the following season. Of the two, 1977 is a short stretch better, a season during which he fashioned an outstanding total of 36 fielding runs. It was the kind of season that attracted Gold Glove attention, though the honors at shortstop that year were given the Reds' Davey Concepcion, another of those super Latino midfielders. DeJesus had the thankless job of filling popular Don Kessinger's shoes, but soon settled in for a five-year stay at Wrigley before being involved in the trade that brought Ryne Sandberg to the Friendly Confines.

David Arthur "Kong" Kingman (OF)

Born: 12-21-1948; Cubs: 1978-1980

1979: 523-97-153, .288 BA; .613 SA; 48 HR; 115 RBI; 131/45 K/BB; 28 BR

The best of "Kong's" 16 major-league seasons was spent in a Cubs uniform in 1979, when he bashed baseballs all over Wrigley Field—and out of it. That summer he tied the record for home runs on the road with 23 and clubbed 48 in all, the third highest single-season home run total in franchise history. Twice he crunched three of those long-distance shots in one game, mostly of the up-up-up-up and away variety. That's the good news. The bad? He also had a 5-for-5 game—5 K's that is. A total of 131 whiffs came along with the Kingman package that summer, as well. But when he did hit 'em, it was a sight to behold. And that happened often enough to liven things up a little on the North Side where, in 1979, it was badly needed!

William Joseph "Billy Buck" Buckner (1B)

Born: 12-14-1949; Cubs: 1977-1984

1982: 657-93-201, .306 BA; 54 EXBH; 105 RBI; 26/36 K/BB; 13 BR; 16 FR

In 1982 Bill Buckner drove home more than 100 runs for the first time in his career (22 years, no less). A real trouper and an accomplished first baseman-outfielder, he was a smart, consistent hitter who led the NL in 1980 with a nifty .324 mark. The combination of run producing and outstanding glove work makes 1982, rather than 1980, his best Cub season. Buckner came to the Windy City from the Dodgers with Ivan DeJesus and spent eight summers before moving on to a number of American League ports of call.

Leon "Bull" Durham (OF, 1B)

Born: 7-31-1957; Cubs: 1981-1988

1982: 539-84-168, .312 BA; .521 SA; 62 EXBH; 90 RBI; 77/66 K/BB; 35 BR

Despite fine seasons by both "Bull" Durham and Bill Buckner, the Cubs went south in '82, finally nestling near the bottom at season's end. That didn't prevent Durham from turning in career highs in batting average, on-base percentage (.389), doubles (33) and stolen bases (28). Three fielding runs prevented more serious consideration for Top 50 summit honors. The big outfielder (he moved to first base in 1984) was in the hunt for batting honors in his best NL season, winding up third behind Al Oliver and Bill Madlock, then with Pittsburgh. Troubled with drug problems, his career, unfortunately, was a level or two below its great potential.

Richard Lee "Rick" - "The Red Baron" Sutcliffe (RHP)

Born: 6-21-1956; Cubs: 1984-1991

1984: 16-1, .941; 20 GS; 7 GC; 155/39 K/BB; .220 OBA; 15 PR; 2.69 ERA

The Cubs set an attendance record in 1984, drawing 2,108,055 to tiny Wrigley Field. One of the reasons was "the Red Baron," a throwback to the older Cub glory days. He was a battler who threw every inch of his 6-foot-7-inch frame into every pitch and every out. And between June 14 and the end of his best season in the bigs he ran up 14 straight wins enroute to a 16-1 whopper. His .941 winning percentage ranks as No. 1 in the franchise's history, and that season brought a Cy Young Award. While it was tough to keep such an effort outside the limits of the Top 50 seasons in Cub history, big Rick's 1984 was, like so many others in these "10 Noteworthy" and "10 Modern Era" lists, an outstanding effort that missed the Top 50 by the thinnest of Total Player Rating margins.

Andre Fernando "Hawk" Dawson (OF)

Born: 7-10-1954; Cubs: 1987-1992

1987: 621-90-178, .287 BA; .568 SA; 137 RBI; 103/32 K/BB; 21 BR; 6 FR

"Hawk" was the NL's MVP for 1987 with league-leading totals in homers (his 49 ranks second to Hack Wilson's Cub topper) and RBIs (137). He was voted the Player of the Month in August, a month he started off with a three-homer salute. More? He hit for the cycle against the Giants on April 29, fielded superbly all summer and wound up with a Gold Glove Award. Those are extreme big-league credentials. They weren't, however, his best numbers in an exceptional career. Those came in Montreal where, between 1980 and '83, he was one of the top five in the NL. That aside, Dawson's '87, '88 and '90 seasons, on a par with one another, were bright spots during otherwise gloomy years on the North Side. He'll be remembered as a professional's pro and the first player to win an MVP title with a last-place ballclub.

Michael Thomas "Mike" Morgan (RHP)

Born: 10-8-1959; Cubs: 1992-1995

1992: 16-8, .667; 34 GS; 123/79 K/BB; .234 OBA; 240 IP; 25 PR; 2 DEF

Near the end of the 1992 season, Mike Morgan threw a 2-0, two-hitter that extended his win record to 15. Another shortly thereafter hiked his total to 16, a career high. That came in his 11th big-league season in a career that kept the bus moving from one team to another in both leagues. And sure enough, Greg Maddux chose that same year to put together his Cy Young numbers. You may also remember 1992 as the year Mike Harkey was finally ready after rehab, then starting out at 4-0, only to reinjure his shoulder doing cartwheels. This and other sad stories of injuries to key players, Sammy Sosa and Shawon Dunston among them, tended to keep Morgan's steady, craftsmanlike season the Cubs' best-kept secret in '92. Make no mistake, Morgan's 16-8 record that season is a worthy entry on our "10 Modern Era Cubs" listing.

Richard D. "Rick" Wilkins (C)

Born: 6-4-1967; Cubs: 1991-1995

1993: 446-78-135, .303 BA; .561 SA; 30 HR; 73 RBI; 30 BR; 2 SB; 7 FR

When Rick Wilkins hit his 30th homer in 1993, it was the first time in more than 20 years that two Cubs had hit that many in a single season. It was, further, the first time a Cub catcher had hit as many as 30 since 1930 when Gabby Hartnett did it. On June 9 he slammed two of his 30 against the Mets to lead the Cubs past the New Yorkers 8-3, and on August 30 he was still at it with a two-out, 11th-inning grand slam that beat the Phils. Hitting wasn't the only reason his '93 was a very good year: His handling of a so-so, 50-50 pitching staff was first rank, and he fielded his position as well as any catcher in the league. He's another of those Cubbie best-kept secrets!

Samuel Peralta "Sammy" Sosa (OF)

Born: 11-10-1968; Cubs: 1992-

1995: 144 GP; 564-89-151, .268 BA; .500 SA; 36 HR; 119 RBI; 34 SB; 21 BR

The punch in Sammy Sosa's stick finally began to manifest itself in 1993 and '94, and in 1995 it paid handsome dividends in an injury-free, 36-homer and 119-RBI season. Patience in the front office, long hours of practice, and Sosa's natural talents had come together to make the Cub investment in his potential a reality. Though he was still whiffing too much, something that caused the White Sox no end of grief when Sosa was with the South Siders, the Cubs stayed the course with the swift and lean slugger. The 1993 campaign was his first 30-30 season, and in '95 he repeated with 36 homers to go with his 34 thefts. Though his 1996 season was, again, curtailed by injury, he managed another 100-RBI season and established himself as a force to be reckoned with in the Bruins' lineup.

APPENDIX A

PITCHING RUNS AND PITCHER DEFENSE

Two sabermetric measures of pitching skill are pitching runs and pitcher defense. These rating categories are explained once again below. Here is the list of the top 20 in pitching runs and pitcher defense:

PITCHING RUNS			PITCHER DEFENSE		
Rank	**Name**	**No/Yr**	**Rank**	**Name**	**No/Yr**
1)	John Clarkson	67, 1885	1)	John Clarkson	9, 1887
2)	Clark Griffith	63, 1898	2)	Greg Maddux	8, 1990
3)	Bill Hutchison	58, 1890	3)	Larry Jackson	7, 1964
4)	Jack Taylor	52, 1902	4)	Larry Corcoran	6, 1880
5)	Ed Reulbach	51, 1905		Clark Griffith	6, 1899
6)	Pete Alexander	50, 1920	5)	Nixey Callahan	5, 1899
7)	Mordecai Brown	49, 1906		Fred Goldsmith	5, 1881
8)	Lon Warneke	46, 1932		Bill Hutchison	5, 1888
9)	Claude Passeau	42, 1940		Rick Reuschel	5, 1974
10)	John Blake	41, 1928		Johnny Schmitz	5, 1948
11)	Greg Maddux	39, 1992	6)	Ted Abernathy	4, 1965
12)	Larry Corcoran	38, 1882		Pete Alexander	4, 1923
	Dick Ellsworth	38, 1963		Mordecai Brown	4, 1907
13)	Bill Hands	37, 1969		Guy Bush	4, 1925
	Bill Lee	37, 1938		Virgil Garvin	4, 1900
	Orrie Overall	37, 1909		Glen Hobbie	4, 1958
14)	Nixie Callahan	35, 1898		Ed Reulbach	4, 1909
	Virgil Garvin	35, 1900		Al Spalding	4, 1876
	Johnny Schmitz	35, 1948		Rick Sutcliffe	4, 1987
	Hank Wyse	35, 1945		Jack Taylor	4, 1909
15)	Pat Malone	34, 1929	7)	John Blake	3, 1927
16)	Leonard Cole	33, 1910		Ray Burris	3, 1977
	Al Spalding	33, 1876		Dick Ellsworth	3, 1961
17)	Guy Bush	32, 1929		Willie Hernandez	3, 1977
18)	John Flynn	31, 1886		Burt Hooten	3, 1974
	Jack Pfiester	31, 1906		Fergie Jenkins	3, 1972
	Rick Reuschel	31, 1977		Claude Passeau	3, 1945
	Lew Richie	31, 1911		Jack Pfiester	3, 1909
	Bruce Sutter	31, 1977		Bob Rush	3, 1954
19)	Carl Lundgren	30, 1907		Hippo Vaughn	3, 1917
	Jake Weimer	30, 1903		Rube Waddell	3, 1901
20)	Larry French	29, 1935		Lon Warneke	3, 1933
	Bob Rush	29, 1952		Jake Weimer	3, 1904
				Hank Wyse	3, 1943

Pitching Runs

This sabermetric category is a linear weights measure of runs saved beyond what league-average pitchers might *save* their teams during the course of a season's play (league average = 0). The formula for computing pitching runs is:

Innings pitched in a season times (the league average ERA divided by 9) minus earned runs allowed during the season. Here's an example taken from the strike-shortened season of 1994: (The pitcher is Jim Bullinger of the 1994 Cub pitching staff.)

In 1994, Jim pitched 100 innings and gave up 40 earned runs. The league average ERA was 4.68. 100 times (4.21/9, which equals 0.468), or 46.8, minus 40, or 6.8, rounded out to 7. Thus, in 1994 Jim Bullinger registered 7 pitching runs. That's, of course, considerably below the numbers listed in our top 20.

Now, what is the significance of that linear measure? Pitching runs translate, finally, to additional (or fewer) wins contributed by a pitcher to his team's season total. In Bullinger's case, the 7 PRs amounts to fewer than one win during 1994's strike-shortened season. Consequently, the final season record is neither enhanced nor harmed by his performance. However, in 1994 Greg Maddux logged a superb 60 PRs, which meant an additional six in the Braves' win column. (The math, as you have figured by now, is roughly 10 to 1 PRs to wins.) Meaning: Without Maddux's contribution to the Atlanta cause, the record would have been 62-52, rather than 68-46.

Consequently, our list leaders, John Clarkson and Clark Griffith, whose PRs rank in the top 100 all time, present a formidable challenge for Cub pitchers. Their PRs are indicative of the enormous contributions their pitching meant to the 1885 and 1898 Chicago teams.

For the curious: Hall of Famer Amos Rusie, the New York Giants' ace, registered the highest single-season PR figure in baseball's history: 126 in 1894. Charles Radbourn, 121 in 1884, and Guy Hecker, 108, also in 1884, are in the Nos. 2 and 3 spots, the only hurlers ever to exceed 100 PRs in one season. Modern-era pitchers, who pitched far more infrequently than did the pre-1900 hurlers, have lesser PR totals. Bob Feller (1940) and Lefty Grove (1936) with 63's, and Ron Guidry (1978) with 61 are among the better totals of the more recent pitchers.

Pitcher Defense

This category rates a pitcher's defensive ability by taking into account factors like chances accepted, assists, errors, and putouts, among other things, as a linear measure of the pitcher's capability of assisting in preventing the opposition from scoring. It's the sabermetrician's calculation for rating the skill with which the pitcher carries out his "fifth infielder" responsibilities.

The formula for this category is quite complicated. For the intrepid and you math majors, here it is:

.10 times (putouts + two times number of assists, minus errors + double plays), divided by: the league's putout total for the season minus the total of league strikeouts.

The result of these mental gymnastics will produce a linear measure of the number of runs *saved* by a pitcher over the course of a season's play. You will, quite obviously, need the appropriate statistics to work your way through the formula. But why bother! Pete Palmer and John Thorn have edited *Total Baseball,** an encyclopedia of history, statistics, and other baseball odds and ends, that not only presents the formulas for these and other statistics, but the bottom lines, as well.

Pitcher defense and pitching runs present another way of looking at the capabilities and skills that are part of the pitcher's complete portfolio. Each part of his game contributes to a total picture that, in sum, helps his team win ballgames by preventing runs from being scored in one way or another. The extent to which he is successful is, then, expressed in terms of the numbers quoted throughout our review of the Cub franchises summiteers.

It's more than coincidental that the names in the various lists keep cropping up now and again. Quite simply, that's because the great pitchers are not one-or-two dimensional. They know *all* the ins and outs, the requirements, the skills and the tricks of the trade. That's what makes a John Clarkson, a Fergie Jenkins, a Pete Alexander or a Claude Passeau an exceptional player—in short, a summiteer.

* John Thorn, Pete Palmer, with Michael Gershman, (Ed's.), David Pietrusza, Managing Editor, *Total Baseball*, Fourth Edition, Viking Press, New York. 1995.

APPENDIX B

BATTING RUNS AND FIELDING RUNS

These two linear measures present hitters and fielders from the perspective of their ability to produce more runs than the league-average ballplayer (Batting Runs), or to prevent other teams from scoring more runs than the league-average player does (Fielding Runs). The numbers help to round out the player's total contribution to the team. Here is a list of the top 20 ratings in the Cubs' organization in both categories:

	BATTING RUNS			**FIELDING RUNS**	
Rank	**Name**	**No/Yr**	**Rank**	**Name**	**No/Yr**
1)	Rogers Hornsby	74, 1929	1)	Freddie Maguire	51, 1928
	Hack Wilson	74, 1930	2)	Fritz Pfeffer	46, 1884
2)	Bill Nicholson	50, 1943	3)	Ryne Sandberg	41, 1983
	Ron Santo	50, 1964	4)	Bill Dahlen	36, 1895
	Heinie Zimmerman	50, 1912		Ivan DeJesus	36, 1977
3)	Phil Cavarretta	49, 1945	5)	Tom Daly	33, 1887
4)	Ernie Banks	48, 1958	6)	Billy Jurges	32, 1932
5)	Tully Hartsel	47, 1901	7)	Ron Santo	31, 1967
6)	Ray Grimes	45, 1922	8)	Johnny Evers	30, 1913
7)	Mike Kelly	44, 1886		Joe Tinker	30, 1908
8)	Andy Pafko	43, 1950		Manny Trillo	30, 1977
9)	Jimmy Ryan	41, 1888	9)	Billy Herman	29, 1929
10)	Cap Anson	39, 1886		Rey Sanchez	29, 1994
	Ross Barnes	39, 1876	10)	Earl Adams	28, 1925
	Riggs Stephenson	39, 1929	11)	Mark Grace	27, 1990
11)	Stan Hack	38, 1941	12)	Don Kessinger	25, 1969
	Bill Lange	38, 1895	13)	Clyde Beck	22, 1927
12)	Frank Chance	37, 1902	14)	Bill Buckner	21, 1983
	Bill Dahlen	37, 1896		Bobby Sturgeon	21, 1942
13)	Kiki Cuyler	36, 1930	15)	Shawon Dunston	20, 1986
	Sammy Sosa	36, 1993		Ken Hubbs	20, 1963
14)	Leon Durham	35, 1982		Lou Stringer	20, 1941
	Gabby Hartnett	35, 1930		Zeb Terry	20, 1920
	Jim Hickman	35, 1970	16)	Bill Killifer	18, 1920
	Ryne Sandberg	35, 1992		Lenny Merullo	18, 1946
15)	Solly Hofman	33, 1910		Arnold Statz	18, 1923
16)	Bill Madlock	32, 1976	17)	Gene Baker	17, 1956
	Hank Sauer	32, 1948		Hank Sauer	17, 1952
	Jimmy Sheckard	32, 1911	18)	Bob O'Farrell	16, 1922
	Andy Thornton	32, 1975	19)	Larry Bowa	15, 1983
17)	Frank Demaree	31, 1936		Woody English	15, 1929
	Augie Galan	31, 1935		Gabby Hartnett	15, 1935
	Mark Grace	31, 1993		Andy Pafko	15, 1944
	Harry Steinfeldt	31, 1906		Jimmy Sheckard	15, 1911
18)	Woody English	30, 1930		Bill Sweeney	15, 1914
	Rick Wilkins	30, 1993	20)	Charlie Deal	14, 1921
19)	Johnny Evers	29, 1912		Cliff Heathcote	14, 1925
	Hank Leiber	29, 1939		Zeb Terry	14, 1920
20)	George Altman	28, 1962			
	Dave Kingman	28, 1979			
	Ned Williamson	28, 1884			

Batting Runs

This one is *the* hitter's category, measuring his capability in a given season to contribute runs *beyond* the league-average player (rated at 0). Ultimately, a 74 reading, like Rogers Hornsby's or Hack Wilson's, which top our list of Cub summiteers, can be reduced, through those tortuous formulas discussed previously in pitching runs and pitcher defense, to a meaningful number representing the player's rating, or TPR. That's the ultimate sabermetric number, designating the actual worth of a player's season. Again, it's in the neighborhood of a 10 to 1 Thus, 74 ranks out around the seven mark, for a contribution of approximately seven more wins for the team than the league-average player would contribute. In 1929, the Cubs won the pennant, and the margin of victory over second-place Pittsburgh (by 10 games) could be traced largely to the Rajah's 74 batting runs.

Similarly, if the Cubs had been deprived of Wilson's 74 BRs in 1930, they would have wound up in fourth or fifth place, rather than in the second-place money. The numbers begin to show just how exceptional his 1930 season was, right?

In the all-time listing of batting runs leaders, 74 ranks near the midpoint of the top 100. Bill Nicholson, Ron Santo and Heine Zimmerman, each with 50, rank in the second 100 on this list of overachieving hitters. The all-time leader? You guessed it: The Bambino (he's also No. 2 and No. 3), with 116 in 1923.

Fielding Runs

Formula adjustments are made for the various positions, namely shortstop, or catcher, or pitcher, as well as for each outfielder. In this category we have ratings for the player's fielding ability. They indicate how many runs in a given season a player like Ivan DeJesus or Andy Pafko or Gabby Hartnett can save the Cubs *beyond* the league-average ballplayer. In the long run, that will serve as a barometer of his defensive prowess (or a lack thereof). Players who could really go get 'em or throw 'em out are invaluable to the overall team effort. Those like Mark Grace, Ryne Sandberg or Manny Trillo pile up some impressive FRs in the 25-to-50 range.

Or how about second baseman Freddie Maguire? If you check the record, you will find that Freddie was a Cub for only one season—but what a fielding year he had! In 1928 he led the league in fielding runs with a monstrous 51, good enough, we have to guess, to get him traded off to Boston and the Braves. That 51 ranks as the fifth-highest single-season FR total ever recorded, placing him right up there with more recognizable stars like Glenn Hubbard (first with 62 in 1985), Bill Mazeroski (third with 57) or that old rascal, Rabbit Maranville (52 in 1914).

Oh those Cubbies! You gotta love 'em—even the Maguires!

APPENDIX C

A CHICAGO PITCHING DYNASTY

The Chicago Cubs franchise was blessed with nearly a half-century of exceptionally fine pitching. From its founding forward, Chicago's National League team fielded a pitching staff that dominated NL hitters as few other teams did. Their pitching superiority reached a climax during the 20th Century's first decade.

This appendix charts the pitchers and some of their more significant statistics during that era. Behind each pitcher's name, in the applicable year, you will find his won-loss record, ERA, and opponents' batting average statistics. There is also a comparison of the staff statistics with those of the National League for each season listed. Note how, in the years indicated, both individuals and staff bettered, in many cases by handsome margins, the numbers logged by the league. The staff was, indeed, a superior force to be reckoned with.

	1902	**1903**	**1904**	**1905**	**1906**
Brown				18-12; 2.17; .235	26-6; 1.04; .202
Cole					
Lundgren			17-9; 2.60; .226	13-5; 2.23; .220	17-2; 2.21; .221
Overall					12-3; 1.88; .217
Pfiester					20-8; 1.51; .194
Reulbach				18-14; 1.42; .201	19-4; 1.65; .175
Taylor	23-11;1.33;.227	21-14; 2.45; .235		12-3; 1.83; .223	
Weimer	20-8; 2.30; .225	20-14; 1.91; .204	18-12; 2.26; .229	20-14 ;2.41; .226	
Wicker	20-9; 3.02; .253	17-9; 2.67; .232	13-6; 2.02; .221		
Staff	68-69; 2.21; .254	82-56; 2.77;. 250	93-60; 2.30; .224	92-61; 2.04; .255	116-36; 1.75; .207
League	2.78;. 259	3.26; .269	2.73; .249	2.99; .255	2.62; .244

	1907	**1908**	**1909**	**1910**	**1911**
Brown	20-6; 1.39; .221	29-9; 1.47; .221	27-9; 1.31; .202	25-14; 1.86; .232	21-11; 2.80; .262
Cole					18-7; 3.13; .236
Lundgren	18-7; 1.17; .185				
Overall	23-7; 1.68; .208	15-8; 1.92; .208	20-11; 1.42; .198	12-6; 2.68; .212	
Pfiester	14-9; 1.15; .207		17-6; 2.43; .240		
Reulbach	17-4; 1.69; .217	24-7; 2.03; .214	19-10; 1.78; .212		16-9; 3.13; .236
Taylor					
Weimer					
Staff	107-45; 1.73; .216	99-55; 2.14; .221	104-49; 1.75; .215	104-50; 2.51; .235	92-62; 2.90; .245
League	2.46; .243	2.35; .239	2.59; .244	3.02; .256	3.39; .260

BIBLIOGRAPHY

Adomites, Paul. (1990). *World of Baseball: October's Game*. New York: Redefinition.

Anson, Adrian, C.(1900). *A Ball Player's Career*. Chicago: Era Publishing Company.

Astor, Gerald. (1988). *The Base Ball Hall of Fame's 50th Anniversary Book*. New York:Prentice-Hall.

Banks, Ernie, & Enright, Jim. (1971). *Mr. Cub*. Chicago: Follett.

Benson, John & Blengino, Tony. (1995). *Baseball's Top 100: The Best Individual Seasons of All Time*.
    Wilton, CT: Diamond Library.

Brown, Warren. (1946). *The Chicago Cubs*. New York: Putnam's.

Cairns, Bob. (1992). *Pen Men*. New York: St. Martin's.

Chadwick, Bruce. (1994). *The Chicago Cubs Trivia Book*. New York: St. Martin's.

Coletti, Ned. (1985). *You Gotta Have Heart: Dallas Green's Rebuilding of the Cubs*. South Bend, Ind:
    Diamond Communications.

Curran, William. (1990). *Big Sticks*. New York: Harper Collins.

Dewey, Donald, & Acocella, Nicholas. (1996). *The Ball Clubs*. New York: Harper Collins.

Deutsch, J. A., Cohen, R. M., Johnson, Roland, & Neft, David (1975). *Scrapbook of Baseball History*.
    New York: Bobbs-Merrill.

Gilbert, Bill. (1992). *They Also Served: Base Ball and the Home Front, 1941-1945*. New York: Crown.

Gold, Eddie, & Ahrens, Art. (1985). *The New Era Cubs*. Chicago: Bonus Books.

Golenbock, Peter. (1996).*Wrigleyville*. New York: St. Martin's Press.

Honig, Donald. (1983). *The National League*. New York: Crown.

Mazur, Bill. *Bill Mazur's Amazin' Base Ball Book*. New York: Kensington Publishing Corporation.

Meade, William, B. (1978). *Even the Browns*. New York: Contemporary Books, Inc.

Meade, William B. (1990). *World of Baseball: Low and Outside*. New York: Redefinition.

Neft, David S., & Cohen, Richard. (1996). *The Sports Encyclopedia: Baseball 1996* (6th ed.). New York:
    St. Martin's-Griffin.

Pfeffer, N. Fred. (1889). *Scientific Ball*. Chicago: N. Fred Pfeffer, Pub.

Reach Official Base Ball Guide for 1909. A. J. Reach Company.

Selzer, Jack. (1986). *Baseball in the Ninteenth Century: An Overview*. New York: SABR.

Spalding, A. G. (1911). *Base Ball*. New York: American Sports.

Spalding's Official Baseball Guide. Philadelphia: American Sports Publications.

Talley, Rick. (1989). *The Cubs of 1969*. Chicago: Contemporary Books.

Thorn, John, & Palmer, Pete. (1994, 4th ed.). *Total Baseball*. New York: Viking Press.

Voigt, David Q. (1983). *American Baseball* (Vol.I). Pennsylvannia: The Pennsylvania University Press.

Newspapers Consulted

The Chicago American
The Chicago Inter-Ocean
The Chicago Sun-Times
Chicago Today
The Chicago Tribune
The New York Times
Sporting Life
The Sporting News

Dr. Warren Wilbert is the Dean Emeritus of Lifelong Learning Services at Concordia University, Ann Arbor, Michigan. He has been a Lutheran educator at every level of education, and has served as a football, basketball and baseball coach. He has written for athletic and sports journals, and his latest article, "20 Year Men," appears in the 1996 edition of the *Baseball Research Journal*, a publication of the Society for American Baseball Research.

Wilbert was born in Kohler, Wisconsin, where he played amateur baseball alongside his father, Norman, forming the team's keystone combination. Wilbert and his wife, Ginny, are actively involved in church work, as are their daughters, Karen, Diann and Ellen. He resides at his home in Chelsea, Michigan, where he maintains a lively interest in Adult Education, baseball (especially the White Sox), and his grandchildren.

William Hageman, co-author of *Chicago Cubs: Seasons at the Summit*, is an editor in the Features Department of *The Chicago Tribune*. He previously worked as a sportswriter, editor and columnist for newspapers in Michigan and Delaware, and last year authored a biography of Honus Wagner. He resides in Aurora, Illinois, with his wife and three daughters.